The Great Awakening

A Buddhist Social Theory

David R. Loy

Wisdom Publications • Boston

Wisdom Publications
199 Elm Street
Somerville, MA 02144

Library of Congress Cataloging-in-Publication Data
Loy, David R.
  The great awakening : a Buddhist social theory / David R. Loy.
    p. cm.
  ISBN 0-86171-366-4 (pbk. : alk. paper)
  1. Sociology, Buddhist. 2. Buddhism—Social aspects. 3. Religious life—Buddhism. 4. Buddhism and social problems. I. Title.
  BQ4570.S6L69 2003
  294.3'37—dc21

                                                            2003004783

07 06
6 5 4 3 2

Cover design by Elizabeth Lawrence
Photograph© Christopher Wray-Mccann / Images.com
Interior design by Gopa & Ted2, Inc.

Wisdom Publications' books are printed on acid-free paper and meet the guidelines for permanence and durability of the Committee on Production Guidelines for Book Longevity of the Council on Library Resources.

Printed in Canada

For the liberation of all communities
from institutionalized greed, ill will, and delusion.

Publisher's Acknowledgment

The Publisher gratefully acknowledges the generous help of the Hershey Family Foundation in sponsoring the publication of this book.

The mercy of the West has been social revolution; the mercy of the East has been individual insight into the basic self/void. We need both.

—Gary Snyder, *Buddhist Anarchism* (1961)

Contents

Acknowledgments

I am very grateful to Josh Bartok at Wisdom Publications and copy editor John Leroy, whose suggestions have improved this book in innumerable ways. Thanks to them, this is a much better book than it would otherwise have been. Needless to say, whatever defects remain are my responsibility.

Earlier versions of these chapters have been published in various journals and edited books. Permission from the following journals and publishers to reprint is gratefully acknowledged.

"Buddhism and Poverty" in the *Kyoto Journal* no. 41 (summer 1999); also in *Contemporary Buddhism* vol. 2 no. 1 (2001).

"Shall We Pave the Earth, or Learn to Wear Shoes? A Buddhist Perspective on Greed and Globalization" in Chandra Muzaffar and Paul F. Knitter, ed., *Subverting Greed: Religious Conscience and the Global Economy* (Mary-knoll, New York: Orbis Books, 2002) in association with the Boston Research Center for the 21st Century.

"Can Corporations Become Enlightened? Buddhist reflections on transnational corporations" in *Globalisation: The Perspectives and Experiences of the Religious Traditions of Asia Pacific*, ed. by Joseph Camilleri and Chandra Muzaffar (Petaling Jaya, Malaysia: International Movement for a Just World, 1998).

"The Nonduality of Good and Evil: Buddhist Reflections on the New Holy War" in *Kyoto Journal* no. 51 (Summer 2002).

A condensed version of chapter 6 was published as "Healing Justice: A Buddhist Perspective" in Michael Hadley, ed., *The Spiritual Roots of Restorative Justice* (State University of New York Press, 2000). The full version was published as "How to Reform a Serial Killer: A Buddhist Perspective on Restorative Justice" in the on-line *Journal of Buddhist Ethics,* vol. 7 (2000).

An earlier version of "Zen and the Art of War" was published as "Is Zen Buddhism?" in *The Eastern Buddhist* Vol. 28 no. 2 (Autumn 1995).

"Remaking Ourselves?" in the *Wild Duck Review* vol. 5 no. 2 (summer 1999); a revised version in Casey Walker, ed., *Made Not Born* (Sierra Club Books, 2000).

"Loving the World as our own Body: The Nondualist Ethics of Taoism, Buddhism and deep ecology" in *Worldviews: environment, culture, religion* vol. 1 no. 3 (December 1997); also in *Asian and Jungian Views of Ethics,* ed. Carl B. Becker (New York and London: Greenwood Press, 1998).

"The Challenge of Global Capitalism: The Perspective of Eastern Religions" in John H. Dunning, ed., *Making Globalization Good: The Moral Challenges of Global Capitalism* (Oxford University Press, 2003).

CHAPTER 1

Buddhist Social Theory?

BUDDHISM TODAY faces the same challenge that confronts and may yet destroy every traditional religion. Our modern world is so different from the India of Shakyamuni Buddha 2,500 years ago—and, for that matter, from most of Asia until recently—that educated Buddhists cannot avoid the cognitive dissonance between their religious beliefs, which originated in an Iron Age worldview, and the Information Age technologies most of us use daily. Although the Buddha has often and traditionally been regarded as omniscient, there is no good reason to think (and many good reasons to doubt) that Shakyamuni knew anything about the cellular structure of organisms, the genetic code of life, the microbial cause of most diseases, the periodic table of the atomic elements, the structure of the solar system, Newton's laws of motion, the physics of light and electromagnetism, or the theory of relativity, much less possible applications such as the internal combustion engine, antibiotics, the telephone, television, nuclear fission, silicon chips, computers, or the Internet.

Most of us do not know very much about them either, but they have created the world we live in. I may not understand anything about how electricity works, yet I turn on the lights when it gets dark. I do not know how computers work, yet I use e-mail and surf the Net. Although I cannot claim to comprehend $E = mc^2$, I grew up (and still live) in a world haunted by the threat of nuclear war and nuclear accidents. Unlike the teachings of Buddhism, the contemporary world has been shaped by these technologies.

As far as we know, the Buddha was illiterate, literacy being rare in the India of his time. His teachings were orally preserved (and no doubt altered, perhaps considerably) until the first century B.C.E. Shakyamuni therefore could not have known about the extraordinary psychological and social effects of literacy, much less the equally significant consequences of the printing press. He was also unfamiliar with nation-states, corporate capitalism, universities and scientific institutes, high-tech warfare, the United Nations, and the Universal Declaration of Human Rights. He knew nothing about the modern social sciences, including developmental psychology (and psychotherapy), sociology, anthropology, and comparative religion.

It is no use pretending otherwise: these developments have so transformed our world that we cannot evade the question of how relevant the Buddha's teachings can be for us today. Nor can we take the easy route of distinguishing these technologies and institutions from the people who use them. The Buddhist emphasis on the nonduality of self and world just aggravates the dissonance. If our world is so different from the Buddha's, then, to a significant extent, so are we. The Buddhist teaching of *anatta* (no-self) seems to undercut efforts to find an invariant human identity throughout history.

What is perhaps an even more fundamental difference between the Buddha's world and ours has not yet been mentioned here: secularism. The scientific and social innovations that have restructured our world are the result of a shift from supernatural explanations to an empirical rationality that casts doubt on all religious beliefs, including claims of spiritual redemption. Despite a resurgent nostalgia for such sanctuaries in the late twentieth century, the contemporary world seems to have a decreasing need for increasingly dubious forms of transcendence. Our empirical understanding of the natural world leads us to be skeptical about the supernatural, but the dualism we create between the natural and the supernatural is generally alien to premodern societies.

That educated Christians, Muslims, Hindus, Sikhs, and Jews experience much the same cognitive dissonance as Buddhists can be no consolation to any of them in this corrosive modern world where the value of premodern religious perspectives is questioned when it is not dismissed out of hand.

The worst is yet to come, however. We have not touched upon the greatest challenge to premodern ways of thinking, which also undermines much modern thinking: the cluster of related insights usually described as *postmodern*. Postmodernism has had extraordinary individual and social effects that may rival the impact of the printing press—consequences we are just beginning to recognize. Over the last thirty years the miniaturization made possible by the silicon chip has transformed most technologies. An equivalent transformation in the intellectual realm is the postmodern insight into the constructed nature of our truths and therefore our "realities." Our previous innocence about such matters cannot be regained, now that we have begun to lose it. Ways of thinking can be repressed, but as Freud realized, what is repressed does not disappear. It returns to haunt us until we acknowledge it and learn to deal with it.

No social activity is more vulnerable to this realization than religion. The French philosopher Jean-François Lyotard has defined postmodernism as incredulity toward all meta-narratives, and no narratives are more "meta-" (the Greek word for more comprehensive) than religious ones. The postmodern revolution may signify the beginning of the end for traditional religious beliefs, practices, and institutions. This includes Buddhism, of course, insofar as the Buddhist message too has been domesticated into a reassuring worldview—a "sacred canopy"—that provides psychic and social stability. Today all such protective canopies are threatened by the fundamental insight that they are human creations.

Unfortunately, that is just about the last thing we want to be told. Throughout most of history, the canopy provided by religions has been essential for grounding us: for teaching us what this world actually is, and therefore what is really important about it, and therefore how we are to live in it. It is terrifying to learn that this canopy is a fiction we have constructed and then objectified (by "forgetting" that we have made it) in order to dwell comfortably beneath it. This is worse than an earthquake: the ground beneath our feet actually disappears. No wonder we have become so anxious; no wonder we spend so much of our psychic energy denying this dawning realization, or distracting ourselves from it. It signifies the end of humanity's collective childhood. It forces us to grow up, or engage in increasingly desperate attempts to suppress what becomes ever more difficult to ignore.

But is religion *only* a protective, reassuring canopy? Even if reassurance has been its main social function, religion has served and continues to serve another role, now becoming more obvious and more important. Religions are vehicles for self-transformation. Not only do they reassure us, they provide us with principles and precepts and practices that can change us or show us how to change ourselves. Buddhism, of course, is a good example. The original teachings of Shakyamuni are concerned almost solely with such a process: the path he discovered (or rediscovered) that led to his "awakening" (the literal meaning of *Buddha* is "the awakened one").

There is often tension between these two roles—sacred canopy and self-transformation—yet they are not entirely distinguishable. The spiritual path is usually arduous and painful, because we confront the demons that lurk in the shadows of our minds. Having *faith* in this process implies, in practice, believing in a particular worldview that encourages and guides our efforts. According to Buddhism, however, the two roles are connected in another way as well. The deconstruction and reconstruction of the sense of self is necessary to become aware of the most deceptive of meta-narratives: the one we normally do not perceive because it is our ordinary, everyday reality—the "real world" we take for granted but in fact is constructed. The postmodern realization that my self and my world are constructs (and, for Buddhism, realizing that the duality between them is a construct) does not necessarily grant insight into what they are constructed of, how they are constructed, or what the possibilities for reconstruction are. Modern empirical science offers an analytic answer: the world, including ourselves, is an extraordinarily complex machine. But is that reductionistic paradigm just another meta-narrative?

Christianity provides us with a particularly wonderful example of personal transformation: the suffering of a loving god-man, whose death was necessary for a redemptive resurrection. As a model symbolizing the ego-death and transformation that each of us needs to undergo in order to realize our true nature, there is perhaps no more inspiring myth. It is therefore all the more unfortunate, from a Buddhist perspective at least, that Christianity has so often literalized this myth into history, into the story of God's only son, who can save us if we *believe* in him. In place of a path of self-transformation, we are taught to depend on someone else to save us.

Is it a coincidence that the same pattern so often recurs in other religions? In India the notion of a savior God is a relatively late addition to the most important spiritual traditions, including Samhkya-Yoga, Vedanta, and even Buddhism. Mahayana Buddhism developed a pantheon of celestial bodhisattvas devoted to helping us, as well as the promise of a Pure Land accessible to those who appeal to Amitabha Buddha. Psychologically, the early equivalent of a sacred canopy is the security provided by our parents, so it is not surprising that we continue to yearn for the protection of a cosmic father or the maternal love of an all-embracing mother. But as a meta-narrative to rely upon and reside within, this kind of canopy is less and less tenable in a postmodern world.

In contrast, the early Buddhist teachings focus almost exclusively on the path of self-transformation, with a minimum of dogma or metaphysics—in other words, with a rather flimsy canopy, at best, to shelter beneath. These original teachings not only deny a creator God and the salvific value of rituals such as sacrifices, they also emphasize the constructed nature of both the self and the world. For Buddhism there are no self-existing things, since everything, including you and me, interpenetrates (interpermeates) everything else, arising and passing away according to causes and conditions. This interconnectedness—not just an intellectual insight but an experience—was an essential aspect of the Buddha's awakening, and *it is congruent with the essential postmodern realization.* Even more radical then than now, the original Buddhist teachings, not surprisingly, eventually became elaborated into another sacred canopy, focused on a transcendental liberation from this world. What is more surprising is that early Buddhism should have had such deconstructive insights and that they have been preserved in recognizable form for two and a half millennia.

This perspective on the Buddha's awakening deserves our attention because no other religious tradition foregrounds so clearly this crucial insight into our constructedness. There are some parallels with the philosophical realization in ancient Greece that society is a construct that can and should be reconstructed (e.g., Plato's *Republic*). The history of the West since then has incorporated and developed the Greek concern for social transformation. Yet none of the important Greek philosophers proposed what Shakyamuni Buddha taught— the deconstruction and reconstruction of the fictive sense of self.

These resonances between postmodern theory and Buddhist teachings provide the basis for a comparison that is more than merely interesting. Today the postmodern realization about the constructed nature of our canopies, sacred and otherwise, contributes to global crises that we are far from resolving. Indeed, Nietzsche's prescient prediction of a coming age of nihilism suggests that the world's destabilization may be far from over. Some people and perhaps a few institutions are beginning to assimilate the postmodern insight, but although we are becoming more aware of its implications and dangers, we do not yet have a good grasp of the possibilities it opens up.

For the West, the postmodern perspective grows out of, and depends upon, a secular modernity that privileges empirical rationalism over religious superstition. In this regard, too, our attitude derives from the Greeks, whose philosophy originated as a critique of the Olympian deities and the rites associated with them. The Indian situation was quite different. According to one's sympathies, one can see that Indian (including Buddhist) philosophy

never quite escaped the orbit of religious concerns or, more sympathetically, that Indian thought never felt the Western need to differentiate
between them.

What does that difference mean for us? Today we are struggling with the
radical implications of the postmodern realization into how we construct
both the world and ourselves; and the Buddha's similar discovery, in a very
different time and place, offers us another perspective on that realization.
This more religious perspective implies different possibilities. To dismiss that
other perspective and therefore those other possibilities, without considering them, is arrogant and may be costly. Ecologists tell us that many exotic
species are disappearing that have never been catalogued, much less studied;
who knows what possible medical therapies—a drug for cancer?—die with
them? Might the same be true for exotic religio-philosophical teachings?
Might some of them have remedies for our postmodern nihilism?

One reason we may be tempted to reject the Buddhist perspective on our
conditioning is that contemporary Buddhist teachers and institutions do not
always offer it. Instead Buddhism is presented as another belief system,
another sacred canopy under which we can find shelter. More often than not,
its destabilizing path of self-deconstruction has been objectified into a fixed
worldview that paradoxically ends up serving to stabilize and reassure the
sense of self. As this suggests, the tension between the two roles of religion—
sacred canopy and self-transformation—is strong within the Buddhist tradition. Shakyamuni Buddha had nothing to do with funerals, yet in Japan
(where I live), most people identify Buddhism with funerals and memorial
services—that is the only time most Japanese care to visit a temple. The main
social (and economic) function of Buddhist priests is performing these expensive ceremonies. In other words, the primary role of Buddhism in Japan is to
reassure people and give them the rituals they need to cope with the death of
loved ones—an important function, to be sure, but a far cry from the path to
liberation taught by Shakyamuni.

In contrast, the practices in Zen monasteries, such as *zazen* meditation and
focusing on koans, works against such a reappropriation by emphasizing a let-
ting-go of mental phenomena and promoting the direct, unmediated realization of our emptiness *(shunyata)*. Shakyamuni Buddha used the metaphor
of a raft that we can use to ferry ourselves across the river of *samsara;* rather
than carrying that raft on our backs everywhere, we need to know when to let
it go. His teachings are tools, not metaphysical claims.

In short, contemporary Buddhism remains a paradoxical mixture of the premodern (e.g., rituals) and the postmodern (an understanding of constructedness), whose liberative potentials are often obscured. In order to clarify the possibilities contemporary Buddhism offers us, both individually and socially, it is necessary for us to begin the process of discriminating between the essentials of its message and the incidentals of its Iron Age origins. What, for example, do the doctrines of karma and rebirth mean today? How can we (post)moderns understand them?

By asking this, I do not mean to imply that these concepts should now be rejected outright as untenable, but they certainly need to be reevaluated. Should Buddhists accept as literal truth everything the Pali canon says about karma and rebirth, simply because it is in the Pali Canon? One does not need to accept the literal truth of everything in the Bible to be a Christian. Shakyamuni himself emphasized that our faith should not be blind; we really understand something only when we know it for ourselves, from our own experience. Karma and rebirth were common beliefs in Shakyamuni's day, just as the belief in an imminent messiah was common in Jesus' Israel. How literal should our understanding of karma and rebirth be now, given what we now know (or believe we know) about the physical world and human psychology? What science has discovered about the physical structure of the world seems to provide no support for psychic survival after death; yet even if we choose to ignore all religious claims about an afterlife, we must at least consider the growing literature of personal accounts of near-death experiences, which may (or may not) be indicative of some type of survival or continuation. Maybe we cannot yet resolve that tension, but still we should acknowledge it.

There are other important dimensions to karma, aside from those pertaining to psychical and bodily rebirth. Whether or not the law of karma is a moral law of the universe—a kind of psychic equivalent to Newton's third law of motion, that every action has an equal and opposite reaction—the Buddhist emphasis on no-self and intentional action points to a more subtle aspect of karma: that we construct ourselves by what we choose to do. My sense of self is a precipitate of my habitual ways of thinking, feeling, and acting. Just as my body is composed of the food I eat, so my character is built by my conscious decisions. According to this approach, people are "punished" or "rewarded" not for what they have done but for what they have become, and what we intentionally do is what makes us what we are.

This does not necessarily involve an afterlife. According to Spinoza, happiness is not the reward of virtue but virtue itself. In more Buddhist terms, we do not live a certain way for the recompense our meritorious actions will bring us, either in this lifetime or in a future one. Rather, to become a different kind of person is to experience the world in a different kind of way. The six realms of samsara have usually been understood as distinct worlds or planes of existence through which we transmigrate according to our karma, yet they can also describe the different ways we experience this world as our attitude toward it changes. The hell realm is not necessarily a *place* I will be reborn into, due to my hatred and evil actions. It can be the *way this world is experienced* when my mind is dominated by anger and hate. The twelve interlinked factors of *pratitya samutpada* (interdependent origination) do not necessarily refer to different lifetimes; that teaching can be understood as describing the various causes and effects of "my" mental processes right now.

When karma is understood along these lines, the Buddhist emphasis on our constructedness, instead of being an example of premodern supernatural thinking, becomes quite consistent with the postmodern insight. That does not mean this is the only way to interpret karma and samsara; my reflections are merely one example of the possibilities that must be addressed for the contemporary relevance of Buddhism to become more apparent. The challenge, of course, is discriminating between the baby and the bathwater, and that will not be easy. If a contemporary Buddhism is to mature, however, this task cannot be evaded.

In addition to such doctrinal issues, there are institutional ones. Buddhist religious structures in Asia have usually been, and for the most part remain, hierarchical, patriarchal, and complicit with state power. Although Buddhist teachings have sometimes been used to challenge state power, more often than not Buddhist institutions have been implicated in justifying and therefore helping to preserve oppressive social relationships. The sacred canopy can be quite a comfortable place for those with privileged positions in religious hierarchies allied with political hierarchies. This suggests that Buddhism needs the contributions of Western modernity—such as democracy, feminism, and the separation of church and state—to challenge its institutional complacency and liberate its own teachings from such traditional social constraints.

So the encounter between Buddhism and (post)modernity may be valuable for both. The modern world can help Buddhism clarify its basic message, otherwise obscured by premodern enculturations no longer relevant today. In this book, I will attempt to show that Buddhism can also help our postmodern world develop liberative possibilities otherwise obscured by the antireligious bias of so much contemporary social critique. The implication is that the secular suspicion of spiritual perspectives—still deeply rooted in most radical critiques of our social ills—is misplaced, because the collective transformations we need are not possible without the personal transformations that Buddhism, for example, encourages. The purpose of this introductory chapter is to clarify the nature of the possible interaction between (post) modernity and Buddhism, and the purpose of this book is to offer some examples of the contribution that Buddhism can make to a new understanding of our new situation.

Elsewhere I have offered an account of how the Buddhist path deconstructs the sense of self and used that account to outline a Buddhist perspective on the historical development of the West.[1] The present book is an exercise in what might be called Buddhist social theory. What can Buddhism contribute today to our understanding of such crucial issues as corporate globalization, terrorist violence, criminal justice, biotechnology, and ecological crises? The rest of this introduction will outline what I believe to be the distinctive character of Buddhist social theory, and the chapters that follow are essays in the original meaning of the French word *essai:* "attempts" to bring Buddhist principles to bear upon such problems.

CONSTRUCTING THE REAL WORLD

The last few centuries have been a steep downhill slide for human hubris. Copernicus discovered that our planet is not the center of the universe. Darwin realized that *Homo sapiens* can be understood as a result of the same evolutionary process that continues to produce other species, a natural selection that does not require any creator God. And, although Freud's legacy is more controversial, his theory of repression implies that we are not even the masters of our own minds: our supposedly self-sufficient ego-consciousness is not autonomous but irremediably split, buffeted by psychic forces that it cannot control because our consciousness itself is a function of them.

And that was only the beginning. More recently, poststructuralist critiques by Jacques Derrida and others have demonstrated the constructed nature of the subject by emphasizing the differences inherent in language. Our consciousness, like our texts, can never attain a stable self-presence because the continual circulation of signifiers denies meaning any fixed foundation. Michel Foucault has argued quite convincingly that reason itself is mortal: each new epoch finds that the basic framework of its predecessor has become unintelligible; and, furthermore, what we have understood to be knowledge cannot be understood apart from its role in systems of human control.

Some of the postmodern claims remain controversial, but many of them are consistent with developments in other disciplines such as psychology, anthropology, and comparative religion. The discovery that the world contains multiple worldviews, that each of those views has its own logic, and that there is no "master" worldview that subsumes all the others, has led to the realization that knowledge about the world—including our own knowledge about our own individual worlds—is not discovered but constructed. This shifts the focus to *the truth about truth*. Why do we construct the world in the ways that we do? As we become more aware of the factors that influence our constructions, what other constructs become possible?

The earliest ethnographers in the South Pacific—many of them Christian missionaries—encountered non-Western cultures they were unable to understand. This forced them to become more aware of the conceptual categories that they themselves had been taking for granted. The contrast had radical implications. They and their successors could not help but become more self-conscious about the constructed nature of their own cultures—and therefore about the constructed nature of their own selves. Without quite understanding what they were doing, they became engaged in a collective project "amounting to the invention of a new subjectivity, the basis of which appears to be an impulse to experience a state of radical instability of value—or even the instability of selfhood itself."[2] Edmund Leach began his influential *Rethinking Anthropology* by emphasizing the necessity for the cultural anthropologist to undergo "an extremely personal traumatic kind of experience" in order to escape the prejudices of his or her own culture and be able to enter into another.[3] Roy Wagner's version of this reproduces what countless Buddhist teachers have said about realizing the Buddhist teachings: "The anthropologist cannot simply 'learn' the new culture, but must rather 'take it on' so as to experience a transformation of his own world."[4]

What does this ability to take on another world tell us about our own? The cultural anthropologist Ernest Becker focused on this issue, but his writings have not received the attention they deserve, perhaps because his insights make us too uncomfortable:

The world of human aspiration is largely fictitious, and if we do not understand this we understand nothing about man. It is a largely symbolic creation by an ego-controlled animal that permits action in a psychological world, a symbolic-behavioral world removed from the boundaries of the present moment, from the immediate stimuli which enslave all lower organisms. Man's freedom is a fabricated freedom, and he pays a price for it. He must at all times *defend the utter fragility of his delicately constituted fiction, deny its artificiality.* That's why we can speak of "joint theatrical staging," "ritual formulas for social ceremonial," and "enhancing of cultural meaning," with utmost seriousness....

The most astonishing thing of all, about man's fictions, is not that they have from prehistoric times hung like a flimsy canopy over his social world, but that he should have come to discover them at all. It is one of the most remarkable achievements of thought, of self-scrutiny, that the most anxiety-prone animal of all could come to *see through himself* and discover the fictional nature of his action world. Future historians will probably record it as one of the great, liberating breakthroughs of all time, and it happened in ours.[5]

In his last two books, the Pulitzer Prize–winning *The Denial of Death* and the posthumous *Escape from Evil,* Becker located the roots of this fiction in our inability to accept the inevitability of our death. Daniel Liechty summarizes this perspective:

We are born into cultures that provide us with immortality narratives and symbols, and we tame the terror of mortality consciousness by vicarious identification with these narratives and symbols of transcendence.... But to keep ourselves from noticing that these transcending symbols themselves are human artefacts, we begin to treat the artefact as if it really had the power to bestow immortality upon us. It is the only way to keep from consciously doubting its ability to do so.[6]

Traditionally, the most important immortality narratives and symbols have been religious. We cope with the awareness of mortality by collectively reassuring ourselves that we will survive death in a different form or realm. What happens, then, when a whole civilization begins to doubt such afterlife?

The most important element in maintaining the intactness and plausi-
bility of any particular cultural immortality ideology is the fact that everyone around you also believes in it. In modern societies, the constant
confrontation with competing and contradictory cultural immortality
ideologies creates inevitable suspicion and doubt about the transcendent
veracity of any one of them. Hence arises in such societies a cultural
malaise or anomie on one hand, and a frantic, meaning-grabbing com-
pulsiveness on the other hand, as the cultural immortality ideologies no
longer function to keep mortality anxiety at bay.[7]

This crucial insight does not need much tweaking to resonate with the
essential teachings of Buddhism, but, as Liechty reminds us, the breakthrough
that Becker celebrates is a problematic one, because it hurts too much. In
Buddhist terms, it involves *dukkha* (suffering) and how we try to evade it.
Without a shared immortality ideology—even if only the pursuit of wealth—
the meaning of our lives is called into question, people become desperate,
and society begins to fall apart. It remains to be seen how liberating this
insight of Becker's will be for us, or how crazy we will become in trying to
deny it.

It is also possible to overemphasize its novelty. If the fruit of this insight has
finally ripened in our day, it is because this tree has deep roots in European
history. After the French revolution it became difficult to defend the divine
right of kings and the "naturalness" of such a social order. It also became difficult to overlook the implications of history: how societies change over time,
sometimes radically and abruptly. It was only a matter of time before the consequences of this for human knowledge would be noticed. Hegel integrated
the different truths of discrete societies and eras by viewing the course of
human history as the gradual self-realization of Mind. Today it is difficult to
be so optimistic, but, without some such philosophical synthesis, it has also
become difficult for the center to hold against a cultural pluralism that threatens all canopies, sacred and otherwise. First we discovered the cultural water
we swim in; then we began to become aware that that water is our own creation…and to realize that such constructions can be reconstructed.

Again, and predictably, the roots of this breakthrough extend back to classical Greece. In traditional societies social norms are usually maintained by
religious claims that validate social values and power arrangements transcendentally: they cannot be changed because they were created by the gods.

The tensions that developed in the fifth and fourth centuries B.C.E. were due to the Greeks' groundbreaking realization that the social order is not natural in the same way that the physical world is. When *nomos* (convention) became thus distinguished from *phusis* (nature), traditional social structures could be challenged. Without belief in a transcendentally grounded sacred order, the Greek city-states became free to restructure themselves, as we continue to do, or try to do, or want to do; but that freedom comes at a price, as Socrates discovered, at the cost of his own life.

Once one becomes aware of the difference between nature and culture, one can never recover the unselfconscious groundedness that, for better and worse, has been lost. Both individually and collectively, the freedom to determine one's own path is shadowed by an anxiety-producing loss of security due to the disappearance of one's transcendental foundation—a sacred canopy that, whether or not it actually protects us, answers our deepest questions about the structure and meaning of the universe, and where we fit into that. Such answers do more than validate and stabilize the social order. Internalized, they also provide personal identity, a secure grounding for the self. When I accept my culture as natural and therefore inevitable, the meaning of my life is more or less decided for me. But when I accept the freedom to construct my own meaning, I experience a vertigo resulting from the lack of an external—that is, a natural—ground.

The Greeks were great seafarers, colonizing much of the Mediterranean and the Black Sea and becoming familiar with a great variety of cultures. This exposure to different customs and beliefs encouraged skepticism toward their own myths. From a Buddhist perspective, however, what is most striking about the Greek experience is how much it resembles the perennial situation of the anxious individual self, which is dimly aware that it is not self-existing or "natural" but a social and psychological construct.

According to Walter Truett Anderson, anthropology's gift to the world—the realization that human beings create different kinds of cultures, which in turn create different kinds of human beings—is a deeply subversive idea, because if you absorb it you will begin to wonder who created it and why; you reflect on what it does to you, and you think about making some changes. "And the more people there are working their way through some such inner thought process, the more culturally diverse, complex and unstable a society is likely to be."[8]

In other words, globalization means that today we all participate in the Greek loss of ground and crisis of meaning, whether or not we understand what is happening. Most of us know little if anything about postmodern fictions, but accelerated communication and transportation systems ensure that any religious confrontation with modernity is also an accelerated confrontation between premodernities. As the world becomes smaller, we find ourselves rubbing elbows with other people and other cultures often living literally next door. This offers a particularly serious challenge to religions, which have always interacted with each other but in the past have usually had more time and space to develop according to their own internal dynamics. And since religions cannot be distinguished from the people who believe in them and practice them, this is also a serious challenge to our multicultural societies.

The problem of immigration into Western societies, for example, is usually understood in terms of economics (cheap labor, competition for jobs), crime, and occasionally differences in "lifestyle." This overlooks another dimension that in the long run may be more important: the anxiety produced when different worldviews are living next to each other. Historically, worldviews have maintained themselves by avoiding and eliminating competition, which is why medieval heretics and Jews needed to be destroyed or confined to ghettos. The less secure one's worldview, the more threatening is any alternative, but the presence of alternatives is always threatening, because it means we are constantly exposed to models of other possibilities, and because one's own worldview is never secure enough.

Fortunately, inquisitions and pogroms are no longer acceptable, at least not officially. Yet tolerance does not allay the anxiety that results from being surrounded by alien worldviews that must be tolerated. Modern distinctions between private and public, or church and state, do not resolve this basic problem either. Now my sacred canopy becomes more like an umbrella. When everyone has his or her own umbrella, and I walk through a sea of multicolored, differently patterned ones, it becomes increasingly difficult to believe that mine is the only "right" one. To make matters worse, learning how to put up an umbrella shows us how they are constructed.

One response is to cling all the harder to the old "eternal" truths and traditional ways of doing things. Since this occurs in a more crowded and fast-paced globalizing environment, in which we must interact much more with people who do not believe in our beliefs or follow our ways, such a reaction becomes more problematic. It tends to aggravate the "antithetical bonding"[9] that constructs group identity and security by denigrating other groups. We create an in-group by distinguishing ourselves from an out-group that becomes vulnerable to scapegoating.

Although such fundamentalist responses are unlikely to be attractive to those who have read this far, we need to remember that often communities are coping in the only way they can in order to retain their sense of who they are and how to live, in response to the unwelcome transformations being thrust upon them. For those people whose lives and livelihoods are threatened by globalization, such a conservative position is not unreasonable. Rapid social change, even when positive in many ways, is destabilizing and therefore productive of anxiety, especially for those who do not share privileged Western lifestyles or modernity's gospel of social progress.

Nevertheless, neotraditionalism is a defensive response that, however reassuring in the short term, must eventually fail. There is no escaping the corrosive effects of the (post)modern world on premodern worldviews. Today we can no more suppress collective doubts about an afterlife than we can return to a life without electricity. Premodern innocence about one's sacred canopy cannot be regained once we become conscious of its constructedness. So far, of course, such an awareness has not yet penetrated very widely, but unless a global catastrophe reverses the globalization of educational exchange and intellectual interaction, the postmodern insight can only continue to spread and infiltrate traditional cultures.

A more common religious response, in the West at least, has been to compartmentalize one's world—or, more precisely, to accept an increasingly compartmentalized world. We resolve the cognitive dissonance between a traditional religious worldview and modernity by ignoring it. For example, we may live in a premodern world on Sunday mornings and in a modern world the rest of the week. This compartmentalization is actually quite postmodern. Our complicated and specialized societies encourage such a fragmentation. In fact, it has become difficult *not* to compartmentalize. A worldview that tries to make sense of the world as a whole has become the exception, even in—or especially in—academia, where a continuous explosion of knowledge continually discourages attempts to comprehend it all. It is all the easier to accept that fragmentation because of the available technological distractions that fill up our free time. And without the opportunity to reflect on these matters, the challenge for most of us is coping, not understanding.

Nevertheless, religion compartmentalized in this way becomes trivialized and irrelevant. A religious orientation that does not inform our daily lives, infusing day-to-day concerns, is not doing its job. The point of a spiritual worldview is to teach us what is really important about the world, and therefore how to live in it. By surrendering this function to more rationalized and secular institutions—the state, the economy, the media, the university and other scientific institutes—religion is reduced to a shell that ends up providing us with little more than an occasional refuge from an otherwise stressful world, a canopy to duck under when it all becomes too much.

In keeping the worldviews of religion and (post)modernity apart, isolated from each other, we also lose the opportunity to see how each might be able to inform the other. To one such opportunity we now turn.

What Is Buddhist about Buddhist Social Theory?

Unlike some other more aggressive religions, Buddhism has been so successful as a missionary religion because of its adaptability, a flexibility consistent with its own emphasis on impermanence and emptiness (the "selflessness" of everything). In China, for example, a natural affinity between Mahayana and Taoism led to the development of Chan/Zen. In Tibet interaction with the native Bon religion led to a distinctive form of tantric Vajrayana Buddhism. So what is Buddhism adapting to today, as it infiltrates the West?

Although Buddhist-Christian dialogue has been a fruitful site of interreligious conversation, a more important point of entry seems to be Western psychology, especially psychotherapy. There is, however, another significant way in which the West has been interacting with Buddhism, not only assimilating it but influencing it. Historically, the Abrahamic religions—Judaism, Christianity, Islam—have had a strong prophetic dimension concerned to promote social justice, an issue that has not been crucial in the development of Buddhism. Asian Buddhism has focused on individual liberation by transforming the greed, ill will, and delusion in our own minds. The Abrahamic focus on social justice has influenced the history of the West by encouraging a liberation that challenges and reforms oppressive social structures. Does this shared concern for liberation suggest affinity between the two traditions? One fruit of this common focus is socially engaged Buddhism, which has become an important practice for a growing number of Buddhists, in Asia as well as in the West.

What is specifically Buddhist about socially engaged Buddhism? Insofar as Buddhism traditionally focuses on alleviating dukkha rather than speculating on its metaphysical origins, it tends to adopt a pragmatic, hands-on approach that does not worry much about social issues. Nevertheless, the question remains important for helping to determine whether Buddhist social engagement may have something unique to contribute to the concern for compassionate action emphasized by all religions (in theory, at least).

One answer is that the Buddhist emphasis on nonduality between ourselves and the world encourages identification with "others": hence *com*-passion, suffering *with*, because we are not separate from them. Is that what makes Buddhist social engagement Buddhist?

If so, there is a problem that can be expressed by rephrasing the original question: What, if anything, is new about socially engaged Buddhism today? According to the Vietnamese Buddhist teacher Thich Nhat Hanh, all Buddhism is (or should be) socially engaged. Shakyamuni himself never abandoned society. According to the Pali sutras he often gave laypeople advice on their social responsibilities. Kings consulted with him, and on several occasions he intervened to stop battles, albeit not always successfully. If Buddhism has always been socially engaged, perhaps the only new thing is that our more democratic forms of governance allow more direct efforts to challenge the state and reform its policies.

There is much to be said in favor of this perspective, yet it suffers from an important drawback. It does not help us to understand, and therefore respond adequately to, the more complicated causes of human-made dukkha endemic to our contemporary world: the suffering caused or threatened by nuclear bombs and power plants; corporate globalization and a widening gap between rich and poor; terrorism, whether religiously inspired or state promoted; a retributive penal system that is obviously inadequate; global warming and many other ecological catastrophes; and genetically modified organisms, including human clones.

What, if anything, can Buddhism offer to help us understand these problems, most of them unique to our times? In the end, our efforts to reduce contemporary dukkha cannot avoid bumping up against institutional and structural issues. There is much that needs to be done to alleviate homelessness and hunger in U.S. cities, for example, but we also need to address the nature of the economic and political systems that create and tolerate such deprivation in such a fabulously wealthy nation. Does Buddhism have anything special to offer that can help us understand those systems and how they might be reformed?

The pragmatic emphasis of Buddhism encourages some Buddhists to give a negative answer to such questions, but I think that sells Buddhism short. Since the modern world is, for better and worse, mostly a product of the West, there may be considerable value in bringing in the perspective of a mature non-Western tradition. If we do not try to understand the larger historical forces moving the world today, we accede to them. The alternative is either to buy our social theory ready-made, more or less off the rack—e.g., some humanized version of green socialism—or to consider alternatives inspired (or at least informed) by what Buddhism has to say about human dukkha and its causes.

According to the Pali sutras, Shakyamuni Buddha often summarized his teaching into four noble truths: the nature of our problem, the cause of the problem, the end of the problem, and the solution to our problem. Because of this therapeutic approach, Shakyamuni is sometimes called the great physician: he tells us that we are sick, diagnoses our illness, reassures us that it is possible to become healthy, and gives us the regimen for a cure. The same logical format can be employed to examine the nature of our present social dukkha and outline the distinctive contours of Buddhist social theory.

What Is Social Dukkha?

There is no need to devote much space or effort here summarizing the varieties and extent of human dukkha around the globe today. Those inclined to read this book will already be familiar with many of the sobering facts, some of which are mentioned in the following chapters. Here it will suffice to cite a few figures, mostly from recent United Nations Human Development Reports. According to the 1996 report, the world's 358 billionaires were already wealthier than the combined annual income of countries with 45 percent of the world's people. More recently, according to the Institute for Policy Studies, the world's 497 billionaires in 2001 registered a combined wealth of $1.54 trillion, a sum greater than the combined incomes of the poorer half of humanity.

As this suggests, globalization is increasing the gap between rich and poor. According to the Human Development Report for 1999, the champagne glass that reflects the world's distribution of resources is becoming even more top-heavy. In 1992 the top fifth of the world's people consumed 82.7 percent of the world's resources, the bottom fifth only 1.4 percent; by 1999 the top fifth had 86 percent, the poorest fifth 1.3 percent. The average African household now consumes 20 percent less than it did twenty-five years ago. Worldwide, well over a billion people are deprived of basic needs, including many in developed countries. Of the 4.4 billion people in developing countries, almost three-fifths lack basic sanitation, almost a third have no access to clean water, a quarter do not have adequate housing, a fifth have insufficient dietary energy and protein and lack access to modern health services; 2 billion people are anaemic. The revised United Nations human poverty index (HPI-2) also shows that some 7 to 17 percent of the population in industrial countries is poor, and in some countries that percentage is increasing. Sweden, though only thirteenth in average national income, has the least poverty (7 percent), while the United States has both the highest average income and the highest percentage living in poverty.

Meanwhile, the earth's ever-expanding human population continues to place ever greater strains on its ecosystems. Fears that the world would soon exhaust nonrenewable resources such as oil and minerals have proved mostly false, for new reserves have been discovered and there has been a shift toward less material-intensive products and services. Nevertheless, pollution and waste continue to exceed the earth's sink capacities to absorb and recycle them, and there is increasing deterioration of renewables such as water, topsoil, forests, fishing grounds, and species biodiversity.

Other types of social dukkha should not be overlooked, however.

"Suffering," the usual English translation for *dukkha*, is not very enlightening, especially today, when those of us who live in wealthy countries have many ways to entertain and distract ourselves. The point of the Buddhist term is that we nonetheless experience a basic dissatisfaction, a dis-ease, which continues to fester. That there is something inherently frustrating about our lives is not accidental or coincidental. It is the nature of an unawakened mind to be bothered about something. At the core of our being we feel a free-floating anxiety, which has no particular object but can plug into any problematic situation. We may try to evade this anxiety by dulling ourselves with alcohol, tobacco or other drugs, television, consumerism, sex, and so forth, or we may become preoccupied with various goals we pursue, but the anxiety is always there; and when we slow down enough to become sensitive to what is occurring in our minds, we become aware of it—which is one reason we do not like to slow down.

This implies that everything we normally understand as suffering is only a subset—for some of us a relatively small subset—of dukkha. The Pali sutras

distinguish dukkha into three different types.[10] The first, *dukkha-dukkhata,*
includes everything that we usually think of as suffering: all physical, emotional, and mental pain or discomfort, including being separated from people we like to be with, and being stuck with those we do not. This also includes
the types of social dukkha mentioned above.

A second and different type is *viparinama-dukkhata,* the dukkha that arises
from impermanence, from knowing that nothing lasts forever and most
things do not last long. Even when we are thoroughly enjoying ourselves, we
know the moment will not last, and there is something frustrating about that
awareness. However delicious that ice cream may taste, we know the last bite
is coming soon—and even if we buy another cone, it does not taste as good
because we begin to feel sated.

The most problematic dukkha of this type is, of course, death: not the physical pain of dying (that is included in the first type of dukkha) but the awareness that I will die. This awareness of our inevitable end often pervades and
colors everything we do—so thoroughly that it poisons life. Insofar as I am
afraid to die, I also become unable to live. To live fully is not possible when we
are hypersensitive to the fact that danger and maybe death lurk around every
corner, because any little accident could be our last.

Most of us are familiar with the social dukkha-dukkhata described above—
the effects of an increasing worldwide gap between rich and poor, a deteriorating biosphere, and so forth. Is there an equivalent viparinama-dukkhata for
society as a whole? This brings us back to what Ernest Becker wrote about the
collective consequences of death denial, especially in his last book, *Escape from
Evil.* In addition to the more obvious types of increasing suffering summarized in the United Nations Human Development Reports, there are growing
social problems often explained as a consequence of weakening family and
community bonds in the developed world. But is something else, maybe less
evident because more discomforting, implicated in this breakdown? Liechty's
gloss on Becker's thesis, part of which was quoted earlier, continues by reflecting on the social effects of doubting our collective immortality project:

> Hence arises in such societies a cultural malaise or anomie on one hand,
> and a frantic, meaning-grabbing compulsiveness on the other hand, as
> the cultural immortality ideologies no longer function to keep mortality
> anxiety at bay. Lacking any one plausible, widely-accepted immortality
> narrative, any "sacred canopy," many people desperately attach themselves

to ersatz immortality ideologies—fundamentalisms of all sorts, nostalgia politics, technologism, pyrrhic tragedies such as "heroic" school shootings, or, following the truncated, material cultural narrative to its (il)logical conclusion, people begin to pile up (or fantasize about) heretofore insane levels of capitalist accumulation and material display.[11]

All of these are a direct result of decaying immortality ideologies, and Liechty points to something quite important and usually overlooked. The West's gradual loss of belief in an afterlife has often been presented as a sign of our this-worldly maturity; less often do we reflect on its psychic costs, which are collective as well as individual. The twentieth century, by far the most violent in history, supports Nietzsche's prediction of a nihilistic age resulting from our religious skepticism, and it remains to be seen whether the twenty-first century will be any better.

Any account of our increasing social dukkha needs to consider such psychological (or spiritual) factors as well as the more obvious economic and ecological issues. Are they related? Liechty's final comment on insane levels of capitalist accumulation reminds us how obscene it is that 497 people monopolize more of the earth's resources than are available to half of the world's 6.1 billion people. Many critics ask why we support an economic system that allows this to happen; another issue, however, is why anyone would *want* to become so wealthy. (How many meals a day can *you* eat?) If a preoccupation with making much more money than you can possibly spend is neurotic, then there is also something neurotic about a society that encourages this preoccupation by making such people into role models and cultural heroes.

According to Becker our collective fascination with wealth amounts to a new immortality project. "Money becomes the distilled value of all existence…a single immortality symbol, a ready way of relating the increase of oneself to all the important objects and events in one's world."[12] For Buddhism, however, there is a somewhat different way to understand this socially maintained delusion, because another interpretation is implied by the third type of dukkha.

That third type is *sankhara-dukkhata,* dukkha "from conditioned states," although in this case the meaning is not as clear in the early Buddhist texts. "Conditioned states" apparently refers to the *skandha*s, the five components of the self—or, more precisely, those physical and mental processes whose interaction creates our sense of self. So this dukkha has something to do with the doctrine of anatta, the strange but essential Buddhist claim that our sense of subjectivity does not correspond to any real ontological self—or in the (post)modern terms I have been using, the claim that the sense of self is a construct.

Contemporary psychology makes such a doctrine seem somewhat less perverse by providing some homegrown handles on what remains a very counterintuitive claim. In this regard Buddhism seems to have anticipated the more recent and reluctant conclusions of psychoanalysis: guilt and anxiety are not adventitious but intrinsic to the ego. Anatta suggests that our dukkha ultimately derives from a repression even more immediate than death-fear: the suspicion that *I* am not real. For Buddhism, the ego is not a self-existing consciousness but a fragile sense of self that suspects and dreads its own no-thing-ness. This third type of dukkha motivates our conditioned consciousness to try to ground itself—that is, I want to make myself *real.* Since the sense of self is a construct, however, it can real-ize itself (or rather, *try* to realize itself) only by objectifying itself (securing itself as an object) in the world. That makes the ego-self, in effect, a never ending project to objectify itself in some way—something that, unfortunately, our conditioned, ever changing consciousness cannot do, anymore than a hand can grasp itself or an eye see itself.

The consequence of this perpetual failure is that the sense of self is shadowed by a sense of lack. What Freud called "the return of the repressed" in the distorted form of a symptom links this basic yet hopeless project with the symbolic ways we try to make ourselves feel real *in* the world. We experience this deep sense of lack as the feeling that "there is something wrong with me," yet that feeling manifests, and we respond to it, in many different ways: I'm not rich enough, not loved enough, not powerful enough, not published enough (for academics!), and so forth. Our root anxiety is eager to objectify into fear *of* something, because then we have particular ways to cope with particular feared things. The difficulty, however, is that no objectification can ever satisfy us if it is not really an object we want.

In this way Buddhism shifts our focus from the terror of death (our primal repression, according to Becker) to the anguish of a groundlessness experienced here and now. The problem is not so much that we will die, but that we do not feel real now. If so, what does this third type of dukkha imply socially? Is there a communal version of sankhara-dukkhata? In *Escape from Evil* Becker argues that society is a collective immortality project. Can it also be understood as a collective *reality* project, a group effort to ground ourselves? That issue, among others, is addressed in chapter 8. An affirmative answer casts a somewhat different light on the loss of our sacred canopies. If religious worldviews provide us with transcendentally validated projects that promise to make us real (i.e., various types of supernatural salvation), the decline of faith in such collective canopies can only lead to more frantic and desperate attempts to real-ize ourselves.

It needs to be emphasized, however, that this is only *one* interpretation of Buddhist teachings about anatta and dukkha, which takes into account recent psychotherapeutic theory and Becker's existential anthropology. If Buddhism is to thrive as a living tradition in the modern world, rather than simply use traditional categories to repeat traditional claims, then such interdisciplinary attempts are necessary—and the more the merrier! In the encounter between Buddhism and (post)modernity, a diversity of interpretations is to be welcomed. Over time, some will be seen as more viable and helpful than others. Given the variety of Buddhist schools that have flourished in Asia, there is little reason to think that this process will eventually lead to—or that there is need for—only one modern version of Buddhism.

To say it again, perhaps the main reason for Buddhism's successful diversity in Asia has been its pragmatism. Buddhism is not primarily a philosophy, nor even (by some criteria) a religion. It is a path we follow to end our dukkha. The most important thing, therefore, is to present the teachings in a form that encourages people to follow that path and enables them to do so. Cross-culturally we find a certain consistency to human dukkha but great variation in the ways different Buddhist cultures have symbolized it and institutionalized the path for ending it. This practical approach to addressing dukkha may be traced back to Shakyamuni himself. Soon after establishing the *sangha* (community of monks), he declined to formalize his teachings into any official language(e.g., Sanskrit). Instead, he sent out his disciples in different directions, to teach the *Dharma* in whatever language was suitable.

This pragmatism applies to the Buddhist teachings themselves. Many sutras in the Pali canon attest to Shakyamuni's lack of interest in metaphysical speculation. Some questions—Does a Buddha exist after death? Is the universe eternal or infinite?—he declined to answer, declaring that he had only one thing to teach: dukkha and how to end it. Today such an anti-metaphysical attitude toward theory has become quite postmodern. The failure of the structuralist approach in the human sciences has led to another conception of what theory is and what it can do, an approach David Scott has summarized as follows:

> By "theory" (at least what I have been able to make of it) is meant that diverse combination of textual or interpretive (or "reading") strategies— among them, deconstruction, feminism, genealogy, psychoanalysis, post-marxism—that, from about the early 1970s or so had initiated a challenge to the protocols of a general hermeneutics....
>
> Theory, in this sense, offered itself as de-disciplinary, as in fact anti-disciplinary, the virtual undoer of disciplinary self-identities. It offered itself as a mobile and nomadic field of critical operations without a proper name, and therefore without a distinctive domain of objects. Indeed what theory went after was precisely the assumption (common to the disci-plines and their rage for "method") of the authentic self-authoring pres-ence of things, of histories, of cultures, of selves, the assumption of stable essences, in short, that could be made to speak themselves once and for all through the transparency of an unequivocal and analytical language. On theory's account there could be no final description, no end to re-descrip-tion, no ultimate perspective which could terminate once and for all the possibility of another word on the matter. [13]

Since such critical theory cannot pretend to mirror the objective nature of society in categories that reveal without distorting, its own truth becomes an inextricable part of the phenomena it seeks to explain. As Geuss puts it:

> A full-scale social theory...will form part of its own object-domain. That is, a theory is a theory about (among other things) agents' beliefs about their society, but it is itself such a belief. So if a theory of society is to give an exhaustive account of the beliefs agents in the society have, it will have to give an account of itself as one such belief. [14]

This nomadic conception of theory continues to discomfort many in the social sciences. Less known is that a very similar conception of theory as self-reflexive and self-negating has been important to Buddhism from its begin-nings, and essential to Buddhist philosophy since at least the time of Nagarjuna (second century C.E.), the most important Buddhist philosopher and arguably the most important figure in the Buddhist tradition after

Shakyamuni himself. Since it emphasized the contemplative need to let go of concepts, Buddhism could not avoid self-consciousness about its own employment of theoretical constructs. We have already noticed that Shakyamuni compared his own teachings to a raft that, once we have used it to cross the river of birth and death to the far shore of nirvana, we should then abandon.

Nagarjuna went further by declining to present any view of his own. His chapter on the nature of nirvana in the *Mulamadhyamikakarika* concludes that "ultimate serenity is the coming to rest of all ways of taking things, the repose of named things; no truth has been taught by a Buddha for anyone, anywhere."[15] This applies even to the crucial concept of shunyata (emptiness), which Nagarjuna used to deconstruct the self-existence of things. Shunyata too is relative to those supposed things; it is a heuristic term, nothing more than a way to demonstrate "the exhaustion of all theories and views," and those who insist on making shunyata into a theory about the nature of things are said to be incurable.[16]

Nagarjuna's self-negating conception of conception reverberates through subsequent Buddhism. The sixth Zen ancestor Huineng, revered as the greatest of all Zen masters, also refused to offer Buddhism as a transparent, mirrorlike teaching about reality: "If I tell you that I have a system of Dharma [teaching] to transmit to others, I am cheating you. What I do to my disciples is to liberate them from their own bondage with such devices as the case may need."[17] Suitable answers are given according to the temperament of the inquirer. Insofar as truth is a matter of grasping the categories that accurately and finally reflect some objective reality, all truth is error on the Buddhist path.

The crucial issue is whether or not our search for truth—be it the personal, subjective claim about my own "nature" or some structural truth in the human sciences—is an attempt to ground ourselves by fixating on certain concepts. When there is such a compulsion to grasp the truth that grasps reality, certain ideas tend to become seductive—that is, ideologies. The difference between samsara and nirvana is that samsara is the world experienced as a sticky web of attachments that seem to offer something we lack—a grounding for our groundless sense of self. Intellectually, that seductive quality manifests as a battleground of conflicting ideologies (social theories as much as religious beliefs) competing for our allegiance, each of which purports to provide the mind with a sure grasp on the world.

In other words, ideology is another attempt to objectify ourselves, by understanding ourselves objectively. On this account, the need for theory, and the difficulty many have with unanchored critique, is the intellectual's version of the dialectic noticed earlier between security and freedom. The Buddhist alternative, as Huineng makes clear, is not to rid oneself of all thought but to think in a different way, without needing to ground oneself thereby. Such a "non-abiding" wisdom can wander freely among an overlapping plurality of truths without needing to fixate on any of them. As in the traditional Zen dialogues, our inquiry becomes a mobile, nomadic play that works to undo both the supposed objectivity of the objects studied and the supposed self-identities of those subjects—us—who study them.

Such an approach is reflexively aware that it always "forms part of its own object-domain," as Geuss puts it, yet this does not become a problem because such teachings are designed to self-negate. Since Buddhist conceptual systems form only part of a spiritual path that emphasizes meditation and mindfulness—during which one lets go of all conceptualizing—Buddhist practice works to free us from all ideology including itself. Jacques Derrida speaks of the necessity to lodge oneself within traditional conceptuality in order to destroy it, which expresses nicely why Nagarjuna insists that the everyday world must be accepted in order to point to the higher truth that negates it.[18] According to Madhyamika Buddhism, shunyata is like an antidote that expels poison from our bodies and then expels itself, for if the antidote stays inside to poison us, we are no better off than before.

To sum up, Buddhism's pragmatic focus on dukkha is consistent with the postmodern attitude toward theory, because it too is suspicious of any grand theory that purports to offer some final synthesis, a master set of categories that supersedes all others. The basic limitation of all theory is simply that even very good ones do not remove our dukkha. Conceptual systems are heuristic, valid insofar as they are useful to us—for Buddhism, insofar as they help us end our dukkha. The best ones, therefore, are also open to revision, adapting to changing circumstances including new ways of understanding oneself. This psychotherapeutic interpretation of anatta—as a sense of lack that perpetually haunts our constructed, ungrounded sense of self—will survive only if it helps us understand and transform ourselves. If it fails to do that, we need to find new categories employing fresh ways of understanding.

Buddhist theory forms part of its own object-domain, not only because it is a self-reflexive belief about beliefs, but because it is itself an expression of the ungraspable ground that it theorizes about. The ultimate reason why there can be no ultimate theory that represents the whole is because we can never stand outside the world to re-present it objectively. The part can never grasp or contain the whole; nor does it need to. Our concepts are not only part of the world, they are manifestations of it. Buddhist awakening does not grasp or otherwise resolve the essential mysteriousness of our being in the world. It opens us up to that mystery, a mystery that is an essential aspect of the meaning of "sacred." In practice, this means that the broadest context for all our intellectual efforts is a wonder in the face of a world that always exceeds our ideas about it. That excess does not signify any defect in our understanding. Rather, it is the source of our understanding, allowing for a perpetual bubbling-up of insights and images—when we do not cling to the ones that we have already become comfortable with.

What Is the Cause of Social Dukkha?

According to Shakyamuni, the cause of our individual dukkha is *tanha,* usually translated as "craving" but more literally as "thirst." Nothing we drink can ever assuage our tanha, because that thirst is due to an emptiness at the core of our being. It is as if that core were a bottomless pit, something like the black holes that astronomers believe lie at the center of most galaxies. No matter how much we try to fill up our own black hole with this or that, everything is swallowed up and disappears into it.

It is bottomless because our sense of self is an ungroundable construct. Notice, however, that the second noble truth does not identify our problem as groundlessness. The problem is "thirst"—not the emptiness at the core of our being but our incessant efforts to fill that hole up, because we *experience* it as a sense of lack that must be filled up. The problem is not that I am unreal but that I keep trying to make myself real in ways that never work. This implies that there might be another way to experience our groundlessness.

The Buddha taught tanha as a general truth about the human condition, yet the specific ways we try to make ourselves feel more real are culturally conditioned. Traditionally, religion fulfills the role of telling us what our lack is and how to resolve it. For example, Christianity explains it as due to our sins, including the Original Sin that each of us inherits from Adam. The solution to sin is variously understood, but for Christians it involves accepting Christ, who reassures us that our sense of lack will be resolved when we are reunited with God. Whether or not that story persuades us, it has become less important in the modern world, in which we are inclined to seek this-worldly solutions to our sense of lack.

Some of those solutions are individualistic (fame, romance, personal power and wealth), others more collective (nationalism and other ideologies). The events of the last century have discredited Marxism in the eyes of most people, but corporate capitalism (allied with what might be called technologism) is also a this-worldly ideology that promises to resolve our sense of lack with an abundance that can fulfill all our needs. From a Buddhist perspective, what those two materialistic ideologies have in common is more significant than their differences. In response to our skepticism about any supernatural salvation, socialism and capitalism both offer us a naturalistic salvation in the future, when we (or at least some of us) will become happy because our desires are satisfied. The Buddhist emphasis on tanha stands in stark contrast to this. Happiness cannot be gained by satisfying desire, for our thirst means there is no end to it. Happiness can be achieved only by *transforming* desire. Mustn't that also be true for the collective happiness of society? There is a basic level of human need for food, shelter, and medical care that should be provided for everyone, but the Buddhist perspective is that we are otherwise mistaken to strive for an economic solution to human unhappiness.

For Buddhism our basic thirst manifests in different ways, usually organized into what are known as the three roots of evil or the three poisons: *lobha,* greed; *dosa,* ill will; and *moha,* delusion. The familiar Tibetan Buddhist mandala known as the Wheel of Life symbolizes these three as a cock, a snake, and a pig at the axle of a wheel representing samsara, the six worlds of dukkha. The animals are depicted as biting each other because the three roots of evil are interconnected. For example, my greed tends to generate ill will, either in others (when it incites me to take what is theirs) or in myself (when they will not give it to me); this both presupposes and reinforces the basic delusion of separation between us. One way to summarize the Buddhist path is that it involves transforming the evil roots into their positive counterparts: greed into generosity *(dana)*, ill will into compassion *(karuna)*, and delusion into wisdom *(prajna)*.

Buddhism, like the Abrahamic traditions, sometimes personifies evil as a being: Mara the deceiver. Yet Mara's role and signficance as an embodiment has been comparatively limited, because Buddhism emphasizes the *roots* of evil, not the evil itself. This accords with the Buddhist emphasis on causality: all things, including evil deeds, originate (and pass away) according to conditions. Can this traditional approach also provide insight into our probematic social institutions? The following chapters attempt to answer that question.

What Is the End of Social Dukkha?

By no coincidence the chapters in this book circle around the same insights into the ultimate source of our social problems and therefore the nature of any genuine solution. Collectively as well as individually, institutionally as well as personally, greed must be transformed into generosity, ill will into loving-kindness, ignorance into wisdom. The sense of duality between ourselves and the world feeds our insecurity and therefore our preoccupation with power, which we seek in order to secure ourselves. The unfortunate fact that we never feel secure enough is experienced as a lack of sufficient power. The Buddhist solution to this delusion of self is to realize our interpenetrating nonduality with the world, which is wisdom, and actualize it in the way we live, which is love. Yet how does this resolve our sense of lack?

The third ennobling truth is *nirodha,* literally the "cessation" of dukkha, the fact that our dukkha can come to an end. The early Buddhist term more often used to describe this cessation is *nirvana* (*nibbana* in Pali). But what nirvana actually involves is not altogether clear in the early texts. Although mentioned many times in the Pali canon, the Buddha did not say very much about what it is. When asked whether an *arhat* (one who has attained nirvana) survives after death, Shakyamuni declined to answer, saying that the question was not helpful. The implication is that such discussions are a waste of time or, worse, in that they involve intellectual speculation, whereas nirvana cannot be attained by grasping at any theories about it. Most of the descriptions found in the Pali sutras are in negative terms: nirvana as the end of dukkha, the end of tanha, and the like. Evidently the vagueness is intentional. Shakyamuni's attitude seems to have been that if we want to know what nirvana is, there can be no substitute for experiencing it ourselves.

Etymology is again helpful. Literally, *nirvana* means something like "blown out"—but what exactly is it that is blown out? The answer is sometimes expressed nihilistically: there is no more dukkha because the self is blown out, which means an arhat's death is extinction, without the dukkha of any future rebirth. More often, nirvana has been understood as some type of transcendental salvation: an enlightened person attains or realizes some higher reality. Both of these interpretations seem incompatible with what the Buddha himself emphasized: there can be no extinction of the self because there never was a self to be extinguished, and there can be no salvation for the self because there never was a self to be saved.

Perhaps the meaning of "blown out" is better understood in terms of what has already been said about our sense of lack, the "black hole" at the core of our being. The third truth reassures us that something can happen to our black hole, that we are not fated to forever trying to fill a bottomless pit. Although we cannot get rid of the hollowness at our core, we can experience it differently.

It turns out that our hollowness is not so awful after all; it is not something that needs to be filled up. We cannot make our selves real in the ways we have been trying—the bottomless pit swallows up all our efforts—but we can realize something about the nature of the hole that frees us from trying to fill it up. We do not need to make ourselves real, because we have always been real. I do not need to ground myself, because I have always been grounded: not, however, as a separate, skin-encapsulated ego somewhere behind my eyes or between my ears and looking out at the world—for there has never been such a self. Rather, the bottomless, festering black hole can transform into a fountain and become a refreshing spring gushing up at the core of my being. The bottomlessness of this spring means something quite different than before. Now it refers to the fact that I can never understand the source of this spring, for the simple reason that *I am* this spring. It is nothing other than my true nature. And my inability to reflexively grasp that source, to ground and realize myself by filling up that hole, is no longer a problem, because there is no need to grasp it. The point is to *live* that spring, to let my fountain gush forth. My thirst (the second noble truth) is "blown out" because a letting go at the core of my being means my sense of lack evaporates as this fountain springs up.

Instead of being a constant anxiety that haunts me, the nothingness at my core turns out to be my freedom to be this, to do that. This liberation reveals my true nature to be formless. Sometimes the fountain is *just this*. Sometimes it becomes *just that*. The origin of the fountain itself always remains unfathomable, because that source is never fixated or bound by any particular form or activity that I engage in.

There is a problem, however, with this metaphor: the image of a fountain at our core is still dualistic. Our core, our formless ground, seems to become even more separate from the world "outside." The actual experience is just the opposite, because the duality between inside and outside disappears when "I" do not need to try to ground myself by grasping at some phenomenon *in* the world. Of course there are still thoughts, feelings, and so forth, yet they are not the attributes of a self "inside." The fountain gushes forth as the spontaneity of words and acts—not so much as "my" spontaneity as a characteristic of the world of which my particular fountain is an inseparable part.

This transformation includes another aspect of the awakening experience especially emphasized in Mahayana Buddhism: the spontaneous wish for others to wake up and realize their formless true nature. On the one hand, awakening includes the realization that there is nothing that needs to be gained, for nothing has ever been lacking. My bottomless pit never needed filling, inasmuch as my groundlessness just needed to be realized as a different kind of grounding. On the other hand, however, I awaken from my own lack—from my dukkha, from my futile preoccupation with trying to make myself real—into a world full of beings similarly empty but suffering from their delusions of self and from their vain attempts to ground themselves and feel more real. A liberated person naturally wants to help the world, because he or she does not feel separate from it. This point is essential because it also provides the foundation for Buddhist social engagement. As Joanna Macy puts it, there is no need to ask why you take care of your own body.[19]

What are the social implications of such an awakening? Can there be a collective parallel? Historically, the classical and most often cited example of a Buddhist society has been the reign of the Indian king Ashoka in the third century B.C.E. Whether or not he himself was enlightened, he seems to have been genuinely motivated by deep compassion for all living beings. Appalled by the carnage during his conquest of the Kalingas, he converted to Buddhism and instituted reforms that remain exemplary. The most important were his emphases on moral self-conquest (dharmavijaya), nonviolence, social welfare, and religious pluralism. Ashoka's policies, as recorded in his rock-inscribed edicts, encouraged nonviolence toward animals as well as humans. Pillar Edict V gives a long list of animal species under protection and issues hunting bans; Edict I, which records in a touching way his struggle to reduce his consumption of meat, provides some of the earliest historical evidence of vegetarianism. According to other pillars, Ashoka's welfare policies subsidized medicine to the extent of importing doctors and herbs from abroad, building rest houses and hospices for the poor and sick, looking after convicts and their families, dispatching special ministers to investigate judicial harshness or corruption, freeing prisoners, and so forth.

Perhaps the most relevant for our multicultural societies was Ashoka's restraint in not making Buddhism a state religion. He empowered officers to look after the welfare of all spiritual sects, providing an early example of church-state separation. From Edict XII:

> King Priyadarsi [Ashoka] honors men of all faiths, members of religious
> orders and laymen alike, with gifts and various marks of esteem. Yet he
> does not value either gifts or honors as much as growth in the qualities
> essential to religion in men of all faiths. This growth may take many
> forms, but its root is in guarding one's speech to avoid extolling one's own
> faith and disparaging the faith of others improperly, or, when the occasion
> is appropriate, immoderately. The faiths of others all deserve to be hon-
> oured for one reason or another. By honoring them, one exalts one's own
> faith and at the same time performs a service of faith to others…. There-
> fore concord alone is commendable, for through concord men may learn
> and respect the conception of Dharma accepted by others. King Priyadarsi
> desires men of all faiths to know each other's doctrines and to acquire
> sound doctrines…. The objective of these measures is the promotion of
> each man's particular faith and the glorification of the Dharma. [20]

The spirit of open-minded tolerance this edict breathes is remarkable even
today. Nevertheless, the model provided by his India—a king ruling over an
agrarian empire—can be of only limited inspiration to socially engaged Buddhists living in postindustrial Information Age societies. The following chapters offer suggestions for institutional change, but they do not add up to a
vision of what might be called an awakened society. Without pretending to
adumbrate one, let me emphasize three points that I believe are essential to
the construction of any Buddhism-compatible alternative.

First, it is necessary to remember that Buddhism does not offer happiness
through the fulfillment of desire. For that reason, a solution to our dukkha is
not to be found in economic or scientific development, whether it be capitalist, socialist, or some other technocratic version. Since our thirst cannot be
sated, it must be transformed. This means that the social solution we seek
cannot be socially engineered. It also means that our collective preoccupation with economic growth and ever increasing consumption must also be
transformed. But into what?

That brings us to the second point. From a Buddhist perspective, it is essential that any satisfactory social arrangement emphasize meeting the minimal
physical needs of its members for food, shelter, clothing, and medical care—
the traditional four requisites of the *bhikkhu* (monk) and *bhikkhuni* (nun).
Beyond that, however, providing increasing sense gratification is not the most
important function of a social system; on the contrary, a preoccupation with

such desire is problematic because of its negative effects on our dukkha. More important is to encourage what Stephen Batchelor has called a "culture of awakening."[21] As the example of Ashoka shows, this does not mean promoting Buddhism but rather valuing and encouraging ethical, psychological, and spiritual development, which includes self-realization and actualizing that realization in society.

In other words, the primary concern of a culture of awakening would be education. Today the values of a liberal education are increasingly subordinated to, if not swallowed by, the demands of the marketplace. Schooling is becoming little more than exam preparation and job training. This deference to market values reflects our preoccupation with money, which from a Buddhist perspective is upside down. In a spiritually healthy society, the most important institutions, which would receive the greatest social attention and therefore the greatest share of resources, would be schools. Instead of economic development as the ultimate goal or end-in-itself, such a society would evaluate itself according to how well educated (in the broadest sense of the term) its members were and wanted to be. This understanding of education includes culture, not in the sense of entertainment but in the root meaning of self-cultivation.

The technologies already available can and often do provide us, if we are affluent, with a cornucopia of personal possibilities that exceeds our ability to take advantage of them and enjoy them. The fact that we are personally preoccupied with acquiring even more, and collectively preoccupied with further technological and economic advances, indicates not an ever-improving condition of well-being but the lack of any other vision of individual and social development to fill the void left by our fading belief in God and an afterlife.

Third and finally, such a Buddhist vision is not utopian. There is no question of recovering a lost paradise or "Golden Age," because we recognize that there never was one. Lacking an all-knowing, all-powerful, and all-loving God, Buddhism has no need to postulate a Garden of Eden before we sinned, or an ideal human existence before the advent of dukkha. Shakyamuni declared that he could not trace the beginnings of dukkha. Buddhist practice reveals something about myself and the world right here and now. The goal is not to attain something but to realize what we have been ignoring (hence the problem of "ignorance"). The emphasis on transience applies to civilizations as well. Whether or not societies improve, they will not stop changing. For Buddhism the aim is not some new situation to be created in the future, but something to be uncovered about the nature of the present moment when we experience our lives in the world without the three poisons.

What is perhaps most remarkable about this process of letting go of illusions, including the illusion of selfhood, is that when we do it, or rather when we practice in such a way that it happens to us, then extraordinary changes occur in our lives without our trying to fit into some idealized model of what we think we should be. Would the same be true collectively? Perhaps this attitude is consistent with certain anarchist and Green approaches that would remove external authority over local communities and empower them to restructure themselves more spontaneously.

In other words, Buddhist teachings do not imply any particular or detailed vision of the new political and economic relationships that will remedy our institutionalized dukkha. Certain principles are more or less obvious—for example, nonviolence, a basic level of social welfare, emphasis on education—yet these allow for many possible social structures. Even as there is little reason to think that one form of Buddhism will supplant all others in the West, so there is little reason to expect all the world's cultures to follow one model of human development—unless it is forced upon them. Awakened people, and people who value awakening, are free to accept or reconstruct a variety of political and economic arrangements that are consistent with a personal and social emphasis on spiritual awakening.

What Path Can We Follow to End Social Dukkha?

With the last ennobling truth we move from Buddhist social theory to Buddhist social praxis. The fourth truth gives us the way (*marga* in Sanskrit) to wake up, the path we follow in order to realize and liberate the fountain springing up at our core. Shakyamuni taught an eightfold path: right understanding, right intention, right speech, right action, right livelihood, right effort, right mindfulness, and right meditation. Mahayana emphasizes developing the six *paramitas*, literally the six "goings-beyond," because they involve perfecting ourselves to the highest (hence to a "transcendental") degree: perfecting our generosity, morality, patience, effort, meditation, and wisdom. Such perfection does not imply extremism. Buddhism is known as the middle way because it avoids both hedonism (indulging the senses) and asceticism ("starving" the senses). This middle way is not halfway between the two, however. It focuses on the mind rather than the senses, because that is where our basic problem is.

How do mindfulness and meditation lead to awakening, to a "turning around" at the core? As we have seen, Buddhism does not provide us with something to fill up our hole. It shows us how to stop trying to fill it. To be mindful (focusing on one thing at a time) and to meditate (focusing on one's mental processes) both involve no longer trying to satisfy one's thirst. Instead, we slow down and become more aware of that thirst, without evasion and without judgment. When I stop experiencing my emptiness as a problem to be solved, then, mysteriously—because *I* do not do it—something begins to happen to that hole, and therefore to me. Realization happens when I let go of myself, transforming the bottomless hole at my core. The problem—my anguished sense of groundlessness—becomes the solution as something wells up spontaneously from that core.

Can this process of individual transformation be generalized for collective transformation as well?

For those who see the necessity of radical change, the first implication of Buddhist social praxis is the obvious need to work on ourselves as well as the social system. If we have not begun to transform our own greed, ill will, and delusion, our efforts to address their institutionalized forms are likely to be useless, or worse. We may have some success in challenging the sociopolitical order, but that will not lead to an awakened society. Recent history provides us with many examples of revolutionary leaders, often well intentioned, who eventually reproduced the evils they fought against. In the end, one gang of thugs has been replaced by another.

From a Buddhist perspective, there is nothing surprising about that. If I do not struggle with the greed in my own heart, it is quite likely that, once in power, I too will be inclined to take advantage of the situation to serve my own interests. If I do not acknowledge the ill will in my own heart, I am more than likely to project it onto those who obstruct me. If I remain unaware that my sense of duality is a dangerous delusion, I will understand the problem of social change as the need for me to dominate the sociopolitical order. Add a conviction of my good intentions, along with a conviction of my superior understanding of the situation, and one has a recipe for disaster.

This suggests a social principle—the commitment to nonviolence—that for Buddhism is vital, for several reasons. Emphasis on transience implies another nonduality, that between means and ends. Peace is not only the goal, it must also be the way; or as Thich Nhat Hanh and Mahaghosananda have put it, peace is every step. We ourselves must be the peace we want to create.

A model here is Gandhi, who with some justice may be considered a twenti-eth-century Buddha.

There is another good reason to be nonviolent: it is more likely to be effective. The people who administer our economic and political institutions, and who also happen to benefit (in the narrow sense) the most from those arrangements, control an awesomely destructive military power and the instruments of police surveillance. Fantasies of a violent revolution that would replace them with a just social order need to be replaced with the revolutionary realization that the struggle for social change is primarily a spiritual one, a clash of worldviews and moral visions. It is important to avoid the violent backlash that violence invites and, even more imperative to preclude the "moral backlash" that occurs when the focus of a challenge shifts from an untenable worldview to the violence used to challenge it. In the late 1960s and early 1970s the violent posturing of radical groups such as the Weathermen and the Black Panthers was suicidal. We should not have any illusions that nonviolence will make this struggle easy. Our leaders—who might more accurately be called our "rulers"—also have powerful media and persuasive public relations machines to inculcate their worldview. How quickly the presidential coup d'etat in the 2000 U.S. elections was forgotten in the aftermath of September 11! How quickly, again, corporate scandals such as Enron and WorldCom, which threatened to implicate the White House, were forgotten as the focus shifted to invading Saddam's Iraq!

From a Buddhist perspective, the most fundamental problem with present social arrangements is that they do not really make people happy—even those who benefit the most—because they are based on a defective premise, a wrong understanding of how dukkha may be ended. To encourage a culture of awakening, that focus must not be lost. If we become angry and want to act out that anger, Tibetan Buddhism provides an apt metaphor: to become angry at someone and want to injure someone is like trying to hurt someone else by stabbing yourself in the chest. Another Buddhist image is of acting angrily as throwing hot coals at an adversary: regardless of whether you hit your adversary, picking up the coals, you are sure to burn your own hand. A deeper understanding reduces our sense of separation from other people, including those in a position of power relative to us. Gandhi always treated the British authorities in India with respect. He never tried to dehumanize them. The more nasty a person may be, the more he or she is deluded, and it makes no difference whether he or she has any inkling of it. For Buddhism such ignorance is never bliss.

Not to kill is the first of the *five precepts* extracted from the eightfold path. The others are not to steal, not to lie, not to engage in sensuality (usually understood as improper sex), and not to use intoxicating drugs that cause heedlessness. These precepts are not commandments that we are required to follow. They are vows that we take to develop ourselves, in the belief that not to live according to these principles hurts ourselves most of all. The precepts also provide another way to make the Buddhist critique of institutionalized greed, ill will, and delusion, for today it has become more obvious that the precepts have collective implications too.

Today the precept against killing clearly implicates the militarization of contemporary societies, especially in the United States, whereby a large percentage of our resources continues to be devoted to the development, sale, and use of increasingly horrific weapons. The U.S. Defense Department now spends a billion dollars a day, roughly equivalent to the total amount spent on defense by the next fifteen largest military nations. According to a congressional study, in the year 2000 world arms sales grew by 8 percent over the previous year, to nearly $36.9 billion; over half of that, about $18.6 billion, was sold by the United States. Many influential people continue to benefit from the widespread belief that violence is an acceptable way to resolve disagreement. The violence of secretive terrorist groups is minor compared to the large-scale terrorism (also against innocents) that modern states use to enforce their control and extend their influence. But it is not only the death and injury inflicted on humans that violates the Buddhist precept against killing; the precept has always been understood to apply to other sentient beings as well. The imminent collapse of ecosystems and the accelerating extinction of plant and animal species require a more ecologically engaged attempt to embody this precept.

Not stealing has traditionally been defined as "not taking what is not given." Today it is arguable that our economic system is based upon stealing, not only because of the heavy debt burden borne by many of the world's poorest countries, but more fundamentally because corporate globalization is commodifying the whole earth and all its creatures into "natural resources" that it also tends to concentrate in the hands of a global elite.

Not lying seems simple enough to understand, if not to practice, yet today we have what might be considered "systemic lying," insofar as increasingly concentrated corporate media use their enormous influence not to inform and educate but to manipulate for the sake of their true purpose, the profits they earn. The result is that we are continually distracted and diverted by info-tainment and sports spectacles. Our national and international nervous systems are for sale to the highest bidder.

Not engaging in harmful sexual behavior is sometimes defined as "avoiding sex that causes pain to others." Except in Japan (and in some of the Japanese-derived American lineages), Buddhist monks and nuns are traditionally celibate; but celibacy is not prescribed for laypeople. Courtship, marriage, divorce, and birth control are secular matters scarcely addressed in the Buddhist teachings. That all of us have the same Buddha-nature implies not only the liberation and empowerment of women but opposition to all gender-based discrimination, including gay, lesbian, and transsexual rights. The widespread use of sexual imagery in advertising today, and more obviously the burgeoning international sex trades, can be considered violations of this precept.

Not using harmful intoxicants that "cloud the mind" traditionally refers to alcohol, but it applies to many other legal and illegal drugs as well. Today, however, no intoxicant clouds our minds more than the "never-enough" consumerism manipulated by a system that needs to keep creating markets for the goods it keeps overproducing. Thich Nhat Hanh understands this precept as "no abuse of delusion-producing substances," which can include televisions, Walkman stereos, cellular phones, the Internet, and many other technological devices that many of us are addicted to. One effect of silicon chip miniaturization has been to provide more opportunities to distract ourselves anytime and anyplace. If it is painful to stop and look at what our life has become—well, that is no longer a problem, because thanks to the wonders of modern science we can evade that predicament indefinitely.

In this fashion what might be called the five *social* precepts provide another way to evaluate the failure of our institutions. They are also useful because they thereby imply specific criteria for how those institutions need to be reformed: until they no longer violate these precepts. If *not killing* becomes a basic principle for challenging social injustice, what about the others? If it is important to address the forces of militarization nonviolently, are there parallels in the case of the other precepts? Do they also provide us with principles that need to be personally integrated in order to most directly and efficiently question institutionalized greed, ill will, and delusion?

If, for example, the social equivalent of stealing is an economic system that commodifies and monopolizes the earth's resources, following the social precept of *not stealing* involves not only challenging this system but, first of all, nurturing another system in our minds and lives: learning to tread lightly on the earth and its beings. Voluntary simplicity, choosing to reduce our consumption, will not by itself be enough to reform the economic order, yet simplifying our lives in this way is socially powerful because of the time and energy it liberates and, perhaps as important, because the example of this alternative lifestyle to others is important—especially if it is seen to reduce rather than aggravate our dukkha.

A similar approach can be applied to the other precepts. We follow the social precept of *not lying* by, first of all, refusing to allow our nervous systems to become addicted to the channels of communication that maintain the collective trance generally accepted as "social reality." In other words, we accept responsibility for liberating our own attention and clarifying our own awareness.

What is perhaps most remarkable about following these social precepts is that they are quite unremarkable—because many people, most of them not Buddhist, are already trying to live according to them. Gandhi, again, is an obvious and inspirational example. This suggests that the basic issue here might not be Buddhist principles so much as a different type of consciousness and lifestyle of which Buddhism is one example. Whether or not we consider ourselves Buddhists, attempting to embody these precepts encourages the same type of transformation: the sense of alienation between myself and the world (and other people in it) diminishes, and a sense of mutual responsibility naturally matures.

For Buddhism, then—or at least the understanding of Buddhism presented in this introduction—realizing and actualizing such nonduality remains the heart of the issue, because ultimately it is the sense of duality between ourselves and others that shores up the social structures institutionalizing greed, ill will, and delusion. The greatest challenge to those working for social transformation, therefore, is to find creative ways that enable more people to realize this simple truth and to embody it in their lives.

Mahayana Buddhism developed the teaching of *no-self* into the bodhisattva archetype, whose lack of self-preoccupation allows him or her to be wholly devoted to the salvation and welfare of others. As the example of Ashoka reminds us, it is not important that such devotion be characterized as Buddhist. Bodhisattvas and Buddhas do not need to think of themselves as Bodhisattvas and Buddhas; what is important is what they do, including their willingness to risk themselves for a greater good. When the Dalai Lama is asked what his religion is, he often replies, "My religion is compassion." From a Buddhist perspective, what we most need is not Buddhism but the wisdom that realizes our oneness with the world, and the loving-kindness that lives that wisdom.

The chapters that follow develop the above understanding of the four noble truths by considering how the three poisons have become institutionalized. Although there is considerable overlap among the poisons, chapters 2, 3, and 4 mainly address the problem of *institutionalized greed* in globalizing capitalism and the economic development of "undeveloped" societies. Chapters 5, 6, and 7 examine examples of *institutionalized ill will:* the new American "holy war" against terrorism, retributive justice systems, and the curious historical problem of Japanese samurai Zen. Chapters 8 and 9 reflect on two significant cases of *institutionalized delusion:* our collective fascination with biotechnology and our dualistic relationship with the earth.

In chapter 2, "Buddhism and Poverty," I ask whether Buddhism has anything special to contribute to our understanding of how to alleviate poverty. Buddhism is sometimes criticized for encouraging a nonmaterialistic way of life that goes against the grain of our main motivations, but it is actually more realistic than economic theory in the way it understands the sources of human ill-being and well-being. Its approach also reflects the ways most pre-modern communities have understood well-being, and the ways "undeveloped" societies today still do. From a Buddhist perspective, then, it is not surprising that the institutional efforts of the last fifty years have actually aggravated the social problems they were supposed to solve. Far from providing a solution, the conventional approach to development is better understood as the problem itself. Buddhism contextualizes the problem of poverty differently; it questions the assumptions that dominate our thinking about "undeveloped" societies.

Buddhism does not encourage poverty, yet it also recognizes that the single-minded pursuit of material wealth does not make human beings happy or even rich, for a world in which envy and miserliness predominate cannot be considered one in which poverty has been eliminated. When human beings gain an intense acquisitive drive for some object, that object becomes a cause of suffering. Such an object can be compared to the flame of a torch carried against the wind or to a pit of embers: it causes much anxiety but yields little satisfaction—an obvious truth we repress by turning our attention to another craved object. There is a fundamental and inescapable poverty built into a consumer society. For that reason, projects that seek to end poverty by "developing" an economy focused on consumption are grasping a snake by the wrong end. Unless they have been seduced by the utopian dream of a technological cornucopia, most "poor" people never become fixated on fantasies about all the things they might have. Their ends are an expression of the means available to them. It is presumptuous to assume that the only way to become happy is to get on the treadmill of a lifestyle dependent on the market and increasingly preoccupied with consumption.

We are also misled by our delusive thinking. Bipolar categories divide things into pairs of opposites. If I want to live a "pure" life, I will be preoccupied with avoiding impurity. In the same way, desire for wealth is inevitably shadowed by fear of poverty. One implication of this dialectic is that there is no such thing as a "poverty problem" that can be understood separately from a "wealth problem." Rather, we are inflicted with a wealth/poverty dualism. Global poverty is *conceptually* necessary if the world is to be completely commodified and monetarized. Traditional cultures must be redefined as obstacles to be overcome, and local elites must become dissatisfied with them, in order to create a class of more self-interested people as the vanguard of consumption. The poverty of others is also the benchmark by which we measure our own achievements. In other words, among the causes of poverty today are the delusions of the wealthy. Instead of focusing only on poverty, therefore, we also need to address the personal, social, and ecological costs of our obsession with wealth and growth.

We would do better to accept that the world can be enriched by a plurality of understandings about human ill-being and well-being. The neoliberal economic understanding of what happiness is and how to achieve it is only one vision among many. There is a social price to pay for the comforts and commodities neoliberalism promises, a price that we should not impose on others who have their own worldviews and values.

Chapter 3, "Pave the Planet or Wear Shoes?" reflects further on the kind of economic system such an attitude implies. Buddhism, like Christianity, lacks an intrinsic social theory, which means that we cannot look to its traditional texts for perspectives on contemporary issues such as the globalization of capitalism. Yet its teachings do have important economic implications that can help us understand and respond to the new world order being created by globalization.

Since individual and social values cannot be separated, one crucial issue is whether an economic system is conducive to the ethical and spiritual development of its participants. Those who defend capitalism argue that its emphasis on competition and personal gain is grounded in the fact that humans are fundamentally self-interested. Critics of capitalism reply that our human nature is more altruistic, so the general good is better promoted by emphasizing cooperative (e.g., social-democratic) policies. Early Buddhism avoids that debate by taking a different approach. Shakyamuni Buddha emphasized that we all have both wholesome and unwholesome traits *(kusala/akusala-mula)*. What is important is reducing our unwholesome characteristics—including "afflictive emotions" such as anger, pride, lust, greed, and envy—and developing the more wholesome ones.

From that perspective, capitalism seems to promote greed in two ways. The engine of the economic process is a continuous desire for profit, and in order to keep making that profit, consumers must continue wanting to consume more. A traditional Buddhist analogy speaks to this. What should we do about a world strewn with thorns and sharp stones? One solution is to pave over the entire earth, but a simpler alternative is to wear shoes. "Paving the whole planet" seems a good metaphor for our collective technocratic project. Without the wisdom of self-limitation, we may not be satisfied even when all the biosphere's resources have been exhausted. The other solution is to learn how to "wear shoes," so that our collective ends become an expression of the renewable means that the biosphere provides.

Approaching globalization from a non-Western perspective helps us to see that capitalism is neither natural nor inevitable; it is one historically conditioned way to understand and organize our material world. Its commodifications presuppose a sharp duality between humans and the rest of the earth. Value is created by our goals and desires; the rest of the world has no meaning except insofar as it serves human purposes. However natural this dualism now seems to us, for Buddhism it is one of our more probematic delusions, which lies at the heart of our dukkha.

Does this imply that capitalism is incompatible with Buddhism? Historically, Buddhism has been pragmatic and flexible regarding economic institutions. This may seem to be an area where the Buddhist tradition has something to learn from the capitalist emphasis on wealth creation, insofar as the Buddhist concern is eliminating all types of dukkha. Despite all the problems with modern technologies and economic globalization, Buddhism today needs to acknowledge the opportunities that such developments can provide for promoting individual and social happiness. Nevertheless, we need to remember the Buddhist insight that economics and technology cannot by themselves resolve our dukkha, because our basic problem—our sense of lack—is not economic or technological but spiritual.

Chapter 4, "Can Corporations Become Enlightened?" offers a less sanguine perspective on our most important economic institution and the main agent of globalization: transnational corporations. Today 51 of the world's 100 largest economies are not nations but corporations, and the world's 500 largest corporations account for nearly 70 percent of worldwide trade, a percentage that has been steadily increasing over the past twenty years. Many social critics have been addressing the economic and political implications of this development. This short chapter offers a Buddhist perspective on the "empty" (i.e., socially constructed) nature of corporations and what that emptiness (shunyata) means for our globalizing world, currently being reconstructed to meet corporate needs.

History teaches us that since they became important in the sixteenth century, corporations have been implicated in colonial exploitation—a process continuing today under a "neocolonial" economic globalization that continues to transfer wealth from the South to the North. From the very beginning, corporations have also had an incestuous relationship with the state. We distinguish between governments and the economy, yet at their upper levels there is rarely any effective distinction between them.

Today both of these problems are further complicated by the impersonal logic that motivates such enormous but privately owned institutions. Legally, the primary responsibility of a corporation is neither to its employees nor to its customers but to its stockholders. What does it mean, then, when those stockholders are anonymous, scattered here and there, and with no interest in the corporation's activities except insofar as they affect its profitability? The tragic example of Union Carbide's 1984 chemical leak in Bhopal, India—still the world's worst industrial accident—suggests that large corporations cannot be responsible in the way that you or I can be. Corporations are dangerous because they are legal fictions that, being without a physical body, are essentially ungrounded to the earth and its creatures, to the pleasures and responsibilities that derive from being manifestations of its biosphere. As the example of Bhopal shows, a corporation is unable to feel sorry for what it has done (its officers may occasionally apologize, yet that is usually a public relations gambit).

Worst of all, a corporation cannot love, for love is an engagement with others that includes responsibility for them and transcends our own individual self-interest. The impersonal way corporations are owned and structured guarantees that any such responsibility is so diffused that, in the end, it tends to disappear. In short, the problem with greed becomes much worse when it becomes institutionalized in the form of an impersonal corporation that takes on a life of its own.

Chapter 5, "The Nonduality of Good and Evil" originated as an attempt to understand and respond in a Buddhist way to the shock of September 11, 2001. It begins by reflecting on the curious fact that the al-Qaeda understanding of good and evil—mandating a holy war against evil—has also been emphasized by the Bush administration. What Osama bin Laden sees as good—Bush sees as evil. What Bush sees as good—America the defender of freedom and democracy—bin Laden sees as evil. They are two different versions of the same holy war between good and evil.

From a Buddhist perspective, such a black-and-white way of thinking brings more suffering—more evil—into the world. When Bush says that the United States is called upon to rid the world of evil, and bin Laden says that Muslims should engage in a jihad against the evil West, we should remember that this is also what Hitler and Stalin sought to do. Both of them were trying to perfect the world by destroying its evil elements: Jews, gypsies, homosexuals, well-to-do peasants. In other words, among the main causes of evil in this world have been human attempts to eradicate evil.

For Buddhism, evil, like everything else, has no essence or substance; it is a product of impermanent causes and conditions. Nor can we focus only on the second root of evil; ill will cannot be separated from the other two roots, greed and delusion. The animosity of others toward us may be due to their greed, but it may also be a result of our greed. This invites the essential question of *why* so many people in the Middle East, in particular, hate the United States so much.

The role of delusion has a special meaning in Buddhism. The fundamental delusion is our sense of separation from the world we live in, including our alienation from other people. The realization of our interdependence and mutual responsibility implies a deep wisdom about how the cycle of hatred and violence works and how it can be ended. As Shakyamuni Buddha says in The *Dhammapada*, "In this world hatred is never appeased by ill will; ill will is always appeased by love. This is an ancient law."[22]

The duality between good and evil is another example of bipolar thinking. We can't know what is good until we know what is evil, and we don't feel we are good unless we are fighting against that evil. We all love this struggle between good (us) and evil (them), because it is quite satisfying in the way it makes sense of the world. That is why it is the theme of so many paperback novels and Hollywood films, and why truth is the first casualty of all wars: in order to prosecute a war successfully, the media must work with the government to "sell" this story to the public.

What alternative is there, if we try to avoid this simplistic duality? We do better to distinguish between two basic modes of *being in the world*, two ways of responding to the uncertainty—the death-haunted insecurity—of our life in the world. We can try to stabilize ourselves by controlling and fixating the world we are in, so that it becomes less threatening and more amenable to our will, or we can open ourselves up to the world, which requires a greater acceptance of the open-ended impermanence of our existence. Both responses involve a quest for security, but they understand security differently.

How much better it would be if the Israel-Palestine conflict were understood in these terms! Not as a holy war between good and evil, but as a tragic cycle of reciprocal violence and hatred fueled by escalating fear on both sides. This choice between *fear* and *love* also provides us with a modern vocabulary to express one of the basic messages of both Christianity and Buddhism. What were Jesus and the Buddha both teaching their disciples? Don't worry about yourself, about how you will live; just spread the word as best you can and have faith that you will be taken care of. In other words, let go of your fears about yourself and give to the world rather than trying to protect yourself from it.

Chapter 6, "How to Reform a Serial Killer," offers a Buddhist perspective on restorative justice, an alternative to our retributive criminal justice systems. The Buddhist perspective on punishment, like any other approach, cannot be separated from its understanding of human motivation and its vision of human possibility. That makes the problem of justice part of a broader issue: When conflict and violence occur, how can we restore peace, instead of responding in kind?

Traditional Buddhist societies have very different judicial systems, but some similar threads have been used to weave their various patterns. For example, all of us, offenders and victims alike, have the same Buddha-nature, which is not to be confused with our usual sense of self; we are often dominated by our greed, malice, and delusion, but it is possible to change and outgrow them; so the only acceptable reason for punishment is education and reformation.

The chapter begins by considering two Pali sutras that address these issues. Then it examines the Buddhist *vinaya,* the rules and corrective measures that regulate the lives of bhikkhus and bhikkhunis. Finally, it looks to traditional Tibet to see how its criminal justice system embodied these Buddhist perspectives.

The Angulimala Sutra is the most famous Buddhist text on crime and punishment. Angulimala was a serial killer who was converted by the Buddha and became a bhikkhu, soon attaining nirvana. The point of this sutra is not difficult to see; we need only contrast his fate with what our retributive justice system would do to him. The importance of this story within the Buddhist tradition highlights the only reason Buddhism accepts for punishing an offender: to help reform his or her character. Nevertheless, the details of this particular myth are unsatisfactory from a restorative point of view. The sutra says nothing about the families of Angulimala's victims, or the larger social consequences of his crimes.

The Lion's Roar Sutra, also cited in some earlier chapters, presents poverty as the root cause of immoral behavior such as theft, violence, and falsehood. Social decline begins in this story when the king stops helping the poor. The basic point is that the problem of crime should not be addressed apart from its economic and social context. The solution is not to "crack down" harshly with severe punishments but to provide for people's basic needs. Instead of solving the problem, the king's violent attempt at deterrence sets off an explosion of violence that leads to social collapse. The state's violence reinforces the belief that violence works, so we should not be surprised when some of its subjects feel entitled to do the same.

The Vinaya Pitaka is a compendium of the rules that bhikkhus and bhikkhunis are expected to follow. Its attitude toward human weakness is quite realistic. It is the nature of unenlightened human beings to be afflicted by craving, malice, and delusion; that is, all of us are somewhat mad. If we are all somewhat insane, however, the insanity defense is always somewhat applicable. The universality of greed, malice, and delusion means there can be no presumption of unfettered free will. Freedom is not a matter of removing the constraints on individual self-will (often motivated by greed, etc.) but a consequence of self-control and spiritual awakening. This understanding of human weakness and freedom denies the distinction we are usually quick to make between an offender and the rest of us. It is also consistent with the Buddhist attitude toward self-perfection. We improve only gradually, step by step, so the best method of treatment is education. Buddhist emphasis on transience means there is nothing indelible about our unwholesome mental tendencies. If deep-rooted ones are difficult to eradicate, that is because they are a result of past habits. If we are serious about a judicial system that truly heals, we must change our focus from punishing guilt to reforming intention.

Traditional Tibet provides an opportunity to observe how well the above principles can work in lay society. Its legal system presupposed that conflict is engendered by our incorrect vision of situations, itself caused by our mental afflictions. Emphasis was on decisions that restored harmony to disputants rather than harmonizing with abstract legal principles. Such a different perspective, which highlights the difference between Buddhist justice and state justice, enables us to see the history of jurisprudence in a new way. For Buddhism justice grows out of mercy, but our Hobbesian myth about the social contract implies that the state's justice grows out of fear. If fear is the opposite of love, we are faced with contradictory paradigms about the origins and role of justice. We must choose which kind of society we want to live in.

In chapter 7, "Zen and the Art of War" returns to Asian Buddhism to examine a historical issue that has important implications today: the curious phenomenon of samurai Zen, which employed Buddhist principles and practices to teach the Japanese military class how to die and how to kill. Such a violent perversion of a nonviolent religion is hardly unique to Japanese Buddhism. European crusaders, for example, were eager to kill infidel Saracens and later to exterminate Albigensian heretics. Today, however, all but the most benighted Christians would condemn such campaigns as a perversion of Christian teachings, while the Zen samurai spirit continues to be appreciated in Japan and elsewhere as a legitimate expression of Buddhism. What can we learn from this extreme example of distorting spiritual practice to brutal ends?

A basic problem with Japanese Buddhism appeared at the very beginning. Buddhism was imported into Japan by its ruling classes, who understood its rituals magically, as potent means to preserve the nation, including their own privilege. Zen arrived several centuries later, yet it continued a pattern that had been set. Buddhist teachings and prestige were appropriated as an ideology supporting the state and justifying class privilege. If, as the Pali sutras imply, Shakyamuni believed in the equality of human beings and hoped that the ideals of the *sangha* would come to permeate all of society, the issue of social hierarchy is especially problematic for Japanese Buddhism, which came to emphasize devotion to one's feudal lord more than one's personal path of liberation from desire and delusion. Or, more precisely, the two tended to be equated: letting go of oneself was understood to mean identifying with one's superior.

The Buddhist scholar Winston King has pointed to a built-in factor that worked against the Buddhist teaching that life is sacred: a doctrine of karmic destiny. Karma is a complicated issue, and it is too simple to say that Zen simply encourages us to accept our own, yet the repeated exhortation to "become one with" our immediate circumstances implies something similar. The difficulty with accepting one's karmic destiny, which the Japanese understanding of egolessness encouraged, is that a collective ego—maybe we could call it a *wego*—is not intrinsically superior to the individual ego. It may be even more dangerous, depending on how that particular egolessness is channeled.

In sum, insofar as the Zen experience "transcends" concepts and ethics, and emphasizes oneness with one's situation, its practitioners can become more vulnerable to the prevailing ideology and more likely to be co-opted by the dominant social system. Then, instead of providing a moral and spiritual perspective on secular authority, Zen ends up sacralizing such authority. This is an important lesson for globalizing Buddhism today; it reinforces the need for a Buddhist social theory to help avoid such co-option.

Chapter 8, "Remaking Ourselves," takes its title from a remark by Gandhi: "As human beings our greatness lies not so much in being able to remake the world as in being able to remake ourselves." Obviously Gandhi was not thinking about genetic engineering, yet now we have access to that alternative way of remaking ourselves. For many of us, however, excitement about this new way to reduce some types of dukkha is overshadowed by our worries about its dangers. So how shall we evaluate the various possibilities?

So far, at least, we have evaluated them in much the same way that most nascent technologies have been assessed: by distinguishing between nature and human artifact in order to take sides between them, privileging one over the other. This dualism too may be traced back to the classical Greek distinction mentioned earlier between *phusis* and *nomos,* or nature and convention/culture (a distinction that creates the possibility of restructuring society and our natural environment). Ever since then, some of us have been more inclined to celebrate technological progress, others to deplore the losses—but both sides presuppose the dualism.

That bifurcation is related to the conflict between two of our most basic human needs, security and freedom. We feel a need to be free, yet becoming free makes us more anxious—and therefore more inclined to sacrifice that freedom for safety, whereupon we again feel a need to be free.... I also need to feel that I am unique, special in the universe, but then I want the security of being just like everyone else. Is the same dialectic true at the collective level? To accept one's culture as natural is to be grounded in the understanding that one's role in life is more or less determined, while to freely discover or construct one's own meaning is to forfeit such a "natural" ground and the security it offers.

If this dialectic traps our thinking about biotechnology, is there any other approach that might shed light on our ambivalence? One alternative is to remember the three roots of evil and look for the *motivations* behind our eagerness to exploit this new technology. The role of greed is more or less obvious, and to a lesser extent so too is the ill will usually associated with greed. The most problematic factor, however, is again delusion.

What is most striking about our collective plight today is how much it resembles the problem we face as individuals: the sense of separation between an ego-self inside and an objective world outside, a delusion that causes us to seek happiness by manipulating the world in order to get what we want from it, which just tends to reinforce the sense of separation. We have already noticed that our empty (because constructed) sense of self is haunted by a profound insecurity it can never quite resolve, despite all our efforts to make ourselves feel more real.

Are we collectively attempting to self-ground ourselves in a similar fashion, by objectifying and transforming the world technologically? Our freedom to construct our own meaning means we have lost our premodern security, so we cannot collectively manipulate the natural world in a technological attempt to control it and also hope to find in that objectified world a grounding for ourselves.

With biotechnology, the last resistance to commodification is being overcome, and the category of the sacred ceases to correspond to anything in our experience. Nevertheless, this does not necessarily imply that all genetic engineering must be bad. It does not deny the possibility that we may someday have the economic and political conditions to conduct it with more conscious and humble motivations. The essential point, for Buddhism, is not to preserve or return to some pristine natural condition but to reduce our dukkha.

Chapter 9, "Loving the World As Our Own Body," relates the ecological perspectives of Taoism, Buddhism, and deep ecology to their common emphasis on the nonduality of self and world. Today the crucial ethical question has become how to relate not just to our fellow humans but to all beings, including apparently nonsentient "beings" such as tropical rain forests and the ozone layer. At the heart of this issue, again, is the self. The ecological crisis is another consequence of the alienation between myself and my world. This transposes the issue from morality to understanding. The problem is not evil but ignorance, and the solution is a matter not of applying the will but of reaching an insight into the nondual nature of things.

The Taoist critique of the self opposes selfness with the realization of Tao, the dynamic source from which all natural phenomena arise. To experience Tao is to realize that, instead of being the crown of creation, *Homo sapiens* is only one of the ten thousand things that the Tao treats indifferently. The Tao is a great flux in which everything harmonizes, and its spontaneity is not opposed to order but expresses it, since it arises from the unforced unfolding of that natural order.

Buddhism and Taoism are both sensitive to how language causes us to perceive the world as a collection of self-existing objects in objectified space and time. Chinese Buddhism expresses the interconditionality of all phenomena, including us, with the analogy of Indra's net, which stretches infinitely in all directions, with a jewel at each node reflecting all the other jewels. The Buddhist approach to morality follows directly from this interpenetration (or "interpermeation") of reflections. When I discover that I am you, the ethical problem of how to relate to you is transformed. Loss of self-preoccupation entails the ability to respond to others without an ulterior motive that needs to gain something from that encounter.

What are the ecological implications? The first precept enjoins us not to kill any sentient being. Bodhisattvas vow to help all beings become happy and realize their Buddha-nature. Such an attitude developed quite early—for example, in the popular *jatakas*, or "birth stories," that describe the previous lives of Shakyamuni. The Jatakas view the world as a vast field of spiritual effort in which no life-form is outside the path, because each is able to feel compassion for the sufferings of others and act selflessly. Many passages in the Pali scriptures contain expressions of the Buddha's gratitude for trees and other plants.

The subversive ideas of deep ecology also challenge our deeply rooted assumptions about the nonhuman natural world, the human world, and the relationship between the two. This is expressed most famously in the first principle of the Deep Ecology Platform as initially formulated by Arne Naess and George Sessions in 1984: "The well-being and flourishing of human and nonhuman life on earth have values in themselves. These values are independent of the usefulness of the nonhuman world for human purposes." Naess has since developed this into two ultimate norms. The first is *Self-realization,* which goes beyond the self defined as an isolated ego. We must stop seeing ourselves as competing egos and learn to identify with other species and even inanimate objects in the nonhuman world. The second norm is *biocentric equality:* all things in the biosphere have the right to reach their own individual forms of unfolding and self-realization within the larger Self-realization.

Taoism and Buddhism also emphasize "letting things be" in order for them to flourish: not for our sake, and not even for their own sake, but for no sake at all—because questions of utility and justification no longer apply. That challenges the basic principle of our technological and consumerist society, and it also subverts our sense of ego-self. To admit that natural objects (or natural events) have an inherent value independent of any awareness or appreciation by other beings is to question our commonsense dualism between the conscious self and the objective world. The ecological catastrophes that have now become common make it evident that resolving the duality between ourselves and the natural world is necessary if we—not only humans, but the rich diversity that constitutes the biosphere—are to survive and thrive in the new millennium.

CHAPTER 2

Buddhism and Poverty

One thing I teach, and one thing only: *dukkha* and how to end it.
—Shakyamuni Buddha

D OES BUDDHISM have anything special to contribute to our understanding of poverty, and how to alleviate it?

Like other religions, Buddhism is sometimes criticized for its idealism: for
encouraging a nonmaterialistic way of life that goes against the grain of our
main desires and motivations. If we want to reduce poverty, we are referred
instead to the science of economics, which has discovered the laws of economic growth that promote worldly well-being, and to international development agencies that apply those principles to improve the lot of "undeveloped"
societies.

In fact, the opposite is true. Contemporary economics is much more "idealistic" in the sense that it presumes an unrealistic image of human nature
derived from an eighteenth-century ethical system, utilitarianism, which was
not derived from empirical observation but conceived in a philosopher's study.
As a result, economists today tend to live in an idealized, one-dimensional
world of statistics and equations that do not accurately reflect human values
and goals.

In contrast with the calculating individualism that neoliberal economics
presupposes, Buddhism is more down-to-earth in its understanding of the
sources of human ill-being and well-being. Its approach also happens to
correspond more closely to the way most premodern communities have
understood well-being, and how "undeveloped" societies today still do. This
chapter considers the implications of Buddhist teachings for the problems

of their economic development. From a Buddhist perspective, it is not surprising that the institutional efforts of the last fifty years have actually aggravated the social problems they were supposed to solve. Far from providing a solution, the development approach still taken for granted today is better understood as the problem itself. Buddhism can help us envision more viable alternatives.

The previous chapter has used the structure of the four noble truths—ill being *(dukkha)*, its cause, its end, and its cure—as a template that can also serve as the foundation for a Buddhist Social Theory. When we try to understand poverty and economic "underdevelopment" according to this simple model, it helps to illuminate aspects of the issue that tend to be overlooked or ignored.

WHAT IS POVERTY?

Paradoxically, perhaps, the actual obstacles to solving the world's most acute problems are less the cultural traditions of a large number of peoples than our own ingrained belief that the boundless progress which results from technology and the market can somehow liberate us from nature and society.

—Gerard Berthoud

Until recently religion has not played much of a role in development debates because its teachings have usually been perceived as preoccupied with a "higher world" or at least a different dimension of life. Whether or not such a preoccupation is true for some other religions, it is not the case for Buddhism. Far from ignoring or minimizing poverty, Buddhist teachings are sensitive to it, offering both diagnosis and remedies. The most important thing, however, is that Buddhism challenges our understanding of poverty by contextualizing the problem in a different way, one that questions the assumptions that still dominate our thinking about "undeveloped" societies.

According to Buddhism poverty is unacceptable insofar as it involves dukkha. The usual English translations are "suffering, frustration, dissatisfaction," but "ill-being" is perhaps the best in this context, a context that does not imply any significant distinction between worldly dukkha and some other transcendental sort. As a worldview and way of life that advocates eliminating dukkha, Buddhism does not and cannot value poverty that is a source of dukkha. In the Anguttara Nikaya, for example, the Buddha says that for a person who enjoys sense-pleasure, poverty (Pali: *daliddiya*) is miserable, because it leads to borrowing and increasing debts and thus ever-increasing suffering.

Buddhism does value nonattachment toward material goods and it promotes the virtue of having fewer wants, yet that is not the same as encouraging poverty. Poverty, as ordinarily understood in early Buddhism, consists in lacking the basic material requirements for leading a decent life free from hunger, exposure, and disease. Buddhism recognizes the importance of such minimum material needs even in the case of those who aspire to its spiritual goal, and in fact the basic needs of a monk or nun provide a useful benchmark for measuring that level of subsistence below which human beings should not be allowed to fall. The four requisites of a Buddhist renunciant are food sufficient to alleviate hunger and maintain one's health, clothing sufficient to be socially decent and to protect the body, shelter sufficient for serious engagement with cultivating the mind, and health care sufficient to cure and prevent illness. People who voluntarily renounce worldly possessions and pleasures in favor of a life of such minimal needs are viewed very positively in Buddhist texts as belonging to the community of "noble ones."

Although lack of these four requisites seems to be a good definition of human destitution, they are not themselves sufficient to evaluate the situation of those who do not choose to follow a spiritual path of renunciation. For example, education and livelihood are not mentioned, the first because some study of the teachings was usually taken for granted, the second because Buddhist renunciants in South Asia were mendicants who devoted themselves not to production but to contemplation. Shakyamuni's Buddhism assumed both a low-tech culture (making comparatively little impact on its environment), and relative freedom from the external economic (although not political) forces that are ravaging many non-industrial societies today. Because our situation today is in many ways unique, a creative response cannot be simply derived from early Buddhist teachings but must rather be informed by them. The important question is, Who should decide what that response will be?

In any case, there is much in those teachings to inform us. According to the Anguttara Nikaya, the Buddha taught that some people are like the completely blind; they do not have the vision to improve their material circumstances or lead a morally elevated life. Others are like the one-eyed; they have the vision to improve their material conditions, but they do not see the need to live a morally elevated life. The third class have the vision to improve both. Such Buddhist teachings imply that when measuring poverty it is not enough to evaluate the material conditions. For a more comprehensive evaluation of deprivation, it is necessary to take into account the moral quality of people's lives.

But that is not to minimize the importance of a single eye. There is even a causal relationship between material poverty and social deterioration, according to the Lion's Roar Sutra *(Cakkavatti-Sihanada Sutra)*.

In this sutra the Buddha tells the story of a monarch in the distant past who initially venerated and relied upon the Buddhist teachings, following the advice of his sage: "Let no crime prevail in your kingdom, and to those who are in need, give property." Later, however, he began to rule according to his own ideas and did not give property to the needy, with the result that poverty became rife. Due to poverty one man took what was not given and was arrested; when the king asked him why, the man said he had nothing to live on. So the king gave him some property, saying that it would be enough to carry on a business and support his family.

Exactly the same thing happened to another man; and when other people heard about this, they too decided to steal so they would be treated in a similar way. Then the penny finally dropped, and the king realized that if he continued to give property to such men, theft would continue to increase. So he decided to get tough on the next thief: "I had better make an end of him, finish him off once for all, and cut off his head." And he did.

At this point in the story, one might expect a moralistic parable about the importance of deterring crime, but it turns in exactly the opposite direction:

> Hearing about this, people thought: "Now let us get sharp swords made for us, and then we can take from anybody what is not given, we will make an end of them, finish them off once and for all and cut off their heads." So, having procured some sharp swords, they launched murderous assaults on villages, towns and cities, and went in for highway robbery, killing their victims by cutting off their heads.
>
> Thus, from the not giving of property to the needy, poverty became rife, from the growth of poverty, the taking of what was not given increased, from the increase of theft, the use of weapons increased, from the increased use of weapons, the taking of life increased.[23]

Despite some fanciful elements, this myth has important implications. Poverty is presented as a root cause of immoral behavior such as theft, violence, and falsehood. Unlike what we might expect from a supposedly world-denying religion, the Buddhist solution has nothing to do with accepting our (or others') "poverty karma." The problem begins when the king does not give property to the needy—in more modern terms, when the state neglects its responsibility to maintain a minimum of what we today call distributive justice. This influential sutra implies that social breakdown cannot be separated from broader questions about the benevolence of the social order. The solution to poverty-induced crime is not to punish severely but to enable people to provide for their basic needs.

In another sutra, the Buddha speaks of the four kinds of happiness *(sukha)* attained by householders: possessing enough material resources, enjoying those resources, sharing them with relations and friends, and not being in debt. More important than any of them, he emphasizes, is the happiness of leading a blameless life. Elsewhere the Buddha teaches that "the greatest wealth is contentment" *(santutthi paramam dhanam)*. There are said to be seven kinds of noble wealth: faith, moral conduct, the shame of doing something reprehensible, and the fear of doing something reprehensible, developing one's character, sacrificing one's possessions for the benefit of others, and insight into the three characteristics of existence (dukkha, impermanence, and no-self). The Buddha says that in the discipline of the noble ones who follow the Buddhist path, the absence of these seven may be called true poverty, a poverty even more miserable than that resulting from lack of material resources.

By redefining these moral qualities as "noble wealth," Buddhism draws attention to the fact that the single-minded pursuit of material wealth will not make human beings happy or even rich. A world in which envy and miserliness predominate cannot be considered one in which poverty has been eliminated. This follows from the second noble truth of the Buddha: the cause of dukkha is *tanha* craving. When human beings gain an intense acquisitive drive for some object, that object becomes a cause of suffering. Such objects are compared to the flame of a torch carried against the wind, or to a burning pit of embers: they involve much anxiety but very little satisfaction—an obvious truth repressed by turning our attention toward another craved object. For Buddhism a proliferation of unnecessary wants is the basic cause of unnecessary ill-being.

Poverty can never be overcome by generating more and more desires to be satisfied by consuming more and more goods and services. Even when consumerism eliminates or reduces material poverty, it does so at the cost of promoting an even more harmful poverty. In short, there is a fundamental and inescapable poverty built into a consumer society. From a Buddhist point of view we should not be surprised that such efforts in social engineering end up creating more problems than they solve.

This is not a criticism of wealth. As we read in the Bible, not money but love of money is the source of evil; however, wealth must be acquired by righteous means, through one's own efforts without using immoral or exploitative methods. Economic activity involving injury to life or the erosion of moral ideals is unacceptable from a Buddhist perspective, however beneficial it may be according to purely economic criteria.

Is this image of our human nature and its potential too idealistic? Not at all. In fact, it reflects better than economic theory the attitudes of most societies not already conditioned by advertising into believing that happiness is something you purchase. According to the Vietnamese teacher Thich Nhat Hanh, Buddhism is "a clever way to enjoy your life." Confusing the quality of one's life with a quantitative "standard of living" is, in contrast, a foolish way. Many of the Third World peoples we have been so eager to "develop" seem to be more aware of this difference than we are.

The first World Bank definition of poverty was based upon the crude criterion of average national income. Since then the Bank has become more sensitive to differences of income among sectors within a country, and now even within families. For economics, however, lack of income remains the basic criterion of ill-being, perhaps because some such numerical measurement is necessary to satisfy the economist's craving for statistical assessment. Gross National Product is a lot easier to gauge than General Well-Being. As a result, development agencies have been slow to realize what many anthropologists have long since understood: in traditional societies, especially rural communities, income is not the primary criterion of well-being; sometimes it is not even a major one.

One of the things we found in the village which surprised us was people's idea of well-being and how that related to having money. We talked to a family, asking them to rank everybody in the village from the richest to the poorest and asking them why they would rank somebody as being less well off, and someone as poor. And we found that in the analysis money meant very little to the people. The person who was ranked as poorest in the village was a man who was probably the only person who was receiving a salary.[24]

When a master builder in a Bulgarian community was invited to rank people according to wealth, he "spontaneously enlarged the list of well-being criteria emphasizing the importance of children's education, good health, a good-humored nature…. Interestingly, those who were less well off included the most wealthy person in the village—an unhappy, bad-tempered fellow put at the bottom of the pile along with the drunks and the sick." From his study of the relevant literature Robert Chambers concludes: "Income, the reductionist criterion of normal economists, has never, in my experience or in the evidence I have been able to review, been given explicit primacy."[25]

To assume that we in the "developed" world know something about worldly well-being that people in Zambia, Bulgaria, and elsewhere do not is a form of intellectual imperialism that looks increasingly dubious. De-emphasizing income is something difficult for us to understand, since money is, after all, the "pure means" that enables us to obtain anything and everything—or is it? Our obsession with economic growth seems natural to us because we have forgotten the historicity of the "needs" we now take for granted. That includes the need for a monetary income in monetarized and commodified Western societies, where anything can be converted into anything else through a common medium of exchange. Since our needs (or rather our wants) are now taken for granted as defining our common humanity, we are encouraged to forget what for Buddhism is an essential condition of happiness: self-limitation.

According to Buddhism, any formulation of "needs" (beyond avoiding destitution) is as much (if not more) a value judgment as a determination of fact. The fundamental human problem is not the technological and economic issue of meeting all our material wants—something psychologically as well as ecologically impossible—but the psychological and spiritual need to understand the nature of our own minds. Economics cannot avoid reducing *what is good* to *an amount* because it factors all desires into its basic equation of scarcity, which derives from comparing limited means with potentially unlimited wants. Without having been seduced by the utopian dream of a technological cornucopia, however, it would never occur to most "poor" people to become fixated on fantasies about all the things they might acquire. For them, their ends are an expression of the means available to them. We are imposing our own value judgments when we insist on seeing them as poor or as living in a state of scarcity (again, except for the destitute unable to satisfy basic requisites for survival). It is presumptuous to assume that they must be unhappy and need to get on the treadmill of market consumerism.

Why do we assume that "poverty of income or consumption" is the same as ill-being? That brings us to the heart of the matter. For us, material well-being has become increasingly important because of our loss of faith in any other possibility of fulfillment—for example, an afterlife in heaven with God, or for some, the secular heaven of socialism, or even (when despairing over the ecological crisis) the continued existence and "progress" of humankind. Increasing our "standard of living" has become so compulsive for us because it serves as a substitute for traditional religious values—or, more precisely, because it has actually become a kind of secular religion.

If so, our evangelical efforts to economically "develop" other societies, which cherish their own spiritual values and community traditions, may be viewed as a contemporary form of religious imperialism. Does that make the globalization of capitalism a new kind of mission to convert the heathen?

What Are the Causes of Poverty?

With the rise of the modern world, a distinctly modern faith—faith in progress—arose to make sense of, and give ultimate meaning to the new notions and institutions that were now dominant. Our deep reverence for science and technology was inextricably linked up with this faith in progress. The universal enforcement of the nation-state was carried out under the banner of progress. And increasing conformity with the rule of economics, and intensified belief in its laws, are still shadows of this enlightened faith.

—José Maria Sbert

According to the accepted development model, the cause of poverty is not a major issue. Poverty is more or less taken for granted as the normal condition of "undeveloped" peoples, one that plagues all premodern societies, since it can be alleviated only by technological and economic development.

From a Buddhist perspective, however, there is something odd about this indifference to the causes of something we want to cure. This is reinforced by some intriguing discoveries that do not support the assumption that poverty is the normal premodern condition. Studies of "Stone Age economics"— based inferentially on modern anthropological findings—have concluded that the first humans may well have had a life in some ways more leisurely than ours.[26] Anthropological surveys have found that until very recently (before the infiltration of globalization) some hunting-gathering communities survived quite well on a few hours work a day, with a diet more nutritious and varied than the farming settlements that supplanted them.

Agriculture also meant harder work, yet it could support a greater population density and still produce a surplus—the latter advantage usually restricted to those who gained the power to appropriate it. Such appropriation led to the development of classes, a social stratification that could not easily arise within hunting and gathering communities. We view this appropriation as the origin of kings and priesthoods, but it can just as well be seen as the origin of the poor, who are newly deprived of the fruits of their arduous labors.

If social class continues to be our fundamental social problem, it is one that the last fifty years of "development" have done very little to alleviate, for, as many recent studies have shown, the share of human wealth owned by the rich worldwide has increased during this period, and continues to do so. According to the World Bank's own Global Economic Outlook for the year 2000, the number of people living on less than two dollars a day has risen by 50 percent since 1980 to 2.8 billion, almost half the world's population; and recent evidence suggests that the number of people surviving on less than a dollar a day is growing in most regions of the world. This continuing catastrophe is partially due to the fact that in "undeveloped" countries it is the powerful and wealthy classes that continue to benefit most from the efforts of development agencies such as the World Bank; and when projects fail, as many do, it is the poor who suffer most from their failure. For example, between 1980 and 1989 thirty-three African countries received 241 structural adjustment loans from the World Bank. During that same decade, average GDP and food production per capita in those countries both declined. The value of the minimum wage dropped by over 25 percent, government expenditure on education declined from $11 billion to $7 billion, and primary school enrollments dropped from 80 percent in 1980 to 69 percent in 1990. The number of people classified as poor rose from 184 million in 1985 to 216 million in 1990, an increase of 17 percent.[27] If we accept the World Bank's profession that its primary concern is to eliminate poverty, we are forced into the paradoxical conclusion that one of the causes of poverty is the Bank's own efforts to reduce it.

In the same way, a great desire for wealth is inevitably shadowed by and preoccupied with the desire to avoid poverty.

One implication of this is that there is no such thing as a "poverty problem" that can be understood separately from what must also be called a "wealth problem." Rather, we are inflicted with a *wealth/poverty dualism*. This has several facets. One aspect is to recognize the simple point that many critics have made about globalization: although not a zero-sum game, rapid economic growth has also meant rapid impoverishment and rapid increase in inequality, a different aspect of development that development agencies prefer to ignore but that structural adjustment programs have abetted.

To understand why we allow this to happen requires us to apply the wealth/poverty dualism to our collective motivations. Is a concern for "attacking poverty" the flip side of our aggressive preoccupation with the creation and accumulation of wealth? In this way we excuse the negative impacts of economic globalization because, after all, we are trying (or at least intend) to address those problems. More insidiously, we rationalize a way of life preoccupied with economic growth, no matter what its other costs. "Undeveloped" poor people *must* be miserable, because that is how we would experience their circumstances of life. Mesmerized as we are by economic growth, we assume that everyone else must be too—or should be, especially if we are to have access to their resources and their demand for our manufactured products.

In medieval Europe, poverty provided an opportunity to save one's own soul by being generous; today some such generosity is necessary to justify our own acquisitive lifestyle. We can feel good about making a killing on the stock market if we donate some of it to charity. More cynically, poverty programs have been useful for subverting protest. "The goal of assistance," wrote the sociologist George Simmel, "is precisely to mitigate certain extreme manifestations of social differentiation, so that the social structure may continue to be based on this differentiation."[28] Today we have sophisticated economic instruments that allow us to take such assistance a step further and (since we no longer worry about our immortal souls) make a profit from our generosity: the assistance must be returned, with interest, no matter what the social cost to the recipients.

Development institutions have been quick to emphasize that a lasting solution to world poverty requires continued growth—a logical conclusion if one assumes that the only route to follow is the production/consumption example provided by the "developed" countries. This means diverting limited community resources to new economic goals, which requires further consolidation of the power of government agencies and other financial institutions. Such power no longer *forces* anything, now it "helps"—but who needs help, and how that help is to be given, is decided not by the people to be helped but by the helper. In this way our human nature is redefined according to the interests and control of professionals.[29]

Global poverty is thus *conceptually* necessary if the world is to be completely commodified and monetarized. Otherwise one cannot rationalize the profound social reorientation (experienced by most people as social disorganization) that is required. Traditional cultures and lifestyles must be redefined as obstacles to be overcome, and local elites must become dissatisfied with them, in order to create a class of more individualistic and self-interested people that will serve as the vanguard of consumption.

There is another implication of the wealth/poverty dualism that afflicts the psychology of wealthy people and nations. The poverty of others is also necessary because it is the benchmark by which we measure our own achievements. Unless there are losers, we cannot feel like winners. Unless the undeveloped are unhappy about their lot, we may come to doubt our own happiness with what we have, unable to rationalize the things we have had to put up with in order to get where we are, or to excuse the negative consequences of our economic development. In this fashion, too, what we perceive as a poverty problem is due to the tinted lenses of our wealth/poverty spectacles—and what is colored most of all by those lenses is our own self-appearance. To live in a commodified world is to recognize that we too are commodified; and as we know, the value of commodities is determined by price comparison. Who has more, you or me? We can rarely ask this question because it cuts too deeply, right to the source of our self-esteem.

In all these ways, then, we need the poor.

None of the above should be taken as making light of the situation of those many people in the world whose destitution needs to be alleviated as soon as possible. What it does imply, though, is that among the causes of poverty today are the delusions of the wealthy—delusions that have very concrete effects on the well-being of many people, including the wealthy themselves.

If so, we should not allow ourselves to be preoccupied only with the poverty side of the problem; to correct the bias, we should become as concerned about the wealth side: the personal, social, and environmental costs of our obsession with wealth creation and collective growth. Far from ignoring genuine poverty, a Buddhist approach emphasizes the importance of seeing through such dualisms if our efforts to help the destitute are actually to be successful.

WHAT IS THE END OF POVERTY?

> The salvation of the people and of the nations shall come about through binding them ever more tightly to the international market, equated with the world community. There, the poor shall partake of the same substance as the rich. Like any universal truth, adjustment is a purely abstract notion even if its application causes concrete pain. The available choices are reduced to one. There Is No Alternative; we are all bound by a single, compulsory, truth which shall be recognized. Then shall the wayward nations be freed from their errors.
>
> —Susan George and Fabrizio Sabelli

It is, again, curious that development agencies such as the World Bank have said so little about what would constitute the end of poverty. The goal is expressed in negative terms that lack a positive vision of a world without poverty. Whether this lack of articulation is unconscious (because the Bank takes the goal more or less for granted) or conscious (because the Bank does not want to reveal its agenda), there are reasons for concern.

Whether the vision is conscious or unconscious the solution is integration of the poor into the global economy. The difference between the two is what the role of the poor will be in the globalization process.

The first scenario speaks in vague, general terms about the benefits that accrue from linking up with the world economy: a market for one's products; access to loans, seeds, and other resources; an income that enables purchase of consumer goods—all of which open the door to the promised land of capitalism. Sure, one must start at the bottom, but with hard work and some luck you might end up big-time consumers like us.

The second scenario is more realistic about the possibility of ending up like us. If that is the temptation, the promise is false. Insofar as the "undeveloped"

internalize our wealth/poverty syndrome, they are doomed to a life of increasing dukkha, since there is no hope that most of them will be able to mimic our
lifestyle. A world of over six billion car drivers? The earth does not have nearly
enough resources for China's population to live like Americans, nor could it
absorb enough pollutants. An article in the February 2002 issue of *Scientific
American* claims that, in order for the other five billion people to live in the
way that the world's richest billion do, the resources of four more planets like
the earth would be needed. But there is no need to worry about all that, for
in truth the world's poor have a different role to play.

If we imagine aliens from another planet had been observing the World
Bank's actual development practices over the last fifty years, rather than lis-
tening to the rhetoric about its intentions—"helping the undeveloped,"
"attacking poverty," and so forth—what would they conclude about the Bank's
goals? On the basis of his own lengthy experience with Zimbabwe, Professor
Colin Stoneman, an economic statistician at the University of York, decided
that the World Bank is an institution "whose overall intention, and increasingly
effect, is to promote the construction of a single world market, substantially on
the basis of the present world division of labor…[a] role mediated through an
ideology that is claimed to be a value-free science [i.e., economics]." Doug
Hellinger, a former World Bank consultant on urban development now with
the Development Group for Alternative Policies (D-GAP), makes the same
point more cynically: "The Bank is saying that to join the world economy you
have to become more efficient and you have to be able to compete against
imports from around the world. But the purpose is not to develop Brazil or to
develop Ghana. They could give a damn. The U.S. is trying to stay competitive
with Europe and Japan and the Bank is helping to provide the government's
friends in business with cheap labor, a deregulated atmosphere, and export
incentives. It isn't a development strategy, it's a corporate strategy."[30]

If this has indeed been their intention, the World Bank and the IMF have
been quite successful:

> For decades, the World Bank has had a free hand to carry out its policies,
> especially during the 1980s following the onset of the debt crisis. Survey-
> ing the results, some critics make the mistake of proclaiming that devel-
> opment has failed. It hasn't. Development as historically conceived and
> officially practised has been a huge success. It sought to integrate the
> upper echelons, say ten to forty percent, of a given third world population

into the international, westernized, consuming classes and the global market economy. This it has accomplished brilliantly.

A decade or more of structural adjustment has given marked impetus to the process of global integration. Elites everywhere have managed to make their poorer compatriots pay the costs of adjustment, whereas they, on the whole, have profited from it or at the very least have lost, proportionally, far less.[31]

By no coincidence it was just after the Cold War began, in January 1949, that Harry S Truman first enunciated a new doctrine of assistance for "underdeveloped areas." The Soviet Union, as the first noncapitalist power to become industrialized, offered an alternative model for development that could compete for the loyalty of Third World countries. It is also no coincidence that, since the Soviet Union collapsed, economic globalization and corporate penetration have accelerated at the same time as the burden of structural adjustment has increased for most of those same countries, still underdeveloped: these are not two separate developments but two faces of the same global integration.

What is the meaning of this integration? And why is it so problematic? In 1944, the year that the World Bank and the International Monetary Fund were established, the economic historian Karl Polanyi published *The Great Transformation: The Political and Economic Origins of Our Time*. His account of the origins of capitalism does not directly address the globalization that the Bank and IMF have since encouraged, yet it remains the best account of the social consequences of a capitalist economy: a reversal of the traditional relationship between a society and its economy.

In premodern societies, and in nonmodernized ones today, the markets that exist are limited in place, time, and scope. They serve a very circumscribed role because they tend to disrupt social relations. According to Polanyi, precapitalist man "does not act so as to safeguard his individual interest in the possession of material goods; he acts so as to safeguard his social standing, his social claims, his social assets. He values material goods only in so far as they serve this end." [32]

The great story of capitalism is the liberation of markets from such constraints. Today we believe that the freedom to engage in market exchanges benefits all of us, because it leads to the economic growth that satisfies our needs. If it is true, however, that there is no clear distinction between the economic and social spheres, there is another way to understand unfettered markets: as a reversal of the traditional relationship between a society and its economy. Today, "instead of economy being embedded in social relations, social relations are embedded in the economic system."[33]

Where there are no restrictions to protect social relations, commodification tends to occur with every potential resource that can be utilized for economic gain. This includes the very moral fabric of society, woven of innumerable personal relationships, now commodified into "social capital" or "moral capital"—ugly economist terms that describe how market forces rely upon but damage that fabric of interpersonal responsibility.

A basic contradiction of the market is that it requires character traits such as honesty and trust in order to work efficiently, yet it is primarily motivated by a desire for profit that erodes such personal responsibility for others. The last few decades have made this more obvious. In the United States, massive downsizing and a shift to part-timers demonstrate diminishing corporate (and university) concern for employees, while at the top, astronomical salary increases and management buy-outs reveal that the executives entrusted with managing corporations are becoming more adept at exploiting or cannibalizing them for their own benefit. The most recent examples of Enron and Worldcom were only the tip of a massive iceberg. Internationally, the globalizing market has promoted more exploitative relationships with the poor and powerless in "undeveloped" parts of the world, where predatory governments often cooperate in keeping factory wages at subsistence levels. These are examples of how the market itself depletes "moral capital" and therefore depends upon the community to regenerate it in much the same way as it depends upon the biosphere to regenerate natural capital.

How do communities generate moral capital? This brings us back to the role of religion, something development institutions have more often seen as an obstacle than a supporting force. Throughout history, religions have been the main source and repository for society's deepest values and goals, those most essential to a community's harmony and self-understanding. Not all of these are goals we should pursue now or values we want to encourage, but genuine religions have thrived because they have the potential to promote and nurture responsible personal relationships. Aspiring bureaucrats need to learn more than literacy and accountancy skills if they are to be good clerks; they must also be equipped with a moral understanding of their responsibilities to other members of society. Needless to say, this applies all the way up and down the hierarchy of roles. Traditionally, religious values have encouraged this best. In contrast, material values that emphasize income and consumption make it more difficult to resist the corruption of graft and bribes. This is not an abstract problem: it touches on what has been one of the major obstacles to successful development.

If a harmonious society requires the moral capital that religions usually generate and that market capitalism tends to deplete, we should not identify economic reform with market liberation. Instead, the implication works the other way: true social development may require us to reverse the transformation Polanyi wrote about, re-embedding the economy in social relations, rather than letting economic forces determine what happens to our communities. Needless to say, this applies at least as much to the wealthy nations as to the "undeveloped" ones.

Today the new rhetoric emphasizes "attacking poverty" by "empowering the poor," yet this contains a dangerous ambiguity: empowerment for what? Is empowerment a means (enabling the poor to join the world market) or a goal (allowing them to determine for themselves where they want to go)? The entrenched poverty we may see in many "undeveloped" peoples may not be the most important thing about their lives and culture. If traditional societies have their own standards of deprivation and well-being, imposing a foreign one on them is a form of intellectual imperialism. Insofar as that imposition undermines their traditional religious values, it may also be considered a type of religious imperialism.

Although we cannot allow destitution to continue—something everyone can agree on—we should accept that the world is enriched (as well as sometimes damaged) by a plurality of approaches to human ill-being and well-being. This does not mean that they all deserve to be tolerated: racist and totalitarian practices, in particular, should not be. How we are to determine the difference between tolerable and intolerable understandings? Reflecting on this brings us to the necessity for genuine democracy and, just as important, freedom of religious practice. These, rather than military or economic impositions, provide the best ways to make those decisions.

The moral role of religions is difficult for most Western-trained economists to accept, since their discipline is a legacy of the eighteenth-century Enlightenment project that contrasted scientific and social progress with the regressive weight of privileged churches. Today, however, it is necessary to recognize that the neoliberal economic vision of what happiness is, and how that is to be achieved, is only one among many. Like every other vision, it has its strengths and weaknesses. There is a social price to pay for the comforts and commodities neoliberalism cherishes, a price that should not be imposed on others who have their own worldviews and values.

All societies are confronted with the same basic tragedy of life, which for Buddhism is not primarily poverty but illness, old age, and death. Historically, the main human response to this has been religion, which addresses it in various ways. From a perspective informed by the eighteenth-century Enlightenment, most of these responses are superstitious and escapist. From a Buddhist perspective, however, economic growth and consumerism are unsatisfactory alternatives because they are evasions that repress the basic problem of life by distracting us with symbolic substitutes such as money, status, and power. Similar critiques of idolatry are explicit or implicit in all the great religions, and rampant economic globalization makes that message all the more important for our time.

How Do We End Poverty?

> The apostles of new life...are the minority, typically those whose close contact with Western education, Western political thought and Western material living standards has led them to want greater opportunities to practice their knowledge, greater outlets for their ambition, and a better material lot for their countrymen.
> —Eugene Black, president of the World Bank, 1949–63

> If we have to drive our people to paradise with sticks, we will do so for their good and the good of those who come after us.
> —Abel Alier, regional president of Sudan

Here, finally, we must see the strength of the economic paradigm, its ability to devise and implement programs to end poverty—or so one would think. Unfortunately, because the solutions attempted have not been based on an adequate understanding of the three preceding questions—What is poverty? What is its cause? What is its end?—we should not be surprised that the attempts have not been very successful.

The best answer to this last question, *How* do we end poverty? is very simple: let us admit that we do not know. This is not a defect that can be remedied by more or better knowledge; the fact is, we cannot know. In this situation, what we need most is humility—the modesty that follows from acknowledging that we are unable to determine what is the best course for other people and peoples to follow. If we are sensitive to what is happening in our own backyards, we will have enough trouble trying to determine what is best for our "developed" societies, all of which have major social problems.

I am suggesting, quite seriously, that one of the best things we can do for many "undeveloped" peoples is not to "develop" them but to leave them alone. That, at least, is better than many poverty programs that have further diminished the ability of the "poor" to meet their own needs, often because they have involved divesting local people of their own resources (e.g., by diverting agriculture from self-consumption into monoculture for export). This would mean allowing people to manage their own resources and to identify their own opportunities and capabilities. It does not mean simply "doing nothing," however; restoring local self-determination may sometimes require considerable intervention.

This does not always mean that we cannot help other communities decide what they would like to change in their lives. Needless to say, this is an extremely subtle process if the means are not to subvert the ends. Some recent work in development studies has been moving in this direction, and many of those new, more participatory approaches are summarized in Robert Chambers's book *Whose Reality Counts?* Chambers argues persuasively that personal as well as professional and institutional change is necessary in order to promote truly successful development. Several Buddhist-inspired development projects, such as the Sarvodaya movement in Sri Lanka, already exemplify many of these changes.

However, and to say it again, leaving alone is not something that should apply to the problem of genuine destitution, which morally obligates us to provide, at the very least, sufficient food, clothing, basic shelter, and medical care to all the world's people. This, it would seem, immediately brings us back to the onerous problem of devising economic development strategies. In fact, these basic requisites could be met quite easily and inexpensively if our intentions were genuine and our motivation serious. Providing them for the destitute would actually require a very small percentage of the world's annual product. "It is estimated that the additional cost of achieving and maintaining universal access to basic education for all, basic health care for all, reproductive health care for all, adequate food care for all and safe water and sanitation for all is roughly $40 billion a year," according to a United Nations report. "This is less than 4 percent of the combined wealth of the 225 richest people in the world." The same report points out that Americans and Europeans spend $17 billion a year on pet food.[34]

I am reversing the usual metaphor and suggesting that instead of pretending to teach the poor how to fish, we give the most impoverished the fish they need. (Recall that the monarch in the Lion's Roar Sutra got into trouble because he failed to give property to the needy, not because he failed to promote economic growth.) The dismal record of the last fifty years of development reveals the cruelty of the usual slogan: when we have taught the world's poor to fish, the effect has often been that they deplete their fishing grounds for our consumption.

The problem, then, is not that we do not have enough resources to provide for the basic needs of everyone. We have much more than enough. The problem is a lack of enough collective will to overcome the simple fact that the people who have the most say about what happens to the earth's resources do not care to do it. It is just not a priority for them, and insofar as our own preoccupation with wealth accumulation encourages us to acquiesce in this situation, we are complicit with their indifference.

In conclusion, I am suggesting that the solution to poverty is not primarily economic, because its origin is not primarily economic. Some "poverty," especially in rural areas, is not poverty at all, at least not by traditional standards. Often economic globalization, far from solving poverty, actually creates it by dislocating people or divesting them of their own resources. And responding to genuine destitution is, at least in the short term, not so much an economic challenge as a matter of our collective intentions and therefore our values.

This brings us back to religion, and to the need for religious institutions that understand how rampant commodification undermines their fundamental teachings. The corrosive influence of economic globalization and its development institutions on nonmarket human values needs to be challenged. Today the mainstream media are corporations interested only in the bottom line, and our universities are becoming little more than an advanced form of job training. Do revivified religions remain our best hope for challenging the commodification of the world?

CHAPTER 3

Pave the Planet or Wear Shoes?

The greatest wealth is contentment.
—*The Dhammapada*

Acording to the traditional story, Shakyamuni Buddha renounced a privileged life of pleasure and leisure for the arduous life of a forest dweller, yet his ascetic practices did not produce the enlightenment he sought. He went on to discover a "middle way" that does not simply split the difference between sense enjoyment and sense denial. It focuses on calming and understanding the mind, for only insight can liberate us from our usual preoccupation with trying to become happy by satisfying our cravings. The goal is not to eradicate all desires but to experience them in a nonattached way, so that we are not controlled by them. Contrary to the stereotype of Buddhism as a world-denying religion, the Buddhist goal does not necessarily involve transcending this world in order to experience some other one. Rather, the goal is attaining a wisdom that realizes the true nature of this world, including the true nature of oneself, and through this wisdom being liberated from dukkha.

These concerns are reflected in the Buddhist attitude toward wealth and poverty. In the words of Russell Sizemore and Donald Swearer, "a nonattached orientation toward life does not require a flat renunciation of all material possessions. Rather, it specifies an attitude to be cultivated and expressed in whatever material condition one finds oneself. To be nonattached is to possess and use material things but not to be possessed or used by them."[35] In short, the main issue is not how poor or wealthy we are, but how we respond to our situation. The wisdom that develops naturally from nonattachment is knowing how to be content with what we have.

This does not mean that Buddhism encourages poverty or denigrates wealth. The Buddha emphasized many times that the goal of the Buddhist path is to end our dukkha. None of the four ennobling truths implies that material poverty is a desirable state. Rather, poverty is a source of unhappiness in itself and also makes it more difficult to follow a spiritual path.

Nevertheless, Buddhism does not approve of a life devoted to acquiring wealth. The ultimate goal of liberating insight may be more difficult to pursue if we are destitute, yet a life focused on money may be as bad, or worse. Shakyamuni warned repeatedly against that danger: "Few are those people in the world who, when they obtain superior possessions, do not become intoxicated and negligent, yield to greed for sensual pleasures, and mistreat other beings." [36] An intense drive to acquire material riches is one of the main causes of our dukkha. It involves much anxiety but very little real satisfaction. Instead, the Buddha praised those who renounce all attachment to material things in favor of a life devoted wholeheartedly to the path of liberation, by joining the community (sangha) of monks and nuns.

Despite the above, however, Buddhism does not claim that wealth is in itself an obstacle to following the spiritual path. The five basic precepts that all Buddhists are expected to follow—to avoid killing, stealing, lying, sexual misconduct, and intoxicating drugs—mention nothing about abstaining from riches or property, although the precepts do imply much about how we should pursue them. The value of riches cannot be compared with the supreme goal of attaining nirvana, yet properly acquired wealth has traditionally been seen as a sign of virtue, and, properly used, can be a boon for everyone, because wealth creates opportunities to benefit people and to cultivate nonattachment by developing one's generosity. The problem with wealth is not its possession but its abuse. The *Dhammapada* again: "Wealth destroys the foolish, though not those who search for the goal." [37] In short, what is blameworthy is to earn wealth improperly, to become attached to it and not to spend it for the well-being of everyone, to squander it foolishly or use it to cause suffering to others. Right livelihood, the fifth part of the eightfold path, emphasizes that our work should not harm other living beings and specifically prohibits trading in weapons, poisons, intoxicants, or slaves.

That wealth can indicate virtue follows from the Buddhist belief in karma and rebirth, according to which karma is moral cause and effect: what we do to others will be done to us. If karma is a law of the universe, what happens to us later (in this life or in a future lifetime) is largely a result of what we have done in the past and are doing now. True wealth (not just of money) is a consequence of one's own previous generosity, and poverty a result of one's own misbehavior (most likely avarice or seeking wealth in an immoral way). Not all Buddhists accept that karma is so inexorable or understand it so literally, but the traditional belief implies (in the long run, at least) harmony between my morality and my prosperity.

BUDDHIST ECONOMICS

Everything so far concerns attitudes that we as individuals should cultivate or avoid. What kind of economic system do they imply? Since Buddhism lacks an explicit social theory, we cannot look to traditional Buddhist texts for perspectives on specific economic issues such as globalization. However, some Buddhist scriptures do have significant social and economic implications. Perhaps the most relevant is the Lion's Roar Sutra, discussed in the previous chapter, which shows how poverty can lead to social deterioration.

Despite some fanciful elements, this sutra implies that social breakdown cannot be separated from broader questions about the benevolence of the economic order and the role of the state. The solution to poverty-induced crime is not punishment but helping those in poverty to provide for their basic needs. What, if anything, does this imply about the moral imperatives of global capitalism? The sutra encourages economic activity, not welfare: the king evidently reforms the first thieves by giving them enough property to become self-supporting. More important, however, is the sutra's emphasis on the role of the state in addressing poverty. The great economic debate that has preoccupied the West for more than a century—the role of the state versus the role of the private sector—is not addressed directly, of course, but the sutra does emphasize the economic responsibility of rulers, and presumably states today, for the welfare of the economically vulnerable.

If we attempt to translate that emphasis into (for example) contemporary controversies about the structural adjustment plans of the World Bank and the International Monetary Fund, plans that often involve a "temporary" reduction in the quality of life for those already poor, this sutra may be taken to imply that such interventions may be socially dangerous as well as morally questionable. It should be obvious that the economy is not an end in itself: an economic system exists for the sake of people, not vice versa. Proponents of globalizing capitalism argue, as they must, that economic globalization benefits most people, yet it is increasingly difficult to overlook the fact that business interests are usually allowed to trump all others. Whether globalization benefits the poor, it does further enrich the wealthy—those who have capital to invest.

However, notice also what the Lion's Roar Sutra does *not* say. Today we sometimes evaluate such situations by talking about the need for "social justice" and the state's role in "distributive justice." This emphasis on social justice, so important in the Abrahamic religions, is not found in traditional Buddhism. As the above story indicates, the Buddhist emphasis on karma implies a different way of understanding and addressing that social problem. The traditional Buddhist solution to poverty is *dana* (giving or generosity).

Dana is the most important concept in Buddhist thinking about society and economics, because it is the main way nonattachment is cultivated and demonstrated. Buddhists are called upon to show compassion to those who need our help. The doctrine of karma seems quite harsh insofar as it implies that such unfortunates are reaping the fruit of their previous deeds, yet this is not understood in a punitive way. Although they may be victims of their own previous selfishness, the importance of generosity for those walking the Buddhist path does not allow us the luxury of being indifferent to their situation. We are expected, even spiritually required, to lend assistance. This appeal is not to justice for victims of circumstances. Despite the prudential considerations expressed in the sutra—what may happen if we are not generous—it is the morality and spiritual progress of the *giver* that is the main issue. In the language of contemporary ethical theory, this is a "virtue ethics." It offers a different perspective that cuts through the usual political opposition between conservative (right) and liberal (left) economic views. According to Buddhism, no one can evade responsibility for his or her own deeds and efforts. At the same time, generosity is not optional: we are obligated to respond compassionately to those in need. In the Lion's Roar Sutra, the king started the social breakdown when he did not fulfill this obligation.

In modern times, however, the social consequences of dana in Asian Buddhist countries have usually been limited. The popular emphasis has been on "making merit" by supporting the sangha, the community of monks and nuns. The sangha is dependent on that support because monks and nuns are not allowed to work for money. Karma too is often understood in a commodified way, as something that can be accumulated by dana. Since the amount of merit gained is believed to depend not only upon the value of the gift but also upon the worthiness of the recipient, and since members of the Buddhist sangha are by definition the most worthy recipients, one receives more merit from donating food to a well-fed bhikkhu than to a poor and hungry layperson.

This preoccupation with accumulating merit seems incompatible with the Buddhist emphasis on nonattachment, for it is liable to encourage a "spiritual materialism" ultimately at odds with the highest goal of spiritual liberation. The benefits of such merit-making redound to the rest of society, since the sangha is primarily responsible for practicing and propagating the teachings of Buddhism. Nevertheless, I believe that the present economic relationship between the sangha and laypeople needs to be reexamined. Rural Thailand, for example, needs hospitals and clinics more than it needs new temples. According to the popular view, however, a wealthy person gains more merit by funding the construction of a temple—whether or not one already exists in that area. Such a narrow but commonplace understanding of dana as merit-making has worked well to provide for sangha needs, but it cannot be an adequate spiritual response to the challenges provided by globalization.

One possible Buddhist alternative, or supplement, is the bodhisattva ideal emphasized in Mahayana Buddhism. The bodhisattva is a spiritually advanced person wholly devoted to responding to the needs of all living beings, not just those of the sangha. A bodhisattva's entire life is dana, not as a way to accumulate merit but because of the bodhisattva's insight that he or she is not separate from others. According to the usual understanding, a bodhisattva does not follow the eightfold path but a slightly different version that emphasizes perfecting six virtues: dana, *sila* (morality), *ksanti* (patience), *virya* (vigor), *dhyana* (meditation), and *prajna* (wisdom). Dana, the first virtue, is believed to imply all the others.

Of course, such a religious model is not easily institutionalized. Yet that is not the main point. Although dana cannot substitute for social justice, there is also no substitute for the social practice of dana as a fundamental aspect of any healthy society. When those who possess much bear no responsibility for those who have nothing, a social crisis is inevitable.

A BUDDHIST PERSPECTIVE ON GLOBALIZATION

Although traditional Buddhist teachings do not include a developed economic theory, we have already seen that they do have important economic implications. Those implications can be further developed to help us understand and respond to the new world order being created by globalizing capitalism.

As the parable of the unwise king shows, Buddhism does not separate secular issues such as economics from ethical or spiritual ones. The notion that economics is a "social science"—discovering and applying objective, transcultural economic laws—obscures two relevant truths. First, the distributional issue of who gets what, and how they get it, always has moral dimensions, so that issues of production, exchange, and distribution should not be left solely to the dictates of the marketplace. If some people receive much more than they need, and many others receive much less, some sort of redistribution is necessary, as the Lion's Roar Sutra implies. Dana is the traditional, if imperfect, Buddhist way of redistributing. Today that sort of response is obviously inadequate, all the more so because economic globalization is further aggravating the distribution problem between rich and poor. If capitalism can do a better job, as its supporters claim, what reforms are necessary to help it do so?

The other truth is that every system of production and consumption encourages the development of certain personal and social values while discouraging others. People make the system, but the system also makes people. Capitalism tends to reward those who have certain values and to penalize those who do not act according to those values. We need to consider not only what values will encourage and support responsible global capitalism but also what values global capitalism tends to encourage and support. As Phra Payutto, Thailand's most distinguished scholar-monk, has put it:

> It may be asked how it is possible for economics to be free of values when, in fact, it is rooted in the human mind. The economic process begins with want, continues with choice, and ends with satisfaction, all of which are functions of the mind. Abstract values are thus the beginning, the middle and the end of economics, and so it is impossible for economics to be value-free. Yet as it stands, many economists avoid any consideration of values, ethics, or mental qualities, despite the fact that these will always have a bearing on economic concerns. [38]

This clarifies the basic Buddhist approach: individual and social values cannot be dissociated. A crucial issue is whether an economic system is conducive to the ethical and spiritual development of its participants. When we evaluate the characteristics and consequences of global capitalism, therefore, we should consider not only its ecological impact, and how efficiently it produces and distributes goods, but also its effects on human values and the larger social consequences of those values.

In *The Moral Response to Global Capitalism*, John Dunning identifies three moral imperatives for responsible global capitalism: creativity, cooperation, and compassion. The order of their presentation does not seem to be accidental; capitalism prioritizes them in that way. So it is perhaps significant that Buddhism, like many other religious traditions, would prefer to reverse the order. The most important virtue in Buddhism is compassion, and community is also valued; but the capitalist emphasis on creativity receives little emphasis, because wealth creation has not been seen as a solution to the primarily spiritual problem of dukkha. On the other side, however, economists emphasize that economic growth is required for the reduction of our physical dukkha (hunger, inadequate health care, etc.), for they doubt that redistribution of existing wealth could be adequate to meet the needs of everyone even if it became politically possible. If this is true, it suggests more of a role for creativity and entrepreneurship than Buddhism has traditionally emphasized.

THE THREE POISONS

Much of the philosophical reflection on economics has focused on whether economic values are rooted in our basic human nature. Those who defend capitalism have usually argued that its emphasis on competition and personal gain is grounded in the fact that humans are fundamentally self-centered. The Scottish economist Adam Smith argued that, in a capitalist economy, the common good of society is promoted by each person pursuing his own self-interest—as if the whole process were supervised by "an invisible hand." Critics of capitalism have responded by arguing that our human nature is less selfish and more cooperative, so the general good is better promoted by emphasizing social-democratic policies.

Early Buddhism avoids that debate by taking a different approach. Shakyamuni Buddha emphasized that we all have both wholesome and unwholesome traits. What is important is the practical matter of how to reduce our unwholesome characteristics—including "afflictive emotions" such as anger, pride, lust, greed, and envy—and how to develop the more wholesome ones.[39] This process is symbolized by the lotus flower. Although rooted in the mud and muck at the bottom of a pond, the lotus grows upward to bloom on the surface, representing our potential to purify ourselves.

Our unwholesome characteristics are usually described as three poisons or roots of evil: greed, ill will, and delusion. As noted in previous chapters, the Buddhist path transforms all three into their positive counterparts: greed into generosity (dana), ill will into compassion, and delusion into wisdom. If collective economic values cannot be separated from personal moral values, we cannot evade the question: which traits encourage, and are encouraged by, the globalization of capitalism?

Greed / Generosity

Greed is an unpopular word both in corporate boardrooms and in economic theory. The economist's concern with being objective does not allow the moral evaluation of different types of demand. From a Buddhist perspective, however, it is difficult to ignore how capitalism promotes and even requires greed. It does so in two ways: the engine of the economic process is the continual desire for profit, and in order to keep making that profit, consumers must continue wanting to consume more.

These forms of motivation have been extraordinarily successful—depending, of course, on one's definition of success. According to the Worldwatch Institute, more goods and services were consumed in the forty years between 1950 and 1990 (measured in constant dollars) than by all the previous generations in human history.[40] Although such a claim is difficult to verify, it remains relevant and shocking. Significantly, this was not simply a matter of meeting latent demand: according to the United Nations Human Development Report (UNHDR) for 1999, the world spent at least $435 billion the previous year for advertising, not including public relations and marketing.

While this growth has given us opportunities that our grandparents never dreamed of, we have also become more sensitive to its negative consequences, including the staggering ecological impact and the unequal distribution of this new wealth. Whether or not this global maldistribution is worsening or improving, and how much of that maldistribution is a consequence of globalizing capitalism, are controversial issues, yet present inequities are certainly great and seem to be worsening. According to the 1998 UNHDR, in the 1960s the 20 percent of the world's people who live in the richest countries had 30 times the income of the poorest 20 percent; by 1995 that figure had increased to 82 times. The assets of the world's three richest people are greater than the combined GNP of the 48 poorest countries, and in 59 countries, average income is lower than it was 25 years ago.

But these grim facts about "their" dukkha should not keep us from noticing the consequences for "our own" dukkha. From a Buddhist perspective, the fundamental problem with consumerism is the delusion that consuming is the way to become happy. If (as the second noble truth claims) insatiable desires are the source of the dis-ease that we experience in our daily lives, then such consumption, which distracts us and intoxicates us, is not the solution to our unhappiness but one of its main symptoms. That brings us to the final irony of our addiction to consumption: according to the same 1999 report, the percentage of Americans who considered themselves happy peaked in 1957, despite the fact that consumption per person has more than doubled since then. Nevertheless, studies of U.S. households have found that between 1986 and 1994 the amount of money people *think* they need to be happy has doubled. That seems paradoxical, but it is not difficult for Buddhism to explain. Once we define ourselves as consumers, we can never have enough, because consumerism can never really give us what we want from it. It is always the *next* thing we buy that will make us happy.

Higher incomes have enabled many people to be more generous in certain respects, but increased dana charity or philanthropy has not been the main effect because capitalism is based upon a different principle, that extra capital should be used to generate more capital. Rather than redistributing our wealth, as the Buddhist king in the Lion's Roar Sutra was encouraged to do, we prefer to invest that wealth as a means to accumulate more and spend more. That is true regardless of whether or not we need more—a notion that has become rather quaint, since we now take for granted that one can never have too much money. This way of thinking is uncommon, however, in societies, including many Buddhist ones, where advertising has not yet conditioned people into believing that happiness is something you can purchase.

In order for capitalism to successfully globalize, such traditional thinking becomes problematic. To facilitate access to resources and markets, a "money culture" is necessary that emphasizes income and expenditure. But is it a form of cultural imperialism to assume that we in the "developed" world who take such a money culture for granted know more about worldly well-being than "undeveloped" societies do? Our obsession with economic growth seems natural to us because we have forgotten the historicity of many of the "needs" we now take for granted, and we are therefore blind to: the importance of self-limitation, which requires some degree of nonattachment from things and therefore from the markets that buy and sell them.

All this is expressed better with a traditional Buddhist analogy. The world is full of thorns and sharp stones (and now broken glass and other human refuse too); what should we do about this? One solution, at least in principle, is to pave over the entire earth, but a simpler alternative is to wear shoes.[41] "Paving the whole planet" seems a good metaphor for our collective economic globalization project. Without the wisdom of self-limitation, we may not be satisfied even when we have used up all the earth's resources. The other solution is for our minds to learn how to "wear shoes," so that our collective ends become an expression of the renewable means that the biosphere provides.

Why do we assume that lack of money and a restricted range of consumer goods must be dukkha? Perhaps that brings us to the heart of the matter. Has material wealth become increasingly important in the "developed" world because of our eroding faith in any other possibility of salvation? Has increasing our "standard of living" become so compulsive because it substitutes for the sense of security once provided by traditional religious values?

From that perspective, our evangelical efforts to economically "develop" other societies, which cherish their own spiritual values and community traditions, may be viewed as a contemporary form of religious imperialism. Does that make the globalization of capitalism a new kind of mission to convert the heathen?

Ill will / Compassion

Ending our dukkha is the problem that Buddhism addresses, and the major way that Buddhism addresses it is with compassion. That is because our compassion not only increases the happiness of others who receive it, it also increases our own. "For if it is correct," as the Dalai Lama tells us, "that those qualities such as love, patience, tolerance, and forgiveness are what happiness consists in, and if it is correct that compassion is both the source and fruit of these qualities, then the more we are compassionate, the more we provide for our own happiness."[42]

In order to determine the ethical value of an action, Tibetan Buddhism considers its utilitarian consequences less important than the individual's *kun long,* his or her "overall state of heart and mind." Ethically wholesome actions arise naturally when our *kun long* is basically compassionate. "Compassion—which entails ethical conduct—belongs at the heart of all our actions, both individual and social."[43] Insofar as the ultimate goal of economic growth is increasing the sum of human happiness, this key Buddhist insight leads to a crucial question: How much does global capitalism encourage compassion (for example, by increasing opportunities to help people), and how much does it discourage the development of compassion (by emphasizing individual self-interest)?

Conventional economic theory assumes that material resources are limited while our desires are infinitely expandable. Without the norm of self-limitation, this situation becomes a formula for strife. The three poisons do not work independently; greed, ill will, and delusion interact. In 2002, we saw the collapse of the Enron and WorldCom Corporations, the largest bankruptcies in U.S. history. One of the many reasons their collapse is so controversial is the way Enron's top management provided golden parachutes for themselves while allowing the pension funds of ordinary employees to become worthless. This may be an extreme example of how greed works against compassion, yet that sort of story is all too familiar, because it regularly recurs.

As we also know, desire frustrated is a major cause—perhaps the major cause?—of ill will. The Buddha warned against negative feelings such as envy (when we have no opportunity to acquire possessions available to others) and avarice (the selfish enjoyment of goods while greedily guarding them from others). A society in which such psychological tendencies predominate may be materially wealthy but is spiritually poor. A society where people do not feel that they benefit from sharing with each other has already begun to break down.

Delusion / Wisdom

For its proponents, the globalization of market capitalism is a victory for "free trade" over the inefficiency of protectionism and the corruption of special interests. Free trade and capital movement seem to realize in the economic sphere the supreme value that we place on freedom. Freedom optimizes access to resources and markets. What could be wrong with that?

Approaching the issue from a non-Western perspective such as Buddhism makes it easier to see that globalizing capitalism is neither natural nor inevitable. It is one historically conditioned way for us to understand and organize our material world, with disadvantages as well as advantages, since it is based upon certain presuppositions about the nature of that world.

The critical stage in the development of market capitalism occurred during the Industrial Revolution, when new technologies led to the "liberation" of a critical mass of land, labor, and capital, which became understood in a new way: as commodities to be bought and sold. In order for market forces to interact freely and productively, the world had to be converted into extractable resources available for exchange. As Karl Polanyi has shown, there was nothing inevitable about this commodification.[44] In fact, it was disliked and resisted by many people at the time, and was successfully implemented only because of strong government support.

For those who had capital to invest, the Industrial Revolution was quite profitable, yet that was not the way most people experienced market commodification. The biosphere (which from an ecological perspective could be considered our mother as well as our home) became commodified into a collection of resources to be exploited. Human life became commodified into labor, or work-time, and priced according to supply and demand. Family patrimony, the traditional inheritance preserved for one's descendants, became commodified into capital for investment. All three were reduced to *means* that the new economy used to generate more capital for more development for more profit—yielding more capital for more development for more...

From a religious perspective, an alternative way to describe this process of commodification is that the world and its many beings (including humans) have become de-sacralized. Today we see biotechnology doing this to the genetic code of life; soon our awe at the mysteries of reproduction—one of the last bastions of the sacred—will be replaced by the ultimate shopping experience. The "developed world" is now largely secularized, yet elsewhere this social and economic transformation is far from finished. Is that why the International Monetary Fund and the World Trade Organization have become so important? A less sanguine way of viewing their role is that they exist to ensure that nothing stands in the way of converting the rest of the earth—the still "undeveloped world," to use our revealing term for it—into resources and markets.

This commodified understanding presupposes a sharp duality between humans and the rest of the earth. Value is created by our goals and desires; the rest of the world has no meaning or value except insofar as it serves human purposes. However natural this dualistic understanding now seems to us,

Buddhist teachings question it, for it is one of our more problematic delusions, at the heart of our dukkha.

There are different accounts of what Buddha experienced when he became enlightened, but they agree that he realized the nondual interdependence of things. The world is not a collection of things but a web of interacting processes. Nothing has any reality of its own apart from that web, because everything, including us, is dependent on everything else. As the Dalai Lama puts it, "When we consider the matter, we start to see that we cannot finally separate out any phenomena from the context of other phenomena."[45] The Vietnamese Zen master Thich Nhat Hanh has expressed this more poetically:

> If you are a poet, you will see clearly that there is a cloud floating in this sheet of paper. Without a cloud, there will be no rain; without rain, the trees cannot grow, and without trees we cannot make paper. The cloud is essential for the paper to exist. If the cloud is not here, the sheet of paper cannot be here either....
>
> If we look into this sheet of paper even more deeply, we can see the sunshine in it. If the sunshine is not there, the tree cannot grow. In fact, nothing can grow. Even we cannot grow without sunshine. And so, we know that the sunshine is also in this sheet of paper. The paper and the sunshine *inter-are*. And if we continue to look, we can see the logger who cut the tree and brought it to the mill to be transformed into paper. And we see the wheat. We know that the logger cannot exist without his daily bread, and therefore the wheat that became his bread is also in this sheet of paper. And the logger's father and mother are in it too.[46]

He goes on to show that "as thin as this sheet of paper is, it contains everything in the universe in it." Such interdependence challenges our usual sense of separation from the world. The Cartesian sense that I am "in here," inside my head behind my eyes, and the world is "out there," alienates us from the world we are "in." The anatta "no-self" teaching denies this duality, which for Buddhism is seen as psychologically and historically conditioned. Our sense of a self apart from the world is a delusion—what would now be called a construction—because the sense of "I" is an effect of interacting physical and mental processes that are interdependent with the rest of the world. This makes each of us a manifestation of the world. The Buddhist path works by helping us to realize our interdependence and nonduality with the rest of the biosphere, and to live in accordance with that. This path is incompatible, therefore, with any economic system that treats the earth only as a commodity, or that works to reinforce our delusive sense of separation from it and from other people.

Transforming the System

Does the above critique—my extrapolation of basic Buddhist teachings— imply that Buddhism is incompatible with capitalism? The nature and role of corporations is addressed in more detail in the next chapter, which points to some other fundamental problems with these organizations. Yet such extrapolations of Buddhist teachings must be kept in context. To say it again, Buddhism does not itself advocate any particular economic system, and neither does it *prima facie* reject any. Historically, Buddhism has been quite pragmatic and flexible regarding such institutions. Furthermore, this would seem to be an area where the Buddhist tradition has something to learn from modern economics, insofar as its central concern is eliminating dukkha and promoting human happiness. Buddhism arose and developed in cultures where technologies were comparatively primitive, and where the economic opportunities to improve one's lot were usually very limited. Traditionally, Buddhism has focused on mental dukkha—the unhappiness caused by our ways of thinking and feeling—but physical dukkha is also dukkha that needs to be addressed. Despite all the problems with modern technologies and economic globalization, contemporary Buddhism needs to acknowledge the opportunities they can offer for promoting individual and social happiness. Generally, though, that is not a point that needs to be stressed today; rather, there is greater need for the Buddhist insight that economics and technology cannot by themselves resolve our dukkha.

The crucial issue remains the relationship between an economic system and the individual and social values it promotes: in other words, how responsible capitalism is or can become. Many critics emphasize the importance of governments in their supervisory and regulatory role, which is indeed necessary, yet that also highlights the worrisome tendency of some capitalist institutions, especially powerful corporations, to subvert such regulation. The U.S. electoral process is an egregious example, but there are many others. The fact that this subversion is now so obvious also suggests the possibility of a solution, at least in democratic societies.

People create the social system, but the system creates people. This sociological truism implies that we need to work on both levels. Naturally, the main focus of Buddhism has been, and will continue to be, on personal transformation. Yet it is not enough to assume that, if only enough people change themselves the system must and will change to accommodate them. The social forces that mold the ways we think, feel, and act today—especially the state and the mass media, both largely corporate controlled—are so powerful that they cannot just be ignored, as we try to construct a more generous, compassionate, and wise society within the shell of institutionalized greed, ill will, and delusion. In order for the necessary changes to occur, we must take advantage of our relatively democratic institutions to challenge those institutions.

If it is agreed that responsible capitalism is not an end in itself but a means toward a better life and a healthier society, it becomes difficult to avoid the conclusion that today we need more democratic supervision of international markets, which need to become more transparent in their operations. If it is also true that societies do not exist for the sake of markets but vice versa, it is also true that during the last two hundred years the tail has often wagged the dog. Many, perhaps most, people have had to adapt to economic changes that were forced upon them by undemocratic (or only nominally democratic) rulers. If global capitalism is to become truly socially responsible, such forced transformations must be recognized as unacceptable. How can more democratic decision making be encouraged? In two general ways:

Change from the top down. Perhaps the most pressing immediate issue is the public supervision of privately owned corporations, especially transnational ones responsible for an increasing share of the world's economic product. I think that the first concern should be to reduce their influence on public institutions, especially to protect the electoral process from the effects of their "contributions," and to address the role of corporate lobbyists. Another step is to require the boards of large corporations to include employee and environmentalist representatives, to ensure that profit is not the only factor considered in decision making. In the end, I think it will be necessary to redefine the nature of corporations by means of their social umbilical cords: that is, by rewriting their corporate charters to ensure that corporations exist to promote the public good rather than vice versa. Until the late nineteenth century, corporations were usually more closely scrutinized and supervised by state governments, and the penalty of institutional death—revoking charters—

was sometimes applied to those that engaged in illegal activities or otherwise seriously violated the conditions of their charters.

I do not underestimate the difficulty of doing these things, but I also doubt whether our present economic system can ever become truly responsible without such measures.

Change from the bottom up. To start at the bottom is to begin with people's basic values, including religious commitments. Buddhist values, like other Buddhist teachings, are not revealed to us but discovered by those who follow the Buddhist path. Shakyamuni Buddha is not a god; through his own efforts he discovered the nature of reality, the Dharma, and by following in his footsteps we can discover those same truths for ourselves. Buddhist precepts are not moral laws that someone or something else obligates us to follow. Rather, the incentive is that if we live according to them, our karma will improve and our lives will naturally become more happy. This does not require anyone to identify himself or herself as a Buddhist, but it does require our own effort to transform ourselves.

Such a transformation may be in accord with a general spiritual shift in contemporary societies, where fewer people are inclined to identify themselves with religious institutions, yet more people say they are interested in the spiritual dimension of their lives. That can be dismissed as another example of our more self-centered individualism, but I think it is much more than that. Other complementary movements, such as "downshifting" and voluntary simplicity, suggest a change of mood among some in the more affluent nations. It is difficult to determine how widespread this change is—corporate media, dependent on advertising revenues (and thus promoting consumerism), have little incentive to spotlight it—but if this grows into a genuine social movement, it might become the most important example of a bottom-up route to upgrading our collective moral behavior by first upgrading our collective spiritual consciousness.

I emphasize this because from a Buddhist viewpoint, and perhaps from any truly religious viewpoint, the most problematic aspect of capitalism today is its tendency to function as a religious surrogate. If religion teaches us what is really important about the world, and therefore how to live in it, today the most important religion for an increasing number of people all over the world is consumerism. Overproduction has long since shifted the focus from the manufacture of goods to the manufacture of demand—one of the more trenchant examples of how capitalism has remolded society in order to solve its own problems.

How might an "upgraded" spiritual consciousness express itself economically? One possibility is an expanded role for churches and religious (or religious-inspired) NGOs such as charities and pressure groups, which can employ their own economic power as well as the oxygen of publicity to influence the values of global capitalist development. Economic boycotts played an important role in hastening the end of apartheid in South Africa.

Since governments are also deeply implicated in the new "religion of the market"—measuring their success by the GNP—grassroots efforts are also indispensable for influencing the political process. One way to start would be with a movement to restrict the role of advertising, on the grounds that today much of it has become as bad for our psychological and spiritual health as tobacco is for our physical health.

Such a grassroots transformation in consciousness would doubtless empower many such reforms, in the end either making global capitalism much more responsible or, if that fails, working to replace it with something else more responsible to our spiritual concerns.

CHAPTER 4

Can Corporations Become Enlightened?

We have given corporations dominion over the sustaining of our lives. They have become sovereign citizens and we have become consumers. They concentrate power and wealth. They design and shape our society and world. They carve our goals and aspirations. They shape our thoughts and our language. They create the images and metaphors of our time, which our children use to define their world and their lives. In other words: what corporations do well, what corporations are designed to be, is the problem.

—Richard Grossman

D ESPITE their enormous and increasing impact upon all of us, most of us know little about corporations. We read about mergers and hostile takeovers, and what stock price has fallen due to an earnings warning. Periodically we follow the latest CEO scandal, as his (rarely her) once-hyped company collapses into bankruptcy. Yet few of us understand how massive corporations have come to assume such a dominant role in public life, or why they function in the ways that they do. Today corporations are the main agent of globalization and the institutions that have more impact on our daily lives than any other, with the possible exception of government. By 1995, only 49 of the world's 100 largest economies were nations; the other 51 were corporations. For example, Malaysia's economy was number 53, bigger than the Japanese corporation Matsushita (54) but somewhat smaller than IBM (52); Mitsubishi, the largest corporation in the world until the Japanese economic bubble burst, was number 22. Total assets of the top 100 multinationals increased seven times between 1980 and 1995, while the total number of their employees decreased. The combined sales of the top 200 multinational corporations were bigger than the combined GDP of 182 countries (all but the top 9). That is almost 30 percent of world GDP. Yet those corporations employed less than one-third of 1 percent of the world's population, a percentage that has been shrinking.[47]

In the United States six corporations (versus fifty in 1983) now control most of the media. The largest one hundred corporations buy about three-quarters of commercial network time and over half of public television time as well.[48] This means that they decide what is shown on television and what is not—in other words, that TV has more or less become their "private medium" for influencing the rest of us. In short, corporations control the U.S. "nervous system" and increasingly the international one as well.

Many social commentators have been addressing the economic and political implications of this consolidation. The concern of this short chapter is to examine the present role of corporations from a Buddhist perspective. One important aspect, of course, is the question of responsibility. Today, thanks to spreading ideals of democracy, it is increasingly accepted that states are or should be responsible to their citizens, but to whom are transnational corporations responsible? There is also another, perhaps even more fundamental issue that Buddhism can shed some light upon: the "empty" nature of corporations and what their lack of self-being means for our globalizing world, now being reconstructed to meet the needs of these fictive (i.e., socially constructed) institutions.

Whenever we want to understand something, one of the first places to look is at its history, which usually illuminates features that we otherwise overlook or misunderstand. What does their past teach us about corporations and their responsibilities?

Incorporated business enterprises, with their liabilities legally limited, originated in Europe. According to some sources, the earliest record of such a corporation is from Florence in 1532. Both the date and place are significant. Columbus had "discovered" America in 1492. Just as important, Vasco da Gama had sailed around Africa to India in 1498 and returned with cargo worth sixty times the cost of his voyage. A profit of 6,000 percent! You can imagine what effect that had on the dreams of Italian merchants. There were some problems, however. It was extremely expensive to outfit an expedition, so very few people could afford to do so. Voyages were also extremely risky;

the chance of a ship sinking in a storm or being taken by pirates was considerable. Finally, there were debtor's prisons—not only for you but for your family and your descendants—if you lost your ship and could not pay your debts.

The solution to these problems was ingenious: limited liability. Unlike partnerships, where each partner is legally responsible for all business debts, limited liability means you can lose only the amount you invest. Such an arrangement required a special charter from the state, which in Renaissance Italy was usually the local prince. This was convenient not only for the investors but for the prince, because a successful expedition increased the wealth of his territory, and also because he was in line for a cut of the profits for granting the charter.

From the beginning, therefore, corporations have been involved in colonialism and colonial exploitation, a process that continues today under a "neocolonial" economic globalization that continues to transfer wealth from the South to the North. Although they have plenty of help from the World Bank and the International Monetary Fund, corporations continue to be the main institutions that supervise this process.

Corporations have also had an incestuous relationship with the state. In the sixteenth century, nation-states as we know them did not exist. The resources generally available to rulers were too limited for them to exercise the kind of sovereignty that we now take for granted. The self-aggrandizing state that we know today developed along with the royally chartered corporation, because they were dependent on each other—Siamese twins, as it were. The enormous wealth extracted from the New World, in particular, enabled states to become more powerful and ambitious, so rulers assisted the colonization and corporatization process by dispatching their armies and navies to "pacify" foreign lands. As this suggests, there was a third partner, which grew up along with the other two: the modern military. Together they formed an "unholy trinity," thanks to new technologies (gunpowder for aggression, the compass for navigation) and to this clever new type of business organization that minimized the financial risk. In short, the modern nation-state and its military machine matured by feeding on colonial exploitation, in the same way that chartered corporations did.

The United States was born of a revolt against corporations, which had been used as instruments of abusive power by British kings. The new republic was deeply suspicious of both government control and corporate power. Corporations were chartered by the states in order to keep them under close local scrutiny, not by the federal government (the U.S. Constitution does not mention them). The term of corporate charters was limited, and they were automatically dissolved if not renewed or if corporations engaged in activities not granted by their charters. By 1800 there were only about two hundred corporate charters in the United States.

The next century was a period of great struggle between corporations and civil society. The turning point was the Civil War. With huge profits from procurement contracts, corporations were able to take advantage of the disorder and corruption of the times to buy legislatures, judges, and even presidents. Lincoln complained shortly before his death: "Corporations have been enthroned…. An era of corruption in high places will follow and the money power will endeavor to prolong its reign by working on the prejudices of the people…until wealth is aggregated in a few hands…and the republic is destroyed." Rutherford Hayes, who became president in 1876 due to a tainted election and back-room corporate-dominated elections, later declared: "This is a government of the people, by the people and for the people no longer. It is a government of corporations, by corporations, and for corporations."[49]

Corporations gradually gained enough influence to rewrite the laws governing their creation: for example state charters could not be revoked, and corporations could engage in any economic activity without any time limitation, and so forth. Their biggest success was in 1886, when the Supreme Court ruled in *Santa Clara County v. Southern Pacific Railroad* that a private corporation is a "natural person" under the U.S. Constitution and thus entitled to all the protections of the Bill of Rights, including free speech. Given their vast financial resources available for defending and exploiting these rights, this means, in effect, that corporations today are more free than any citizen ever can be.

This incestuous history needs to be emphasized, not only because we are ignorant of it, but because it continues today. We distinguish between the government and the economy, yet at their upper levels there is rarely any effective distinction between them. As Dan Hamburg, a former Democratic representative from California, concluded from his years in the U.S. Congress: "The real government of our country is economic, dominated by large corporations that charter the state to do their bidding. Fostering a secure environment in which corporations and their investors can flourish is the paramount objective of both [political] parties."[50] The same is true internationally. Almost everywhere, globalization means that the interests of politicians who control the destinies of nations are increasingly entwined with the concerns of those who control corporations. In most countries the elite move back and forth quite easily from one to the other, from CEO to cabinet position and back again. Naturally they identify with each other's interests. Think, for example, how much U.S. foreign policy today is determined by the desire to pry open or keep open foreign markets (and raw materials, cheap labor, etc.) for U.S. corporate penetration. Occasionally there have been exceptions to this cozy relationship—genuinely populist leaders like Allende in Chile, for example—but for some reason they tend not to survive very long.

This brings us back to the question of corporate responsibility. A royal charter listed a corporation's privileges and responsibilities. It has been said that corporate history since then is a story of attempts by corporations to increase their privileges and to reduce their responsibilities. One important step in reducing that responsibility was the introduction of the joint stock company. The first English one was chartered in 1553. One's shares in a corporation could now be bought and sold freely, even in a foreign country. The stock market has since become an essential feature of every developed economy, of course, and of many developing ones as well. Consider, however, the effects of this development on corporate responsibility—on the ethical consequences of business activities. Legally, the primary responsibility of a corporation is neither to its employees nor to its customers but to its stockholders; after all, it is the stockholders who own the corporation. What does it mean, then, when those stockholders are anonymous, scattered here and there, and with no interest in the corporation's activities except insofar as they affect its profitability?

Compare the situation of a locally owned business. Suppose you are a master carpenter living in sixteenth-century Italy. When business is good, you employ several other carpenters and apprentices. If you treat them badly— long hours, low wages—it might be difficult for you to escape all the consequences. You and your family live above the workshop, or around the corner. Your wife sees the wives of your senior workers, whether or not she socializes with them. Your children probably play with their children, may even take lessons from the same teachers. You worship in the same church, participate in the same local festivals. In such a situation economic responsibility is also local and not so easily evaded. Everyone in the town knows how you treat your workers, and that affects what other people think about you and how they respond to you.

Contrast that with what happened at Bhopal, India, in 1984, where it is now believed that well over ten thousand people died and another fifty thousand were permanently injured in the world's worst chemical disaster, when a Union Carbide plant leaked toxic gases. Although I do not know who they were, it is safe to assume that the stockholder owners of Union Carbide were elsewhere, living in various places around the world, and that the large majority of them felt no individual responsibility for what happened (although, exceptionally, a few were outraged enough to protest). Needless to say, the people most responsible for managing Union Carbide also lived and worked far away from Bhopal. Whatever legal liability a corporation may have—usually only financial—is quite different from having to *live* with the consequences, and this difference has a great impact upon the way that impersonal institutions like corporations can conduct their business.

It is important to understand that Union Carbide's problem at Bhopal was not primarily a technological one, (and it is important not to think that such debacles are are one of the "unavoidable dangers" of modern life), but a matter of corporate irresponsibility—or rather, as I prefer to put it, of corporate *immorality*. The gas that escaped is so volatile and dangerous that normally it is not stored but immediately made into a more stable compound. At the Bhopal plant it was stored improperly, without being refrigerated. The emergency release valve was not working. There had been prior problems and accidents, yet recommendations resulting from those incidents had not been implemented. There were no plans or exercises for emergency evacuation; no information or training had been provided to the municipality about the gas or how to respond to such an accident.

Consider this simple change to the scenario: If the CEO of Union Carbide had been living next door to that plant, with his family, would those dangerous conditions have been permitted to continue?

Moreover, the Union Carbide corporation never apologized for the accident, evidently because of the legal implications of such an apology. Instead, company executives in India spread rumors that a disgruntled employee had caused the disaster, although no evidence to support this was ever provided. This inability to apologize is precisely my point: it is intrinsic to the nature of impersonal corporations, with limited liability, that they cannot be responsible in the way that you and I can be. Dr. Rosalie Bertell, who directed the International Medical Commission to Bhopal in January 1994, was asked how the Bhopal disaster has changed the way multinationals operate abroad.

Her reply is sobering: "I don't think it has, and that's scary. I think that most of them think that Union Carbide got away with it, and maybe they could get away with it. I think the effect has been minimal." In the end the accident cost Union Carbide nothing. Union Carbide settled all claims for $470,000,000, which was covered by its insurance.[51]

We begin to understand how "a principle purpose of corporations is to shield the managers and directors who run them, and shareholders who profit, from responsibility for what the corporation actually does."[52] This also explains why we should speak of *transnational* corporations rather than multinational ones. Early corporations transcended local communities; today the largest, most powerful corporations transcend responsibility even to nation-states and their citizens. In their preoccupation with profitability, they have learned to play off communities and nations against each other in order to obtain the most favorable operating conditions—the biggest tax breaks, the least environmental regulation, and so forth. This has been a significant development: although corporations and nation-states grew up together, in important respects they have separated. Today corporations are freer than nation-states, which remain bound (at least in principle) by their responsibilities to their own borders and peoples. Corporations have no such fixed obligations. They can reinvent themselves completely, in a different location and even in a different business, when it is convenient for them to do so.

Emptiness, Inc.

So what makes a corporation a corporation? To become "incorporated" (from the Latin *corpus, corporis,* "body") does not mean, of course, that a corporation gains a physical body. You cannot point to a corporation, because its "being" is not material. It is created by a government charter, issued in response to filing an official document and paying a (usually nominal) fee. In principle, at least, such bodiless corporations are now immortal. You can point to a building that is owned or used by a corporation, yet that building can be sold without affecting the legal status of that corporation. In fact, everything can be replaced—all the people working for it, all the material resources owned by it, the activities it engages in, even its name—while it remains essentially the same corporation.

Viewed from another angle, corporations are not things but processes. Despite not having physical bodies, corporations are dissipative systems. That is, a corporation takes in energy from the outside (e.g., raw materials), which it processes in various ways (manufacturing). In order to continue "living" indefinitely, its income must not be less than its expenditures. In addition, and as with organic beings, this process is subject to the law of entropy: although value-added products may be produced (manufactured goods), energy is consumed in the process.

There is an important parallel here with human beings. Of course, our physical bodies are also dissipative systems that absorb energy and use it for physical and mental activities. From a Buddhist perspective, however, the parallel is deeper, for like corporations humans are constructions, according to the Buddhist doctrine of anatta. Buddhism teaches that our sense of self is a delusion because the feeling that there is a "me" apart from the world is mistaken.

This similarity between corporations and people—both being dissipative yet integrated constructs—raises the question as to whether corporations are subject to the same type of problems. According to the second noble truth of the Buddha, the primary cause of human dissatisfaction is tanha, or craving; sometimes ignorance is emphasized as well. Is this also the problem with corporations? It seems to be a natural tendency of our minds never to be satisfied with what we have, but always to want more. The tendency of corporations to expand and seek ever greater profits implies a similar problem. When we consider the Buddhist solution to this problem, however, we realize the difference between corporations and us.

The difference is that corporations are legal fictions, social constructs, and that is why they are so dangerous: without a body, they are essentially ungrounded to the earth and its creatures, to the pleasures and responsibilities that derive from being manifestations of the earth's biosphere. You may prefer to say that corporations are unable to be spiritual, because they lack a soul, but I think it amounts to the same thing. As the example of Bhopal shows, a corporation is unable to feel sorry for what it has done (it may occasionally apologize, but that is public relations, not sorrow). A corporation cannot laugh or cry; it cannot enjoy the world or suffer with it.

Most important of all, a corporation cannot love. Love implies realizing our interconnectedness with others and living in a way that embodies our concern for their well-being. Love is not an emotion but a genuine engagement with others that includes responsibility for them, a responsibility that transcends our own individual self-interest. If that sense of responsibility is not there, one's love is not real. Corporations cannot experience such love or live according to it, not only because they are immaterial, but because their primary responsibility is to create wealth for the shareholders who own them. A CEO who tries to subordinate his company's profitability to his love for the world will lose his position, for he is not fulfilling his financial responsibility to its shareholders.

To make the same point in more Buddhist terms: despite the talk we occasionally hear about "enlightened" corporations, a corporation cannot actually become enlightened in the Buddhist sense of the word. Buddhist enlightenment includes realizing that my sense of being a self apart from the world is a delusion that causes suffering for the world and for me. To realize that I am the world—that I am one of the many ways the world manifests—is the cognitive side of the love that an enlightened person feels for the world and its creatures. The realization and the love are two sides of the same coin, which is why Buddhism emphasizes that genuine enlightenment is accompanied by a spontaneous welling-up of compassion for all other sentient beings. Legal fictions such as corporations cannot experience this any more than robots or computers can.

What most concerns me about corporations, and about a globalization realized primarily by and for them, is that corporations are "fueled" by, and reinforce, not wisdom or compassion but a very different human trait: namely, greed. As we saw in the previous chapter, our corporate-dominated economy *requires* greed in at least two ways: a desire for ever more profit is the engine of the economic process; and in order for the economy to keep expanding, consumers must be conditioned into always wanting more. Buddhism, like most religious traditions, acknowledges the power of greed, yet rather than erect an economic system based upon it, Buddhism emphasizes the need to control it.

Corporations, however, rationalize and "naturalize" our constant desire for more than we already have. The problem with greed magnifies when it is institutionalized in an impersonal corporation that functions quite independently of the values of the people employed by it. For corporations, the world (which, again, is our mother as much as our home) can be meaningful only as a source of raw materials or as a market for its products—in other words, as commodified. The result is that a modern corporation tends to function as a socially constructed vehicle of *institutionalized greed.*

The stock market is a good example. With few exceptions, it tends to function as an ethical "black hole" that dilutes and renders anonymous the responsibility for the actual consequences of the collective greed that now fuels economic growth. At the one end of that hole, investors want increasing returns in the form of dividends and higher stock prices. At the other end, this anonymous expectation translates into a generalized, impersonal pressure for profitability and growth, preferably in the short run. However well intended they may otherwise be, CEOs unable to meet this demand will not last long. The globalization of market capitalism means that such profitability and growth are becoming increasingly important as the engine of world economic activity. Everything else, including the environment, employment, and the quality of life, tends to become subordinated to this anonymous demand that-is-never-satisfied.

Who is responsible for this pressure for growth? The system has attained a life of its own. We all participate in this process, as workers, employers, consumers, and investors, yet with little or no personal sense of moral responsibility for what happens, because such responsibility has been diffused so completely that it is lost in the impersonality of the corporate economic system.

In an important sense, that total loss of responsibility sums up the tragedy of economic globalization today. Increasingly, the destiny of the earth is in the hands of impersonal corporations that, because of the way they are structured, are unmoved by concern for the well-being of the earth's inhabitants and are driven by desire for their own profit and growth. This, of course, is hardly a new insight. Henry Demarest Lloyd expressed it well in 1894: "We are calling upon [those who wield corporate] power and property, as mankind called upon kings of their day, to be good and kind, wise and sweet, and we are calling in vain. We are asking them not to be what we have made them to be." It is intrinsic to the nature of corporations that they cannot be responsible in the ways that we need them to be. The impersonal way they are structured guarantees that such responsibility is so diluted and diffused that, ultimately, it tends to disappear.

One might argue, in reply, that there are good corporations that take good care of their employees, are concerned about their products and their effect on the environment, and so forth. The same argument can be made for slavery: there were some good slave owners who took good care of their slaves, and so on. This does not refute the fact that the institution of slavery is intolerable. "It is intolerable that the most important issues about human livelihood will be decided solely on the basis of profit for transnational corporations."[53] And it is just as intolerable that today the earth's limited resources are being allocated primarily according to what is profitable for transnational corporations.

My Buddhist conclusion is that transnational corporations are defective economic institutions due to the basic way they are structured. We cannot solve the problems they keep creating by addressing the conduct of this or that particular corporation, because the institution itself is the problem. It is difficult to see how, given their present structure, they can be simply patched up to make them better vehicles for our economic needs. We need to consider whether it is possible to reform them in some fundamental way—perhaps by rewriting corporate charters, their social umbilical cords—or whether they should be replaced by other economic and political institutions, ones that are more responsible to the communities they function in and are motivated by service to the earth and the beings who dwell on it. For example, corporate charters could contain a clause emphasizing that their concern for profit will not take precedence over the social and environmental effects of their activities. This prescription could be subject to yearly review by a board composed of public citizens as well as state officials. The general concern is to find ways to legally codify, as well as to emphasize in the public consciousness, that corporations are allowed to exist only insofar as they promote the common good.

The alternative is to promote the public good with smaller, more localized economic institutions that are more easily regulated. As long as corporations in their present form are allowed to remain the primary instruments of economic globalization, they will endanger the future of our children and the world they will live in.

A final caveat: This Buddhist critique does not imply that large corporations are *the* economic problem. The ecological and social devastation wrought by the economic policies of the Soviet Union and Mao's China remind us forcefully that corporations have no monopoly on greed. The collapse of communism has augmented the global reach and influence of corporations, but we should have no delusions that curtailing them will be enough to solve our economic problems. Human greed can take many forms.

The Nonduality of Good and Evil

Buddhist Reflections on the New Holy War

> If only it were all so simple! If only there were evil people somewhere, insidiously committing evil deeds, and it were necessary only to separate them from the rest of us and destroy them. But the line dividing good and evil cuts through the heart of every human being. And who is willing to destroy a piece of his own heart?
>
> —Alexander Solzhenitsyn

I N HIS AUTOBIOGRAPHY Gandhi writes that "those who say that religion has nothing to do with politics do not know what religion means."[54] Perhaps this is more obvious to us after September 11, 2001, but it should always have been obvious—religion is about how we should live, and politics is about deciding together how we will live. The main reason it has not been obvious is because most modern societies have been careful to distinguish the secular public sphere from the personal and private world of religious belief. This distinction has been essential for creating a multicultural climate of religious tolerance, but it comes at a price: such tolerance effectively "displaces morality" by "asking you to inhabit your own moral convictions loosely and be ready to withdraw from them whenever pursuing them would impinge on the activities and choices of others."[55] Most of us would prefer that Osama bin Laden inhabited his moral convictions more loosely, but the downside of loose convictions has been an increasingly amoral public sphere. In two other ways, however, Gandhi's comment seems especially important now.

First, the terrorists who attacked the World Trade Center and the Pentagon were engaged in a political act that was religiously inspired, not withstanding whether they may have misunderstood their religion. In fact, it is difficult to think of any other motivation that can inspire people to sacrifice themselves, and others, so willingly. (The kamikaze pilots of World War II were not exceptions to this motivation; at that time the Japanese emperor was a god, so he was a religious leader as much as a political one.) Although they left no suicide notes, the September 11 hijackers seem to have understood themselves as engaged in a jihad defending Islam against the globalizing West.

And that brings us to another aspect of Gandhi's statement, the one that I wish to focus on: the intersection of religion and politics in the way we perceive good and evil. Our understanding of good and evil cannot be simply identified with any religious worldview, but the two are intimately related. The new war against terrorism, like the long-standing tension between Israel and the Palestinians, and like many earlier conflicts among Jews, Christians, and Muslims, can be viewed as an Abrahamic civil war. These encounters are violent and difficult to resolve, not only because they draw on old historical tensions, but because the opponents seem to share some very similar views about the struggle between good and evil. This essay originates in the curious fact that the al-Qaeda understanding of good and evil—the need for a holy war against evil—is also shared by the administration of George W. Bush.

Three days after the September attacks, President Bush declared that the United States had been called to a new worldwide mission "to rid the world of evil," and two days later he said that the U.S. government was determined to "rid the world of evil-doers." America, the defender of freedom, now has a responsibility to rid the world of its evil. We may no longer have an "evil empire" to defeat, but we have found a more sinister evil that will require a protracted, all-out war to destroy it. Later Bush unwisely referred to this war as a "crusade," and in his 2002 State of the Union address he identified a new "axis of evil," especially Iraq, Iran, and North Korea.

If anything is evil, the terrorist attacks on September 11 were evil. That must not be forgotten in what follows. At the same time, however, I think we need to take a close look at the rhetoric of good-and-evil. When Bush says he wants to rid the world of evil, alarm bells should go off for us—because that is also what Hitler and Stalin wanted to do.

What was the problem with Jews that required a "final solution"? The earth could be made pure for the Aryan race only by exterminating the Jews, gypsies, homosexuals, the mentally defective, and the like—all the impure vermin who contaminate it. Stalin needed to exterminate well-to-do Russian peasants in order to establish his ideal society of collective farmers. Both of these great villains were trying to perfect the world by eliminating its impurities. The world can be made good only by destroying its evil elements.

In other words, one of the main causes of evil in this world has been human attempts to eradicate evil. In Buddhist terms, much of the world's suffering has been a result of our way of thinking about good and evil.

On the same day that Bush made his first pronouncement about ridding the world of evil, the *Washington Post* quoted Joshua Teitelbaum, a scholar who has studied the al-Qaeda movement: "Osama bin Laden looks at the world in very stark, black-and-white terms. For him, the U.S. represents the forces of evil that are bringing corruption and domination into the Islamic world."

What is the difference between bin Laden's view and Bush's? They are opposites, of course—in fact, *mirror* opposites. Let's look at that Teitelbaum quote again, changing only a few names: "George W. Bush looks at the world in very stark, black-and-white terms. For him, al-Qaeda represents the forces of evil that are bringing corruption and domination into the Western world." As President Bush says, "You're either with us or against us."

What bin Laden sees as good—an Islamic jihad against an impious imperialism—Bush sees as evil. What Bush sees as good—America the defender of freedom and democracy—bin Laden sees as evil. That makes them two different versions of the same holy war between good and evil.

This is not to equate Bush's actions with those of bin Laden (although I can appreciate why such an argument might be attempted, considering the large number of civilian casualties in Afghanistan). Rather, I am making a point about our ways of looking at the world, at the lenses through which bin Laden and Bush—and we too—use to understand what happens in it. From a Buddhist perspective, there is something delusive about both sides of this mirror image, and it is important to understand how this black-and-white way of thinking brings more suffering, more evil, into the world.

This dualism of good versus evil is attractive because it is a simple way of looking at the world, and there will be more to say about that later. Although it is certainly not unique to the Abrahamic religions, I think this dualism is one of the reasons why the conflicts among them have been so difficult to resolve peacefully: believers tend to identify their own religion as good and may subtly or grossly demonize other faiths and their adherents.

It is difficult to turn the other cheek when viewing the world in this way, because this dualism rationalizes the opposite principle of an eye for an eye.

If the world is a battleground of good and evil forces, the evil that is in the world must be fought and defeated by any means necessary.

I am not saying that this attitude represents the best of the Abrahamic religions but am only drawing attention to the sometimes dichotomous pull within them. There is another way to understand the war between good and evil: to turn within and understand its psychological roots as the struggle that occurs within each of us when we try to live up to the ideals of our own religion. This is the "greater jihad" or "internal jihad" that most Muslims emphasize more than any externalized one. Nevertheless, it is a tragic fact that many religious people—or many people who believe themselves to be religious—have projected this struggle as a struggle in the external world between objectified good and evil.

The secularization of the modern West has not eliminated this tendency. In some ways it has intensified it, because we can no longer rely on a supernatural resolution. We have to depend upon ourselves to bring about the final victory of good over evil, as Hitler, Stalin, and Mao Zedong tried to do. It is unclear how much help bin Laden and Bush have expected from God.

Perhaps the basic problem with this simplistic good-versus-evil way of understanding conflict is that, since it tends to preclude further examination, it keeps us from looking deeper, from trying to discover causes. Once something has been identified as evil, it is time to fight it. Bin Laden and Bush seem to share this tendency. This is where we can benefit from the different perspective of an Asian religious tradition.

For Buddhism, evil, like everything else, has no essence or substance of its own; it is a product of impermanent causes and conditions. Buddhism places less emphasis on the *concept* of evil than on its *roots:* three causes of evil, also known as the three poisons—greed, ill will, and delusion. I wonder if the Abrahamic religions emphasize the struggle between good and evil because the basic issue for them is usually understood to be our will—i.e., which side are we on? In contrast, Buddhism emphasizes ignorance and enlightenment because the basic issue depends on our self-knowledge—i.e., do we really understand what motivates us?

One way to summarize the basic Buddhist teaching is that we suffer, and cause others to suffer, because of greed, ill will, and delusion. Karma implies that when our actions are motivated by these roots of evil, their negative consequences tend to rebound upon us in obvious or less obvious ways. That is true for everyone. However, the Buddhist solution to suffering does not

involve requiting violence with violence, any more than it involves responding to greed with greed, or to delusion with delusion. From a Buddhist perspective, the deaths of some three thousand innocent people in New York and
Washington cannot justify a bombing campaign that leads to the deaths of an
even larger number of innocent Afghanis. Rather, the Buddhist solution
involves breaking that cycle by transforming greed into generosity, ill will into
loving-kindness, and delusions into wisdom.

What do these teachings imply now, in the aftermath of the September
2001 attacks?

To begin with, we cannot focus only on the second root of evil, the hatred
and violence that were directed against the United States. The three roots are
intertwined. Ill will cannot be separated from greed and delusion; the ill will
of others may be due to their greed, but it may also be a reaction to our greed.
This points us toward an essential question that some of us prefer to brush
away: Why do so many people in the Middle East, in particular, hate the
United States so much? What have we done to encourage that hatred? These
are crucial questions that all the simpleminded rhetoric about "evil" has
tended to ignore or downplay. Undoubtedly, some fundamentalist versions of
Islam are also important factors; yet they are not the only ones. We Americans
usually think of America as the most ardent defender of freedom and justice,
but obviously that is not the way many Muslims in the Middle East perceive
us. Are they misinformed? Are we? Or are both of us?

As the social critic Micah Sifry writes, "Does anybody think that we can send
the USS New Jersey to lob Volkswagen-sized shells into Lebanese villages—
Reagan, 1983—or loose 'smart bombs' on civilians seeking shelter in a Baghdad
bunker—Bush, 1991—or fire cruise missiles on a Sudanese pharmaceutical factory—Clinton, 1999—and not receive, someday, our share in kind?"[56]

More precisely, how much of U.S. foreign policy in the Middle East has been
motivated by our love of freedom and democracy, and how much by our
need—our greed—for its oil? (How did "our" oil get into their wells?) If the
main priority has been securing oil supplies, and if we have sacrificed other,
more democratic concerns for access to that resource, does it mean that our
petroleum-based economy is one of the causes of the September 11 attacks?

Buddhist teachings imply that we should focus especially on the role of delusion in creating this situation. Delusion has a special meaning in Buddhism.
The fundamental delusion is our sense of separation from the world we live
in, including our separation from other people. Insofar as we feel separate

from others, we are more inclined to manipulate them to get what we want. This naturally breeds resentment: both from others, who do not like to be used, and within ourselves, when we do not get what we want.... Isn't this also true at the collective level of corporations, cultures, and countries?

The delusion of separation becomes wisdom when we realize that no one is an island. We are interdependent because we are all part of each other, different facets of the same jewel we call the earth. This world is a not a collection of objects but a community of subjects, a web of interacting processes. Our "interpermeation" means we cannot avoid responsibility for each other. This is true not only for the residents of lower Manhattan, many of whom worked together in response to the World Trade Center catastrophe, but for all people in the world, however hate-filled and deluded they may be...including even the terrorists who did these horrific acts, and all those who supported them.

Christians are urged to distinguish the sinner from the sin. This attitude is also quite Buddhist. I do not know how greedy bin Laden and the other al-Qaeda leaders are, but they certainly seem to be extreme examples of how ill will and delusion can overwhelm the mind. Nevertheless, from a Buddhist perspective they still have the capacity to understand how evil their actions have been, and to atone for them. We know that such an awakening is unlikely to occur, and in fact bin Laden and most of the other al-Qaeda leaders may be dead by the time you read these words. That fate, however, is not something for Buddhists to celebrate, but will be yet another occasion to mourn, in that case for the karmic consequences for themselves, too, of their ignorance and deadly hatred.

Do not misunderstand me here. Of course those responsible for the attacks must be found and brought to justice. That is part of our responsibility to those who have suffered, and we also have a duty to stop all other deluded and hate-filled terrorists. If, however, we want to stop this cycle of hatred and violence, we must realize that our responsibility is much broader.

Realizing our interdependence and mutual responsibility for each other implies something more than just an insight or an intellectual awareness. Trying to *live* this interdependence is *love*. Such love is much more than a feeling; perhaps it is best understood as a mode of being in the world. Buddhist texts emphasize compassion, generosity, and loving-kindness—which are essentially different aspects of love. Such love is sometimes mocked as weak and ineffectual, yet it can be very powerful, as Gandhi showed. It embodies a deep wisdom about how the cycle of hatred and violence works, and about how that cycle can be ended. An eye for an eye makes the whole world blind, but there is an alternative. Twenty-five hundred years ago Shakyamuni Buddha said:

> "He abused me, he beat me, he defeated me, he robbed me"
> —for those who harbour such thoughts ill-will never ceases.

> "He abused me, he beat me, he defeated me, he robbed me"
> —for those who do not harbour such thoughts ill-will ceases.

> In this world hatred is never appeased by ill-will;
> ill-will is always appeased by love. This is an ancient law.[57]

The present Dalai Lama emphasizes the necessity for "internal disarmament."[58] For genuine peace—which is much more than the absence of overt violence—such internal disarmament is as important as external disarmament, and this involves taming the greed, ill will, and delusion in the minds of all those involved, starting with ourselves. It is not possible to work toward peace in a confrontational, antagonistic way.

Certainly, this insight is not unique to Buddhism. It was not the Buddha who gave us the powerful image of turning the other cheek when we have been struck. In the Abrahamic religions the tradition of a holy war between good and evil coexists with this "ancient law" about the power of love. That does not mean all the world's religions have emphasized this law to the same extent. Maybe this is one way to measure the maturity of a religion, or at least its continuing relevance for us now: How much is the transformative truth of this law about love acknowledged and encouraged? Given our much greater technological powers today, our much greater ability to destroy each other, we need this truth more than ever.

What does all this imply about the new situation created by the terrorist attacks? We are at a historical turning point. A desire for vengeance and violent retaliation has arisen, fanned by a leader caught up in his own rhetoric of a holy war to purify the world of evil…. Now, please consider: Does the previous sentence describe bin Laden, or President Bush; does it describe the al-Qaeda network, or the response of the U.S. government?

Many people wanted retaliation and vengeance—we should also reflect on the fact that that seems to be what the terrorists also wanted. If we continue along the path of large-scale violence, bin Laden's war and Bush's war will become two sides of the same escalating holy war.

No one can foresee all the consequences of such a war. They are likely to spin out of control and take on a life of their own. However, one sobering effect is clearly implied by the Buddha's "ancient law": it is already apparent that massive retaliation by the United States is spawning a new generation of suicidal terrorists who will be eager to do their part in this holy war.

Yet widespread violence is not the only possibility. If this time of crisis encourages us to see through the rhetoric of a war to exterminate evil, and if we seek to understand the intertwined roots of this evil, including our own responsibilities, then perhaps something good may yet come out of this horrific tragedy.

Good versus Evil

More or less everything above is from a "Buddhist response" I e-mailed to many people a week after the September 11 attacks. Afterward I found myself reflecting more generally on the problematic duality between good and evil: first considering how that way of thinking deludes us, and then asking what alternative perspective might give us better insight into the cycle of suffering, ill will, and ignorance.

I observed in earlier chapters that because enlightenment or "awakening" requires mindfulness of our ways of thinking, Buddhism encourages us to be wary of antithetical concepts: good and evil, success and failure, rich and poor, and even enlightenment and delusion. We usually distinguish between such opposing terms because we want one rather than the other, yet psychologically as well as logically we cannot have one without the other, since the meaning of each *depends* upon the other. That sounds abstract, but such dualities are actually quite troublesome for us. For example, if it is important for me to live a pure life (however purity is understood), then my life will be preoccupied with (avoiding) impurity. If becoming wealthy is the most important thing for me, then I am equally worried by the prospect of poverty. We cannot take one without the other, and together they filter and distort our experience of the world: because we focus too much on some aspects, we are unable to perceive and appreciate others. If "wealth/poverty" becomes the most important pair of categories I use to understand and react to the world, I tend to see all situations in those terms.

What does this mean for the duality of good versus evil? Their interdependence means that we don't know what is good until we know what is evil, and we don't feel we are good unless we are fighting against that evil. We can feel comfortable and secure in our own goodness only by attacking and destroying the evil outside us. St. George needed that dragon in order to *be* St. George. His heroic identity required it. And, sad to say but true, this is why so many of us like wars: they cut through the petty problems of daily life and unite us good guys here against the bad guys over there. There is fear in that, of course, but it is also exhilarating. The meaning of life seems clearer. The problems with my life, and yours, are now over *there*.

That is one of the main reasons the end of the Cold War created a big problem in the United States, and not only in the military: once Reagan's "evil empire" was history, people whose "goodness" depended on its "badness" felt adrift. A new enemy was needed, but Grenada, Panama, and the war on drugs didn't really fill the bill. This new holy war on worldwide terrorism is much more promising, especially since it seems that we won't ever be able to tell when or if we've won.

In mid-October 2001 the U.S. Secretary of Defense Donald Rumsfeld (or, as he is now called in the alternative media, Secretary of War Rumsfeld) said that the fight against terror:

> undoubtedly will prove to be a lot more like a cold war than a hot war. If you think about it, in the cold war it took 50 years, plus or minus. It did not involve major battles. It involved continuous pressure. It involved cooperation by a host of nations. It involved the willingness of populations in many countries to invest in it and sustain it. It took leadership at the top from a number of countries that were willing to be principled and to be courageous and to put things at risk; and when it ended, it ended not with a bang, but through internal collapse.[59]

Is there some nostalgia in this comparison? Despite all the problems involved, Rumsfeld seems to be saying, it is reassuring to return to the good old days. Now we know what needs to be done: to be courageous and aggressive attacking the evil that is outside and threatens us.

Everyone loves this struggle between good (us) and evil (them), because it is, in its own fashion, quite satisfying. It makes sense of the world. Think of the plot of every James Bond film, every *Star Wars* film, every Indiana Jones film. The bad guys are caricatures: they're ruthless, maniacal, without remorse—and so they must be stopped by any means necessary. We are meant to feel that it's okay—even pleasurable—to see violence inflicted upon them. Because the villains like to hurt people, it's okay to hurt them. Because they like to kill people, it's okay to kill them. After all, they are evil, and evil must be destroyed.

This kind of story seems to be teaching us that if you want to hurt someone, it is important to demonize them first: in other words, to fit them into your good-versus-evil script. Even school bullies usually begin by looking for some petty offense (often a perceived insult) that they can use to justify their own violence. That is why it's said that the first casualty of all wars is truth: the media must "sell" this script to the people.

Such stories are much more than entertainment. In order to live, we need air, water, food, clothes, shelter, friends—and we need these stories, because they teach us what is important in life. They are our mythic tales. They give us models of how to live in a complicated and confusing world. Until the last hundred years or so, the most important stories for most people have been religious: the life of Jesus or Mohammed or the Buddha, and the lives of their followers. Theologians and philosophers may like to argue over concepts and dogmas, but for most people it is the stories that are important: the Easter passion, the Prophet in exile, the future Buddha deciding to leave home.

Today, however, the issue is not usually whether a story is an ennobling tale or a good myth to live by, but the bottom line: Will it sell? You don't need to be religious to wonder how much of an improvement that is.

Disney's very successful—that is, very profitable—film *The Lion King* is a clear example of this kind of dualistic myth-making; it contrasts the noble ruler of the animals, his loving wife, and their innocent cub Simba, all on the good side, with Simba's evil uncle. The uncle hatches a plot to kill the king and eliminate Simba, who escapes but eventually returns to fight the uncle. All very predictable and boring, although often beautiful visually.

In Japan *The Lion King* was featured in cinemas at the same time as *Princess Mononoke*, an animated film by Hayao Miyazaki. (*Princess Mononoke* turned out to be more popular, breaking all attendance records.) One of the striking things about this film—in fact about many of Miyazaki's wonderful films—is the way it avoids any simple duality between good and evil. In *Princess Mononoke*, for example, people do bad things, not because their nature is evil, but because they are complicated: sometimes selfish and greedy, and sometimes just so narrowly focused on what they are doing that they do not see the wider implications of their actions.

I do not know if Miyazaki considers himself a Buddhist, but many of his films seem very Buddhistic to me. Compare the following passage from the Sutta Nipata, an early Buddhist sutra, where Ajita asks of the Buddha, "What is it that smothers the world? What makes the world so hard to see? What would you say pollutes the world and threatens it most?" Notice that the Buddha's response makes no reference to evil:

"It is ignorance which smothers," the Buddha replies, "and it is heedlessness and greed which make the world invisible. The hunger of desire pollutes the world, and the great source of fear is the pain of suffering."

"In every direction," said Ajita, "the rivers of desire are running. How can we dam them, and what will hold them back? What can we use to close the flood-gates?"

"Any such river can be halted with the dam of mindful awareness," said the Buddha. "I call it the flood-stopper. And with wisdom you can close the flood-gates." [60]

A Better Duality?

What alternative is there, if we try to avoid the simplistic duality between good and evil as our way of understanding and evaluating the world? Is it enough to talk about the three roots of evil, or can we say something more about their origins? If greed, ill will, and delusion can be transformed into generosity, loving-kindness, and wisdom, it seems to suggest that these two ways of living are different angles on the same thing, divergent responses to the same situation. What is that situation?

I think we will do better to distinguish between two basic modes of *being in the world*, two different ways of responding to the uncertainty—the death-haunted insecurity—of our life in the world. This insecurity involves not only the impermanence of our circumstances (the fact that everything is changing all the time) but the fragility of our own constructed identities (that "everything changing all the time" includes our sense of self).

One mode of being in the world involves trying to stabilize ourselves by controlling and fixating the world we are in, so that it becomes less threatening and more amenable to our will. The other mode involves a very different strategy: giving priority to opening ourselves up to the world and a greater acceptance of the open-ended impermanence of our existence. That means not allowing our concern for *controlling* the world to dominate the way we *respond* to the world.

Both modes of being involve a quest for security, but they seek that security in very different ways. The word *security* derives from the Latin *se* plus *cura*—meaning, literally, "without care," and connoting a condition where my life is not preoccupied with worrying about my life. We can try to achieve such a condition by completely controlling our world, yet there are other ways to be "without care," which involve a greater trust or faith in the world itself. The first way is more dualistic: I try to manipulate the world in order to fixate my situation, including my own sense of who I am. The second way is more nondual: greater openness to the world is possible because that world is perceived as less threatening and more welcoming, so my own boundaries can be more permeable.

The best terms that I can think of for these two modes of being are *fear* and *love*. Notice that, despite the tension between them in our lives, they are not antitheses in the way that good/evil, rich/poor, and high/low are; the meaning of each is not the opposite of the other. The choice between these two most basic modes of being in the world, or the proportion between them, is the basic challenge that confronts each of us as we mature. This choice is nothing new to psychologists, of course, and a contemporary psychotherapist, Mel Schwartz, has expressed it aptly:

> Contrary to what we may believe, there are only two authentic core emotions; they are love and fear. Other emotions are secondary and are typically masks for fear. Of these, anger is very common. Although we may have come to regard anger as a source emotion, it is really a smokescreen for fear. When we look at our anger, we can always find fear buried beneath it. In our culture we are trained to believe that it's unwise to show fear. We erroneously believe that expressing such vulnerability will permit others to take advantage of us. Yet the fear is there nonetheless.[61]

In the film *Princess Mononoke* the main protagonists display plenty of greed, ill will, and delusion, but it is not difficult to detect the underlying fear. The major conflict is between two powerful women, both sympathetically presented, who want to kill each other. Lady Eboshi, the benevolent ruler of Irontown, is destroying the forest to mine the iron ore she needs for making muskets and bullets; these weapons are both Irontown's source of income and its means of defense against predatory warlords. Young Mononoke, raised by an enormous white wolf god, wants to kill Eboshi to defend against the rape of the forest. *Each side fears what the other side is trying to do to them.* Like Bush and bin Laden, the hatred and aggression of each is a mirror image of the other. During the climax, an extraordinarily violent battle between them, another warlord also attacks Irontown, encouraged by the emperor, who craves the head of the Great Forest Spirit, because a legend says that the spirit's head can confer immortality on whoever gets it. This last motivation is not much developed in the film, but it reminds us of perhaps our greatest fear, and perhaps the one that interferes most with our ability to be open to the world.

How much better it would be, for example, if the Israel-Palestine conflict were understood in these terms! Not as a holy war between good and evil, but as a tragic cycle of reciprocal violence and hatred fueled by a vicious cycle of escalating fear on both sides. Israelis fear that they will never be able to live at peace, believing that Palestinians are determined to destroy them. Palestinians, impoverished by Israeli control over their own communities and dominated by its U.S.-supplied military, also fear that they will never be able to live at peace and believe that Israelis are determined to destroy them, so they strike back in the only way they can.

Needless to say, Schwartz's point about anger as a smoke screen for fear is also very pertinent for understanding the aftermath of September 11. The United States is not used to being attacked, and the disempowering fear that ensued was not something most people were prepared to cope with. In such a case, the collective conversion into national anger, and a reciprocal act of aggression against Afghanistan or some such country, was inevitable. Somebody was going to get bombed.

And what is al-Qaeda's anger a smoke screen for? What fear cowers behind their horrific desire for violence and mass destruction? It has been widely reported that bin Laden is offended by the U.S. military presence in Saudi Arabia, Islam's holy land, yet that is only the tip of a much more problematic iceberg. Al-Qaeda has widespread support among poor Muslims because it is seen as defending Islam against the globalizing West.

Although the relationship between Islam and Western-led modernity is a complicated issue, it is difficult to avoid the conclusion that Islam needs to reform in order to become more compatible with the modern world. That is not the only conclusion to be drawn, however. Of all the major religions, Islam is probably the most concerned with social justice, and therefore the most sensitive to the great social injustices of Western colonialism and domination. Allah is a merciful God but He is also a God of justice and will judge us harshly if we do not accept personal and collective responsibility for the less fortunate. Islam believes that everything really belongs to God, and material things should be used as God wishes them to be used. This means not hoarding but sharing with others who need them. That is why the capitalist idea of using capital to gain ever more capital—you can never have too much!—is foreign and even reprehensible to many devout Muslims. For example, the often-quoted Surah 102:1 of the Qur'an declares that "the mutual rivalry for piling up (the good things of this world) diverts you (from the more serious things)" and Surah 92:18 praises "those who spend their wealth for increase in self-purification."

By adapting so well to the modern world of secular nationalism, capitalism, and consumerism, Christianity in the West has learned to finesse such concerns. Islam is less willing to accept such equivocations, because it recognizes no God above Allah. And recent controversies over the World Trade Organization and other institutions of economic globalization remind us that the era of colonialism is far from over. Bin Laden's own Saudi Arabia is a good example: created by the British after the First World War, and now within the U.S. "sphere of interest," it has one of the most oppressive, undemocratic, and hypocritical governments in the world—but we in the United States hear almost nothing about that reality, and we never will, until the day the U.S. government decides it is necessary to replace that government to keep the oil flowing.

So do poor Muslims around the world have reason to fear and hate the United States? Of course they do, and all the more after the aggression in Afghanistan. That military reaction to September 11 invites the same response as in the Middle East, where every Israeli assassination invites a Palestinian suicide attack, and vice versa.

Needless to say, viewing the conflict in these terms—not good versus evil but reciprocal cycles of escalating aggression driven by fear—does not offer us any simple solution. Mutual fear and hatred between Israelis and Palestinians has been brewing for generations and will not easily be defused. Yet this perspective offers us the hope for a solution, which present policies of mutual retaliation obviously do not. What has been created can also be undone—if each side makes efforts for "internal disarmament" and accepts responsibility for addressing the fear in the heart of the other side.

The same is true for the new holy war between aggrieved Muslims and the United States. In this case, I think it will become necessary to address the even larger issue of social justice around the world, and whether the United States is going to be part of the solution rather than part of the problem.

We may wonder if this is a realistic possibility in the foreseeable future, especially given the quality of most leadership today. From a Buddhist perspective, then, perhaps the immediate issue becomes whether the duality of good versus evil can be more widely perceived as delusive, and whether the more insightful duality between fear and love can become more widely acknowledged.

The Basic Message?

Does this choice between fear and love also provide us with a modern vocabulary to express the basic message of both Christianity and Buddhism?

The Sangha, or the community of monks and nuns, founded by Shakyamuni Buddha eventually became settled and wealthy, but originally they were a motley crew of wandering mendicants, with almost no possessions except robes and begging bowls. The Buddha sent them out one by one in all directions to preach the Dharma, in a manner strikingly reminiscent of the way Jesus charged his apostles to go out and preach that "the Kingdom of Heaven is at hand": "Take nothing for your journey, no staff, nor bag, nor bread, nor money, and do not have two tunics" (Matthew 9:3). What were both teachers saying? Don't worry about yourself, about how you will live, what you will eat; let go of your fears about yourself. Just do the best you can spreading the word, and have faith that you will be taken care of. Open up to the world and live a life of love focused on giving to the world rather than taking from it, trusting in the world rather than always trying to protect yourself from it.

There are many such passages in the Gospels, especially in the Sermon on the Mount. "Do not lay up for yourselves treasures on earth" (Matthew 6:19); "do not be anxious about your life, what you shall eat or what you shall drink, nor about your body, what you shall put on.... Look at the birds of the air: they neither sow nor reap nor gather into barns.... Consider the lilies of the field, how they grow; they neither toil nor spin, and yet your heavenly Father takes care of them" (Matthew 6:25–29). And what did Jesus tell the rich young man? "If you would be perfect, go, sell what you possess and give it to the poor, and you will have treasure in heaven; and come, follow me. But the young man went away sorrowful, for he was very rich" (Matthew 19:16–22).

Perhaps the most remarkable Gospel passage of all, from a Buddhist perspective, elaborates upon this teaching of salvation through insecurity. Jesus declares that any disciple who loves his father or mother or son or daughter more than him is not worthy of him; even family attachments should not keep us from following the path. (Becoming a monk in Buddhism is also known as "leaving home.") This apparently cruel verse is immediately followed by one of the most wonderful verses of all: "He who finds his life will lose it, and he who loses his life for my sake will find it" (Matthew 10:37–39). This encourages us to follow the personal example of Jesus, who undertook to "empty" himself (*kenosis;* Philippians 2:5–11).

There are different ways to understand that emptying, but as a Zen Buddhist I am reminded of the thirteenth-century Japanese Zen master Dogen, who wrote something that resonates in a similar way: "To study Buddhism is to study yourself; to study yourself is to forget yourself; to forget yourself is to be awakened and realize your intimacy with all things." The fruit of the Buddhist path, the end of a life organized around fear, is to lose and empty yourself by forgetting yourself, which is also to find your true self: not an alienated self threatened by the world and seeking security from anxiety, but a nondual self that knows itself to be an expression or a manifestation of the world.

Both religious traditions encourage us to live in this way, and not necessarily because of what will happen to us after we die. This encouragement is often understood in terms of some heavenly reward that we can get in an afterlife (better karma in a future rebirth, or an eternity with God in heaven), which caters to our fear of mortality. But there is another way to understand both nirvana and the kingdom of heaven. If, as Augustine put it, God is closer to me than I am to myself, then forgetting/losing myself is a way to realize the Buddha-nature or divinity at the core of my being right now, so that "not I but Christ lives in me" (Galatians 2:20). From the usual perspective obsessed with securing ourselves, forgetting myself or losing myself seems the supreme foolishness; but from a spiritual viewpoint it can lead to the greatest security, a life "without care," because if we have truly emptied ourselves and already died to ourselves then there is no longer anyone still to die, no longer any alienated self to worry about death.

Then we should live a life of love, not because of hope for some afterlife reward, but because (as Spinoza would put it) a way of life oriented on love is its own reward. Both modes of living—fear and love—involve reinforcing feedback systems that tend to incorporate other people. The more I manipulate the world to get what I want from it, the more I will feel separate and alienated from it; and the more others recognize that they have been manipulated, the more they will feel separate from me. This mutual distrust encourages both sides to manipulate more. On the other hand, the more I can relax and open up to the world—trusting it and responding to its needs, which is what loving means—the more I will feel a part of it, at one with other people, and the more others will be inclined to trust and open up to me.

The final word I have to offer on this choice is neither Christian nor Buddhist, reminding us that no religious traditions have a monopoly on this wisdom. It is an uncredited story (I could not trace its source) that was included in an e-mail I received after September 11.

> A Native American grandfather was talking to his grandson about how he felt about the tragedy of September 11.
>
> He said, "I feel as if I have two wolves fighting in my heart. One wolf is vengeful, angry, violent. The other wolf is loving, forgiving, compassionate."
>
> The grandson asked him, "Which wolf will win the fight in your heart?"
> The grandfather answered, "The one I feed."

This is our choice, too: Which one will we feed?

CHAPTER 6

How to Reform a Serial Killer

The history of punishment is in some respects like the history of war; it seems to accompany the human condition almost universally, to enjoy periods of glorification, to be commonly regarded as justified in many instances, and yet to run counter to our ultimate vision of what human society should be.

—Deirdre Golash

WHY DO WE PUNISH? It may seem an odd question, but only until we try to answer it. To punish is to harm, and harming must be justified. (Etymologically, *punish* derives from same proto-Indo-European root as *pain*.) Three types of justification are usually offered: the harm of punishment is outweighed by some greater good (for example, it deters others); punishment does not really harm offenders (because it reforms them); and harming offenders is good in itself (because retribution somehow "annuls the crime"—to borrow a phrase from Hegel). However, each of these reasons becomes problematic when we examine it.

The first argument is a utilitarian one, and the usual objections against utilitarianism are all the more pointed when the issue is justice. It seems immoral to harm someone because we want to influence others' behavior; such a principle could also be used—and has been—to justify the scapegoating of innocents. This is not just an abstract refutation, for there is the uncomfortable possibility that offenders today have become our scapegoats for larger social problems. And from a practical point of view this justification does not seem to be working. If punishment warns other would-be offenders, why does the United States, which punishes a larger percentage of its population than any other major country, continue to have such an extraordinarily high incidence of crime?

The second argument, that punishment does not really harm the offender, has some force but is not usually true today. The Quakers may have intended the penitentiary to be a place of penitence, yet that meaning has long been lost and there is little doubt that incarceration makes most offenders worse. The RAND Corporation report *Prisons versus Probation in California* found that recidivism is actually higher for offenders sent to prison than for similar offenders put on probation. That should not surprise us. Shakyamuni emphasized the importance of good friends—that is, wholesome company—but the predatory societies that prisons encourage make most of them more like hell than places to repent and reform. Prison settings dehumanize; they offer no way for prisoners to deal with their feelings of guilt and their need for forgiveness. Many prisoners feel that they have been treated badly (as many have), and this diverts their attention from what they have done to their victims, who also lose the opportunity to work toward closure. Moreover, prison reinforces the low self-confidence and sense of failure that lead many prisoners to offend.[62] As often happens, an institution that does not fulfill its original purpose continues to exist for other reasons—in this case because, to tell the truth, we do not know what else to do with most offenders except to remove them to places where they will be unable to offend again.

The third argument, that harming offenders is good in itself, is more complicated because it incorporates several types of justifications. Historically the most common, and (although we don't like to admit it) perhaps still prevalent, is the desire for vengeance. In many cases, the wish for revenge is understandable, but it is nevertheless morally unacceptable and socially destructive, undoubtedly "counter to our ultimate vision of what a human society should be," as Deirdre Golash observes. Another version of this argument sees punishment as God's retribution; the Buddhist equivalent understands punishment more impersonally, as an effect of one's karma. However, this is not a good argument for *human* punishment. Neither an omnipotent deity nor the law of karma needs our (all too human) help, especially since it is inevitable that human authorities will occasionally make mistakes (e.g., execute innocents). In traditional Tibet—seemingly as Buddhist as any society has been—karma was never used to justify punishment.

There are more philosophical versions of this argument, such as Kant's deontological view of punishment as rationally needed to maintain the cosmic order, and Hegel's idealist view that punishment "annuls the crime." Challenging such views would involve evaluating the metaphysical systems they are part of, which is not my aim in this book. The important point for our purposes is that all versions of this third justification build upon our intuitive belief that something must be done to "make right" the harm that offenses cause to victims and to the social fabric. From that perspective, the basic problem with our present judicial systems is that they are not working well enough to make things right, a problem so deeply rooted that it may be beneficial to consider the judicial perspectives of other religious and cultural traditions. "The failure of contemporary criminal justice is not one of technique but of purpose; what is needed is not simply new programs but new patterns of thinking."[63] Our understanding of justice may be connected with a social paradigm that we have difficulty identifying because we are part of it. We sense that something may be wrong with our atomistic understanding of the social contract and its presumptions about how to pursue the good life, but we're not sure where to look for an alternative paradigm—in which case it may be important to get perspectives on our paradigm that can only be provided by the worldviews and values of other cultures.

The Buddhist approach to punishment, like other approaches, cannot really be separated from its understanding of human psychology (especially motivation and intention), from its conception of the relationship between the individual and society, and from its vision of human possibility, of what a good life is or can be. This suggests that the problem of how to have a good criminal justice system is not solely a secular concern, for issues of fairness and justice cannot be completely separated from the religious perspectives they historically derive from. In the past, and even today for the vast majority of humankind, ideas about justice are inextricably bound up with religious views and customs. Justice is one of those ultimate questions (like "the meaning of life") that bridge whatever distinctions we try to make between the sacred and the secular. It is no historical accident that restorative justice programs have so often been promoted by Christian groups (e.g., Quakers and Mennonites).

Harold Pepinsky, in a discussion of Buddhism, has pointed out that the problem of justice is part of a broader issue: how can all our relationships be just and peaceful—or more generally, how can humans get along? When conflict occurs, how can we restore peace instead of responding in kind? If this is the main problem, the issue of a good criminal justice system must be viewed as subordinate to our larger vision of how people are to relate to one another. Buddhist teachings agree with Pepinsky that conflict is inevitable as long as we are the kind of people we are; the issue, then, is how to learn from these conflicts.

> Unless we can make peace in the privacy of our own homes, men with women, adults with children and with older people, we cannot build peace outside in our other workplaces and in our nations. Research on peacemaking in criminology thus becomes the study of how and where people manage to make peace, under the assumption that the principles that create or destroy peace are the same from the Smith family kitchen to the Pentagon and the prison.[64]

That, however, is not the focus of our present criminal justice systems.

Then do the presence of these defects in our judicial system manifest a wider social failure? As many have observed, perhaps criminal justice cannot be achieved without social justice. Expressed another way, if we punish offenders so they will pay their "debt to society," we should also consider whether society is meeting its obligation to them to ensure that they are educated, not abused, and so forth. We cannot hope to reintegrate offenders back into the community when there are so few communities left to integrate back into, and this lack means that many victims also face similar problems in trying to heal the harm they have experienced. Maybe our criminal justice system is a barometer of our social failure in these respects: ultimately, of our inadequate vision of what personal and social possibilities there are, which many people today experience as a loss of vision and hope.

This would explain our uncomfortable suspicion that criminals often become scapegoats, their offenses easily exploited by ambitious politicians trying to get (re)elected (a fourth justification for punishment, unfortunately). Crime reminds us that something is wrong with society, but that is something we do not like to think about, so it is tempting to banish the problem by blaming "them" for what we don't like. Yet the interdependence between "us" and "them" can be turned around and transformed into a source of hope: the increasingly obvious failure of our criminal justice system can be used as a focal point to address this larger crisis. A successful reformation of judicial systems could have important implications for many other social problems.

It is difficult to generalize about crime, because there are many different types of crime, committed by many different types of people, which may require many different kinds of responses. Since this chapter is concerned to present a Buddhist perspective, the first thing to emphasize is that the same is true for Buddhism itself. Buddhist countries (more precisely, countries with a predominant number of Buddhists) such as Thailand, Tibet, China, and Japan have had and continue to have very different judicial as well as political systems. Despite their important differences, however, some very similar threads have been used to weave their various judicial patterns. The predominant threads that will recur in the following sections are, first, that offenders should be treated sympathetically because all of us, offenders and victims alike, have the same Buddha-nature; second, we are usually dominated by our greed, malice, and delusion, but it is possible for all of us to change and outgrow them; hence, third, the only acceptable reason for punishment is education and reformation.

We begin with the two Pali sutras that directly address these issues: the Angulimala Sutra, the most famous Buddhist text on crime and punishment, about the reform of a serial killer; and the Lion's Roar Sutra (already discussed in earlier chapters), which considers the role of a ruler in avoiding crime and violence.[65] Although the first may be based upon a true incident, both are obviously mythic—but this does not reduce their interest for us, since our concern is not historical fact but Buddhist attitudes. Then we look at the Buddhist vinaya, the rules and corrective measures that regulate the lives of Buddhist bhikkhus and bhikkhunis (monks and nuns). Since the Buddhist Sangha is a voluntary order, the direct relevance of these regulations is limited, yet they have many implications for our psychological understanding of motivation, education, and reform. Finally, we turn to traditional Tibet to see how its criminal justice system embodied these Buddhist perspectives. Tibet too seems to be of limited value to us, since its lack of church/state separation means it is not a model that a modern secular and pluralistic society can duplicate. I conclude with some reflections on the role of the state. Does our usual distinction between religious and civil spheres merely obscure the fact that the state has become a "secular god" for us? Is that why our present criminal justice system serves the purposes of the state (to maintain its power) better than the needs of offenders and their victims?

THE ANGULIMALA SUTRA

Angulimala was a merciless bandit, who single-handedly laid waste to villages, towns, and even whole districts, murdering people and wearing their fingers as a garland (hence his name, literally "finger-garland"). The commentaries give a rather implausible account of how he became a killer, obviously intended to persuade us that he was not really such a bad guy after all. Although warned about him, the Blessed One walks silently into his territory. When Angulimala tries to catch him, however, Shakyamuni Buddha performs a feat of supernatural power: Angulimala, walking as fast as he can, cannot catch up with him, even though the Buddha is walking at his normal pace. Astonished, Angulimala calls out, "Stop, recluse!"

Still walking, the Buddha answers: "I have stopped, Angulimala; you stop too." In response to Angulimala's puzzlement, he explains: "I have stopped forever, abstaining from violence toward living beings; but you have no restraint toward things that live." This impresses Angulimala so much that he renounces evil forever and asks to join the Sangha, and the Buddha welcomes him as a new bhikkhu.

Meanwhile, great crowds of people had gathered at the gates of King Pasenadi's palace, demanding that Angulimala be stopped. King Pasenadi goes forth to capture him with a cavalry of five hundred men. When he meets the Buddha and explains his quest, the Buddha responds: if you were to see that he is now a good bhikkhu, who abstains from killing living beings and so forth, how would you treat him?

The king replies that he would pay homage to him as a good bhikkhu, and is surprised when the Buddha points out Angulimala seated nearby. After offering him robes, almsfood, and other requisites, the king marvels that the Buddha was able to tame the untamed and bring peace to the unpeaceful. "Venerable sir, we ourselves could not tame him with force or weapons, yet the Blessed One has tamed him without force or weapons." Then he departs, after paying homage to the Buddha.

Soon after, the venerable Angulimala, diligent and resolute, realizes for himself the supreme goal of the holy life and becomes an *arahant* (one who has attained nirvana). Later, however, during an almsround, he is attacked and beaten by townspeople. The Buddha tells him to bear it, for it is a result of his past karma. The sutra concludes with some verses Angulimala utters while experiencing the bliss of deliverance—for example:

Who checks the evil deeds he did
By doing wholesome deeds instead,
He illuminates the world
Like the moon freed from a cloud.

The point of this sutra is not difficult to see: we need only contrast the fate of Angulimala with what our retributive justice system would do to him. The importance of this story within the Buddhist tradition highlights the only reason Buddhism accepts for punishing an offender: to help reform his or her character. There is no reason to punish someone who has already reformed. The sutra makes no mention of punishment as a deterrent. On the contrary, the case of Angulimala may be seen as setting a negative example, implying that one can escape punishment by becoming a bhikkhu, as if the Buddhist Sangha were something like the French foreign legion, which accepts new recruits with no questions asked.

There is also no hint that punishment is needed to "annul the crime," although Angulimala does suffer karmic consequences that even his condition of spiritual perfection cannot escape. Note that in this case the judicial role of secular authority is unnecessary, or is rather superseded: the king defers to the Buddha as an alternative spiritual authority. This text may have been used politically to make exactly that point: the Sangha as a religious community is exempt from civil control. If so, it seems to have been somewhat successful, at least initially, since Indian rulers often left the Sangha alone. Yet that should not divert us from the main point: once someone has realized the error of his ways, what further reason is there to punish? More generally, determining what judicial response is right or wrong—what is just—cannot be abstracted from the particular situation of the offender.

Nevertheless, this myth is unsatisfactory from a restorative point of view. The sutra says nothing about the families of Angulimala's victims, or the larger social consequences of his crimes, except for the crowds at King Pasenadi's gate. That the humble monk Angulimala is stoned by villagers indicates more than bad karma. It implies that there has been no attempt at restorative or transformative justice that takes account of his effects on society. The social fabric of the community has been rent, yet there is no attempt to "make things right." The particular situation of the offender is addressed by abstracting him from his social context, from those affected by his offense. It would be unfair to take this as indicating an early Buddhist indifference to society; many other sutras demonstrate a wider social concern, including the Lion's Roar Sutra. Yet it does seem to exemplify something about the early Buddhist attitude to spiritual salvation: liberation is an individual matter, and the path to achieving it involves leaving society, rather than transforming it.

THE LION'S ROAR SUTRA

The Lion's Roar on the Turning of the Wheel addresses the relationship between criminal justice and social justice, especially the connection between poverty and violence. Earlier chapters have discussed its implications for addressing poverty; here we focus on its implications for understanding violence and crime. In accordance with the usual Buddhist approach to remedying problems, the way to control crime naturally follows from the correct understanding of the causes of crime, and this sutra considers those causes.

The Buddha tells the story of a righteous monarch in the distant past who initially venerated and relied upon the Dharma, following the advice of his sage: "Let no crime prevail in your kingdom, and to those who are in need, give property." Later, however, he did not give property to the needy. One man took what was not given and was arrested; when the king asked him why, the man said he had nothing to live on. So the king gave him some property, saying that it would be enough to carry on a business and support his family.

When other people heard about this policy, they too decided to steal so that they would be treated the same way. So he decided to get tough on the next thief: "I had better make an end of him, finish him off once and for all, and cut his head off."

What we might expect to be a moralistic parable about the importance of deterring crime suddenly turns in the opposite direction:

> Hearing about this, people thought: "Now let us get sharp swords made for us, and then we can take from anybody what is not given, we will make an end of them, finish them off once and for all and cut off their heads." So, having procured some sharp swords, they launched murderous assaults on villages, towns and cities, and went in for highway-robbery, killing their victims by cutting off their heads.
>
> Thus, from the not giving of property to the needy, poverty became rife, from the growth of poverty, the taking of what was not given

increased, from the increase of theft, the use of weapons increased, from the increased use of weapons, the taking of life increased.[66]

As if these ills were not enough, they in turn lead to deliberate lying, speaking evil of others, adultery, harsh speech and idle chatter, covetousness and hatred, false opinions, incest, excessive greed, and—evidently the last straw—lack of respect for one's parents, for ascetics, and for the head of one's clan.

In spite of some fanciful elements, this myth has important implications for our understanding of crime and punishment. The first point is that poverty is presented as the root cause of immoral behavior such as theft, violence, and falsehood. According to this sutra, crime, violence, and immorality cannot be separated from broader questions about the justice or injustice of the social order. Much the same point is made in the Kutadanta Sutra, in which a chaplain tells a king that there is much lawlessness and civil disorder in his kingdom, making property insecure. The king is advised to deal with this not by taxation, or by attempting to suppress it forcibly, but by improving the people's lot directly:

> Suppose Your Majesty were to think: "I will get rid of this plague of robbers by executions and imprisonment, or by confiscation, threats and banishment," the plague would not be properly ended.... To those in the kingdom who are engaged in cultivating crops and raising cattle, let Your Majesty distribute grain and fodder; to those in trade, give capital; to those in government service assign proper living wages. Then these people, being intent on their own occupations, will not harm the kingdom. Your Majesty's revenues will be great, the land will be tranquil and not beset by thieves, and the people, with joy in their hearts, will play with their children, and will dwell in open houses.[67]

We may be inclined to view this as an outmoded perspective from an ancient culture that never experienced the benefits of capitalism's invisible hand, yet it raises some sharp questions about a state's economic responsibilities to its people. The basic point of both these sutras is that the problem of crime should not be addressed apart from its economic and social context. The solution is not to "crack down" harshly with severe punishments but to provide for people's basic needs. "The aim would be, not to create a society in which people in general were afraid to break the law, but one in which they could live sufficiently rewarding lives without doing so."[68] We prefer to throw our money at "wars on crime," although the results suggest what the king belatedly realized: that no one wins such wars.

That brings us to the second point of the Lion's Roar Sutra, its understanding of the causes of violence. Instead of solving the problem, the king's violent attempt at deterrence sets off an explosion of violence that leads to social collapse. The sutra emphasizes this by using exactly the same words to present both the king's intentions and the intentions of the people who decide to become criminals. If punishment is sometimes a mirror image of the crime (something exponents of retributive justice propose), in this case the crime is a mirror image of the punishment. Psychologically, the latter makes as much sense as the former. The state's violence reinforces the belief that violence works. When the state uses violence against those who do things it does not permit, we should not be surprised when some of its citizens feel entitled to do the same. Such retributive violence "tends to confirm the outlook and life experiences of many offenders. Wrongs must be repaid by wrong and those who offend deserve vengeance. Many crimes are committed by people 'punishing' their family, the neighbors, their acquaintances.... Apparently the message some potential offenders receive is not that killing is wrong, but that those who wrong us deserve to die."[69] The emphasis on nonviolence within so much of the Buddhist tradition is not because of some otherworldly preoccupations; it is based upon the psychological insight that violence breeds violence. This is a clear example of the maxim that means cannot be divorced from ends. There is no way *to* peace; peace itself is the way. If the state is not exempt from this truth, we must find some way to incorporate it into our judicial systems.

THE VINAYA

For our purposes the details of the Vinaya Pitaka, the compendium of rules for bhikkhus and bhikkhunis, are less important than what they imply about the early Buddhist understanding of punishment and reformation. The vinaya is based upon *shila* (morality), which provides the ethical foundation for all Buddhists, both renunciants and laypeople. The five basic precepts are to abstain from killing, stealing, lying, improper sexual behavior, and intoxicants. As we already noticed, the fundamental goal of these precepts is to help us transform *lobha* (lust), *dosa* (ill will), and *moha* (delusion), the three roots of evil that afflict all of us except those who are awakened. "As lust, malice and delusion are the basis of all undesirable volitional activity done by means of thoughts, word and body, the disciplinary code or Buddhist Laws are regarded as a means established for the rise of detached actions which finally result in pure expressions of body, speech and thought."[70]

Although rigidly codified and in some respects outdated, the vinaya is in fact quite practical in its approach. In almost all cases a rule originates from an actual event (what today is called *case law*) rather than from a hypothetical possibility of wrongdoing. "The spirit of the law suggests that the laws act more or less as sign-posts or 'danger zones' indicating that one should be careful here, keeping in mind the example or examples of individuals who fell into trouble by this or that stratagem."[71] Since not derived from God or any other absolute authority, these rules are always open to revision, and on his deathbed the Buddha emphasized that all the rules that had evolved during his lifetime could be revised except for the major ones—probably (although controversially) meaning the four fundamental *parajikas* (that bhikkhus must not have sexual intercourse, steal, kill a human being, or lie about their spiritual attainment), which constitute automatic "defeat" and self-expulsion from the Sangha. Following the rules well is not in itself the goal; the reason for rules is that they are conducive to personal development and spiritual progress.

The vinaya approach is very practical in another way: its realistic attitude toward human weakness. It is the nature of unenlightened human beings to be afflicted by craving, malice, and delusion; that is, all of us are somewhat insane. As long as human beings are unenlightened, then, there will be crime. The extent of crime can be reduced by improving social and economic conditions, but no human society will ever be able to eradicate crime completely. This is consistent with the Buddhist attitude toward self-perfection: we improve only gradually, step by step (the example of Angulimala notwithstanding).

If we are all somewhat insane, then the insanity defense is always somewhat applicable. The universality of greed, malice, and delusion means there can be no presumption of unfettered free will or simple self-determination. Freedom is not a matter of the individual will (often characterized by greed, malice, and/or delusion), but a result of overcoming that kind of willfulness— not gained by removing external restraints, but a consequence of self-control and spiritual awakening. This denies the distinction we are usually quick to make between an offender and the rest of us. According to Buddhism the best method of treatment is education. "Education by example or depicting concrete occasions suited the Buddhist tradition best." The best antidote to criminal behavior is helping people to realize the full consequences of their actions, in which case they will want to refrain from them.[72]

In determining the nature of an offense against the vinaya and how to respond, everything about an offender's situation is taken into consideration: past actions, character and intelligence, friends and associates, and whether or not he or she has confessed. This may be contrasted to our own judicial preoccupation with the black-or-white question of guilty/not guilty. "Degrees of severity of the offense may vary, but in the end there are no degrees of guilt. One is guilty or not guilty." Such either-or situations, Howard Zehr observes, teach "the hidden message that people can be evaluated in simple dichotomies."

> The question of guilt is the hub of the entire criminal justice process. Establishing guilt is the central activity, and everything moves toward or flows from that event…. The centrality of guilt means that the actual outcome of the case receives less attention. Legal training concentrates on rules and processes related to guilt, and law students receive little training in sentence-negotiation or design.[73]

From a perspective that takes the offender's self-reformation seriously, such an approach is seriously flawed:

> Offenders are constantly confronted with the terminology of guilt, but denied the language and clarity of meaning to make sense of it…. Western laws and values are often predicated on a belief in the individual as a free moral agent. If someone commits a crime, she has done so willfully. Punishment is thus deserved because it is freely chosen. Individuals are personally and individually accountable. Guilt is individual…. Much evidence suggests that offenders often do not act freely or at least do not perceive themselves as capable of free action…. Ideas of human freedom and thus responsibility necessarily take on a different hue in such a context.[74]

The vinaya supports this notion that our preoccupation with guilt is based on an erroneous understanding of human nature and an erroneous conclusion about the best way to change human nature. "Guilt says something about the quality of the person who did this and has a 'sticky,' indelible quality. Guilt adheres to a person more or less permanently, with few known solvents. It often becomes a primary, definitional characteristic of a person."[75] In contrast, Buddhist emphasis on the transience of everything means there is nothing indelible about our unwholesome mental tendencies. When deep-rooted ones are difficult to eradicate, that is because they are a result of past habits, not an "essential" part of us.

If free will is not presumed, and encouraging self-reformation is the most important task, the main concern shifts from ruling on the suspect's guilt to determining his or her intention. This is the emphasis of the vinaya. The intention of an accused person is always crucial, because one's intention decides the nature of the offense. If one does not consent to commit an act, one is not guilty of it, and the lighter the intention, the less grave the offense.[76]

Intention is also the most important factor in the operation of the law of karma, which according to Buddhism is created by volitional action. Karma is essential to the Buddhist understanding of justice, but how literally or metaphorically we understand it should have little if any effect on the moral code that a sincere Buddhist tries to follow. What is most important in either case is the basic teaching that "I am the result of my own deed; heir to deed; deeds are material; deeds are kin; deeds are foundation; whatever deed I do, whether good or bad, I shall become heir to it."[77] One modern approach to karma is to understand it in terms of what Buddhism calls *sankharas*, our "mental formations," especially our habitual tendencies. These are best understood not as tendencies we have but as tendencies we *are*. Instead of being "my" habits, their interaction is what constitutes my sense of "me." Yet that does not mean they are ineradicable: unwholesome sankharas are to be differentiated from the liberatory possibilities that are available to all of us if we follow the path of replacing them with more wholesome mental tendencies.

The point of this interpretation is that we are punished not *for* our sins but *by* them. People suffer or benefit not for what they have done but for what they have become, and what we intentionally do is what makes us what we are. This conflation makes little sense if karma is understood dualistically as a kind of moral dirt attached to me, yet it makes a great deal of sense if I am my habitual intentions, for then the important spiritual issue is the development of those intentions. In that case my actions and my intentions build/rebuild my character, just as food is assimilated to build/rebuild my physical body. If karma is this psychological truth about how we construct ourselves—about

how my sense of self is constructed by "my" greed, ill will, and delusion—
then we can no longer accept the juridical presupposition of a completely
self-determined subject wholly responsible for its own actions. Again, we can
no longer justify punishment as retributive, but must shift the focus of criminal justice to education and reformation.

The system of punishments used within the Sangha shows how these principles work in practice. Needless to say, there is no physical punishment. The
emphasis is always on creating a situation that will help a bhikkhu or
bhikkhuni to remember and reflect upon the offense, in order to overcome
the mental tendencies that produced it. The Pali word for punishment, danda,
also means "restraint." "What was necessary was to establish restraint because
the volitional activity of the offender, undesirable in nature, has resulted in the
commission of this serious offense."[78]

A great variety of penalties were used to do this. An act of censure involved
reproving a disputatious "maker of strife" in a Sangha meeting and instruct-
ing him to mend his ways. An act of guidance placed an offender under the
authority of a teacher, to study the teachings. An act of banishment expelled
an offender from a particular location/environment. An act of suspension
could be used when an offender did not accept that his act was an offense;
this prohibited the accused from associating with other monks. One of the
most interesting punishments is the act of reconciliation, which could be used
when a bhikkhu did something to disturb cordial relations with the laity. It
required the bhikkhu to seek the pardon of the layperson toward whom he had
behaved incorrectly.[79] (In our public judicial system as well, couldn't it sometimes be appropriate to require the offender to seek the pardon of his victim?)

Most of these acts involved what we now call probation. Probation is usually regarded as a modern method of treatment derived from English common law, but it has been widely used in Buddhism for twenty-five hundred
years, because it is consistent with the Buddhist concern to reform an offender's
intentions rather than to punish. With the exception of the four parajikas and
the most minor offenses, all could be dealt with by probation. According to
the Vinaya Pitaka, "A monk under probation should conduct himself properly...he should not fall into that same offense for which he was granted probation, nor into another that is similar, nor into one that is worse, he should
not find fault with the act [or]...with those who carry out the act."[80]

In most instances, the probation automatically ended after a fixed period
of time. In other cases, an offender who accepted the penalties and mended

his ways could apply to be rehabilitated; a Sangha meeting would be called and the act could be revoked. Once the probation was successfully finished, the monk returned to his previous position and status, so "the social image of the offender was not harmed. After the penalty, he was received back and he enjoyed the identical position he had earlier without stigma or contempt. Human dignity thus was always regarded as important in the court and in the society, while under a penalty or after rehabilitation."[81]

There are some important similarities between this approach and what John Braithwaite has called "reintegrative shaming." Daniel Van Ness and Karen Strong's description of this approach to reformation could serve just as well as a summary of the Buddhist approach:

> Reintegration requires that we view ourselves (and others) as a complex measure of good and evil, injuries and strengths, and that while we resist and disparage the evil and compensate for our weaknesses, we also recognize and welcome the good and utilize our strengths. [Braithwaite] noted that Japanese culture values apology as a gesture in which people divide themselves into good and bad parts with the good part renouncing the bad.[82]

This is very similar to the Buddhist view of human nature, which does not presuppose a unitary soul or self-determining subject, but understands the self to be a composite of unwholesome and wholesome mental tendencies.

To sum up, the vinaya approach suggests that if we are serious in our desire for a judicial system that truly heals, we must find a way to divert our focus from punishing guilt to reforming intention.

TIBETAN JUSTICE

Traditional Tibet provides an opportunity to observe how well the above principles can operate in lay society. The presupposition of its legal system was that conflict is engendered by our incorrect vision of situations, itself caused by our mental afflictions. In Tibetan Buddhist teachings there are six root afflictions (desire, anger, pride, ignorance, doubt, and incorrect view) and twenty secondary afflictions (including belligerence, resentment, spite, jealousy, and deceit) that cause us to perceive the world in an illusory way and engage in disputes. Again, there is a Socratic understanding of human conflict: our immoral behavior is ultimately due to our wrong understanding, which only a spiritual awakening can wholly purify.

As long as our vision is incorrect and our minds are afflicted, there is no question of free will, and Tibet's judicial system does not presuppose it. "The goal of a legal proceeding," according to Rebecca French, "was to calm the minds and relieve the anger of the disputants and then—through catharsis, expiation, restitution, and appeasement—to rebalance the natural order."[83]

A primary purpose of trial procedure was to uncover mental states if possible, and punishment was understood in terms of its effect upon the mind of the defendant. In a profound way, Tibetans saw no possible resolution to a conflict without calming the mind to the point at which the individuals involved could sincerely agree to conclude the strife.

This included the disputants attempting to reharmonize their relations after a court settlement. For example, the law codes specified a "getting-together payment" to finance a meeting where all the parties would drink and eat together, to promote a reconciliation. Generally, coercion was considered ineffective, for no one could be forced to follow a moral path. The disputants had to work out their own difficulties to find a true solution and end the conflict. Therefore even a decision accepted by all parties would lose its finality whenever they no longer agreed to it, and cases could be reopened at any later date.[84]

This emphasis on reharmonizing was embodied both in the legal philosophy and in the different types of judicial process used to settle problems. Legal analysis identified two basic forms of causation: the immediate cause and the root cause, both of them deriving from Buddhist scriptures. The root cause was usually considered more important, because the source of animosity had to be addressed to resolve the strife. The most common type of judicial process was internal settlement by the parties themselves. If that did not work, conciliation, using private and unofficial conciliators could be tried; this was usually preferred because it was informal, saved reputations, allowed flexible compromises, and was much less expensive. A third process involved visiting judges at home to get their informal opinion of the best way to proceed. Official court proceedings were a last resort.

This emphasis on consensus and calming the mind also presupposed something generally accepted in Tibet but less acceptable in the West today: a belief that it is only the mind, not material possessions or status, that can bring us happiness. In more conventional Buddhist terms, it is my state of mind that determines whether I attain nirvana or suffer in one of the hells. This helps us to see the more individualistic assumptions operative in our own judicial system, which emphasizes the personal pursuit of happiness, freedom from outside restraint, and the right to enjoy one's property without interference.

Tibetan officials were careful to distinguish religious beliefs from secular legal views when it came to settling a case. Crimes and disputes had to be settled in this world, without referring to ultimate karmic causes or effects, which are unknowable. Nonetheless, Tibetan culture was permeated with a spiritual mentality, and the moral standards of the Buddha and his vinaya influenced every part of the legal system. The law codes even cited them as the source of Tibetan law: "The Buddha preached the Ten Nonvirtuous Acts [killing, stealing, and engaging in sexual misconduct; engaging in lying, abusive, gossiping, or slanderous speech; harboring craving, malice, and wrong views] and their antidotes, the Ten Virtuous Acts. By relying on these, the ancient kings made the secular laws from the Ten Virtuous Acts."[85] The example of the Buddha provided an immutable standard of how to live:

> Stories, parables, and jataka tales (accounts of the Buddha's former lives) offered countless social examples of how the virtuous and the nonvirtuous actor operated in the daily world and provided Tibetans with a concrete understanding of proper action. Each Tibetan knew that the moral Buddhist cared more for the welfare of others than for his or her own welfare, gave to others rather than amassed a fortune, rigorously tried to prevent harm to others, never engaged in any of the nonvirtuous acts, had complete devotion to the Buddha and his path, worked to eliminate anger and desire for material goods, accepted problems with patience and endurance, and remained an enthusiastic perseverer in the quest for truth and enlightenment. As there was no confusion about this ideal, there was little ambiguity about how the moral actor would deal with a particular daily situation. Even though the average Tibetan may not have been any more likely to follow the moral path than a person in any other society, his or her understanding of that ideal path remained strong. Moreover, that understanding prevailed in reasoning about legal cases, even over reasoning connected with community standards.[86]

Since all societies require models of how to live, norms as well as sanctions, we may ask what comparable standards prevail in Western cultures. Although we have a plurality of models, our standards tend to be more competitive and atomistic. In U.S. law, for example, "the question becomes 'Would a reason-able person leave ice on the sidewalk and foresee harm to a passerby?' The court and the individuals are not expected to know or to ask the moral ques-tion 'What would a correctly acting moral human have done under the same circumstances?'" In Tibet the accepted standard was not "a reasonable man" but the moral person exercising self-control. The members of a Tibetan vil-lage or neighborhood recognized that they had responsibility for other mem-bers of the group; unless there are special circumstances, a U.S. adult has no legal duty or responsibility to help others. "Tibetans find such an attitude repulsive and inhuman."[87]

This emphasis on ending strife and calming the mind even implied dif-ferent attitudes toward legal truth and the use of legal precedents. Truthful-ness and honesty were universally employed terms, but as Rebecca French observes, the Tibetan understanding of how to determine truth was quite different from ours. "Whereas the American view is that legal truth emerges from the clash of opposing forces asserting their interests, Tibetans saw lit-tle value in weathering such a process with all its extremity, anger, and pas-sion. Truth was understood in one of two ways: as an ideal and separate standard (hence normally unattainable), or as consensus—that is, the result when disagreeing parties reach a similar view of what happened and what should be done."[88] The necessity of consent so preoccupied the whole decision-making process that if the disputants could not agree, truth could not be reached.

The search for consensus also reduced reliance on previous legal decisions as precedents. The need to work out the best way to end conflict meant that emphasis was on decisions harmonizing the group, rather than on decisions harmonizing with more abstract legal principles. As a result, Tibetan jurispru-dence evolved a core of five factors to be considered: the uniqueness of each case (requiring a sensitivity to its particular features); the suitability of pun-ishment (avoiding fixed punishments or statutory guidelines for sentencing); considerations of karma (orienting punishment toward improving the offender's future life); the correct purposes of punishment (bringing the community, the victim, and the gods into harmony and making offenders mindful of the seriousness of their offenses and of the need not to repeat them); and the correct types of punishment (usually foregoing incarceration, for lack of facilities). Economic sanctions such as fines and damages were the most common, followed by physical punishment and forced labor; others included ostracism, publication of the offense, and reduction of official rank or loss of occupational status. Capital punishment was also used, although apparently not often. In general, local and nongovernmental decision makers were believed to be more likely to find solutions that would actually rectify behavior and work within the community to restore harmony.[89]

To sum up, Tibet provides an example of a country whose judicial system was organized according to those principles very different from that of Western law. Nevertheless, any attempt we might make to incorporate those principles into Western criminal justice would seem to be vitiated by one obvious problem: Buddhist Tibet was not a secular society. As French emphasizes, Tibet had no autonomous legal system, for its framework of "legal cosmology" was derived from the Tibetan worldview, and this almost entirely embedded in a Buddhist cultural base. For a Tibetan, then, there was no clear division between religion and the state.[90] Such a judicial system is difficult to harmonize with our Western legal systems, which have evolved to fit secular and pluralistic societies. For the West, a distinction between religious commitment and civil authority is essential.

Or is it? Is our judicial system an enlightened secular alternative to such a religiously based legal cosmology, or is it merely unaware of its own religious origins and commitments? "Law," writes Jerold Auerbach, "is our national religion; lawyers constitute our priesthood; the courtroom is our cathedral, where contemporary passion plays are enacted." [91] There is nothing unique about Tibet's legal system being derived from its worldview; that is true of any legal system. Ours too is embedded in a particular worldview, which we take for granted just as much as Tibetans take for granted a Buddhist cosmology. The concluding section of this chapter will suggest that, for us, the role of the Buddha is now assumed in part, by the state. This implies a rather different understanding of what is wrong with Western criminal justice systems.

A GENEALOGY OF JUSTICE

Our understanding of justice, like every understanding of justice, is historically constructed. If we want to reconstruct justice, then, it is important to understand how we got where we are. But there is no perspectiveless perspective. A Buddhist concern for restorative justice enables us to see the history of jurisprudence in a new way.

In premodern Anglo-Saxon and Germanic law, the notion of a wrong to a person or his family was primary, that of an offense against the "common weal" secondary. In other words, our distinction between civil and criminal law hardly existed, even for the gravest of offenses. The conception that, for example, killing is a crime—an offense against the community—did not exist until the state gained the power to enforce the penalties for such offenses. As monarchies grew more powerful, private settlements of crimes that were regarded as public wrongs were not permitted, because they were understood to undermine the Crown's authority. Centralization of the Crown's power meant that kings could assume the judicial role and enforce their judgments. This was justified by their new role as personifying society: "the king, in whom centers the whole majesty of the community, is supposed by law to be the person injured by every infraction of the public rights belonging to that community."[92]

This development intersected with another in the religious sphere. Initially, Christian practice had emphasized accepting and forgiving wrongdoing. Like Buddhism, it was focused on the importance of reconciliation and directed toward spiritual salvation. Beginning in the eleventh century, however, theology and common law began to redefine crime as an offense against the metaphysical order, one that had caused a moral imbalance and needed to be righted. Crime became a sin against God, and it was the responsibility of the church to purge such transgressions.[93]

These developments intersected in the sixteenth and seventeenth centuries, when the Reformation initiated a social crisis that culminated in the birth of the "self-subsisting" nation-state as we know it today. The schism within Christendom increased the leverage of civil rulers, and the balance of power between church (moral authority) and state (secular authority) shifted to the latter. This allowed some rulers to appropriate the church's mantle of spiritual charisma. Their power became absolute because they filled the new vacuum of spiritual authority by becoming, in effect, "secular gods" accountable only to God. Thanks to reformers such as Luther and Calvin, who postulated a vast gap between corrupt humanity and God's righteousness, the Christian deity was now too far away to interfere with their rule. Luther and Calvin also endorsed the punitive role of the state, which took over God's role in administering punishment. The eventual overthrow of absolute rulers did not decentralize their power; it merely freed state institutions from responsibility to anything outside themselves, since now they "embodied the people."

This gives us a different perspective on the state's new role as the legal victim of all crimes, with a monopoly on justice. Instead of viewing the nation-state as a solely secular institution, we should understand that our historically conditioned allegiance to it is due to the fact that it took over some of the authority of a schismatic and somewhat discredited Christianity. The impersonality of state justice led to an emphasis on formal law and due process, which meant a focus on the bureaucratic result (and thus on legal precedent), with little regard for the effects of this process on its participants.[94] The objectivity of bureaucratic procedure engendered trust in the institution, which took the form of law and respect for law. But at a price. Peter Cordella observes that "as trust diminishes among individuals, bureaucracies, particularly legal bureaucracies, become more integral to the maintenance of social order and ultimately to the existence of society itself. In this context, law can be viewed as being inversely related to personal trust. With respect to trust, bureaucracy can be viewed as the antithesis of community."[95]

The local breakdown of traditional communities created "mobile and atomized populations whose claim to humanity rests more and more on the assertion of individual rights vis-à-vis an impersonal, distant and highly bureaucratized government apparatus."[96]

The Anabaptists (Mennonites, Amish, Hutterites, etc.) understood that such a state is inherently coercive and reacted against it. They rejected the Lutheran/Calvinist accommodation with the new nation-state by refusing to engage in its civil affairs, because state authority was antithetical to their own mutualist vision of community. In short, they saw the basic problem that the rest of us are just beginning to understand: if the nation-state is a god, it is a very problematical one—an idol that should not be worshiped.

Hobbes' social contract theory is not reliable as a historical claim, but its understanding of the state's origins is nonetheless revealing. For Hobbes the most distinctive quality of human beings is our egoism, more precisely our "perpetual and restless desire for power after power." The clash of our egoisms causes a social chaos whose only antidote is "that mortal God," a sovereign who is able to establish order because it is to the advantage of all others to submit to his authority. "The state, created *ex nihilo*, was an artificial ordering of individual parts, not bound together by cohesion, as an organic community, but united by fear." This gets at the heart of the issue: the contrast between the mutuality that makes a genuine community and the fear that motivates Hobbes's contractual state composed of competing individuals.

The state's order is externally imposed and supervised because in a social contract the self-interest of others is perceived as a constant threat to one's own self-interest. As Hobbes says, "Except that they be restrained through fear of some coercive power, every man will dread and distrust each other."[97]

What does all this have to do with restorative justice? The all-important issue here is the social *context* of justice. In a revelatory passage, Zehr discusses the relationship between biblical justice and love:

> We tend to assume that love and mercy are different from or opposite to justice. A judge pronounces a sentence. Then as an act of mercy, she may mitigate the penalty. Biblical justice, however, grows out of love. Such justice is in fact an act of love which seeks to make things right. Love and justice are not opposites, nor are they in conflict. Instead, love provides for a justice which seeks first to make things right.[98]

The same is true for Buddhism: Buddhist justice grows out of a compassion for everyone involved when someone hurts another.

Logically, the opposite of love is hatred, but in the previous chapter I suggested that the *psychological* opposite of love is fear. As Hobbes makes clear, fear is the origin of the state, because the state is the only thing that can protect my self-interest from yours. Whether or not this is true historically, it has become our myth: we legitimize the state's justice insofar as we accept that it is needed to protect us from each other.

This implies a sharp and perhaps an irreconcilable conflict between biblical/Buddhist justice and state justice. Our usual understanding of justice and mercy distinguishes them. In Zehr's biblical understanding and my Buddhist one, justice grows out of mercy, but our myth about the social contract implies that the state's justice grows out of fear. If fear is indeed the opposite of love, we are faced with two contradictory paradigms about the origins and role of justice, and two different ways a society might embody it.

That leaves us with the question: Which kind of society do we want to live in?

CHAPTER 7

Zen and the Art of War

It may be considered strange that Zen has in any way been affiliated with the spirit of the military classes of Japan. Whatever form Buddhism takes in the various countries where it flourishes, it is a religion of compassion, and in its varied history it has never been found engaged in warlike activities. How is it, then, that Zen has come to activate the fighting spirit of the Japanese warrior?

—D. T. Suzuki

THE TWO PREVIOUS CHAPTERS argue that the Buddhist understanding of the second poison, ill will, gives us insight into what is wrong with the dualism between good and evil (chapter 5) and what is wrong with our failing retributive justice systems (chapter 6). In line with this, one would expect (or at least hope) that Buddhism has also played an important role in reducing violence in the cultures that have adopted it. To some extent this has been the case. An example is Tibet, which became less violent when Buddhism became widely accepted. But there have also been significant exceptions, most notably Japan. The samurai appropriation of Zen provides an important lesson in how Buddhist teachings can be adopted to other ends, a cautionary tale that highlights the need for a Buddhist social theory sensitive to such distortions.

Suzuki's question, above, remains perhaps the most problematic one for understanding the place of Zen within Buddhism and comparative religion generally. In his provocative study *Zen and the Way of the Sword: Arming the Samurai Psyche,* Winston L. King raises this issue on the first page and reminds us that perversions of moral and religious ideals are not found only in Japan. We need only consider "how the simple otherworldly ethic of Jesus, the carpenter of Nazareth, to love those who hate us and turn the other cheek to those who strike us could have been transformed into the Crusaders' gospel of killing infidel Saracens or into a church of bitterly feuding and even warring sects. The answers to all such questions are always complex and unsatisfactory."[99] This response too, valid as it is, overlooks an important issue: the difference between the religious ideology of the crusaders (which nowadays would be thought benighted by all but the most benighted Christians) and the Zen samurai spirit, as understood by contemporary Japanese and those most likely to read this book. The problem, then, is not only how a militaristic perversion of Buddhism occurred, but why samurai Zen continues to be accepted as a legitimate form of Buddhism.

Zen and the Way of the Sword never addresses this question squarely, mainly because King is better on the sword than on Zen. It includes many quotations from the writings of D. T. Suzuki, which raise problems that King does not address, since we can no longer accept Suzuki's version of Zen uncritically. King does not shrink from making some telling criticisms of Suzuki, which will be discussed later, but this critique is limited by the fact that King's book depends on Suzuki for setting the terms of the discussion. Suzuki's usual bifurcations are central to King's explanations: the intellectual, cerebral, conceptual, conscious, and deliberate is bad; the existential, visceral, intuitive, unconscious, and instinctive is good. Given how much Suzuki criticized dualism, it is difficult to overlook how problematic these distinctions are. For one thing, such binary oppositions have a history and a context within Western thought that tends to be lost when they are translated into such a different language as Japanese, and a similar loss occurs when Japanese conceptual distinctions are rendered in English: so we must be cautious about understanding the Japanese conception of Zen in such terms. That Suzuki's command of English was excellent, far from alleviating the problem, aggravates it: How much do his English writings skillfully adapt Zen to Western sensibilities? That is, how much did he tell us what we wanted to hear?

Another problem with such categories is that they conveniently valorize characteristics that just happen to be Japanese. For example: "Zen wants to act, and the most effective act, once the mind is made up, is to go on without looking backward. In this respect, Zen is indeed the religion of the samurai warrior."[100] This emphasis on action exemplifies a general trait that Robert

Bellah considers the most important of Japanese society: its goal-oriented behavior. According to Nakamura Hajime, "Japanese Buddhists came to maintain the view that one should repudiate traditional disciplines *in the name of disciplines for the promotion of productive activities*."[101] To make the same point from the other perspective, Japanese culture is less interested than Indian in abstract theory and universalized principles. This raises again the old question, How much of Zen is Buddhist and how much Japanese? Is Zen anti-intellectualism an aspect of Buddhist enlightenment, of the Japanese version of enlightenment, or of the Japanese understanding of enlightenment?

Raising such questions about the differences between Pali Buddhism (the ancient Buddhism of India based exclusively on the Pali texts) and Japanese Buddhism brings us back to the most important issue, the relationship between Zen and the samurai spirit.

Sacralizing the Secular

Nearly fifty years ago, Paul Demieville observed a curious paradox: "The Hinayana [i.e. Pali Buddhism], which tends to condemn life, has remained strict in the prohibition of killing; and it is the Mahayana [e.g. Zen], which extols life, that has ended up by finding excuses for killing and even for its glorification." [102]

Whether or not Pali Buddhism condemns (or devalues) life, it is strict in its prohibition against taking life. The eightfold path includes right action (not destroying living beings, etc.) and right livelihood (not making one's living through a profession that brings harm to others, such as trading in arms and weapons, soldiering, killing animals, etc.). The *Dhammapada* expresses the psychological dimension of such an attitude: "The victor breeds hatred, and the defeated lie down in misery. He who renounces both victory and defeat is happy and peaceful."[103]

Depending on how one understands life and killing, it is possible to take these prohibitions in more subtle ways: for example, "when we transcend the dualism of life and death, we realize that no one kills, and no one is killed." The danger with this, however, is a sophistry that can end up rationalizing Buddhism itself away. In his persuasive study "The Modern State and Warfare: Is There a Buddhist Position?" and more recently in *Zen at War*, Brian Victoria finds "no evidence in what are generally considered to be the fundamental tenets of Buddhism (centered on the Four Noble Truths and

Holy Eight-fold Path) that would condone an adherent's participation in the killing of other human beings for any reason whatsoever. Thus, Buddhism, at least in its earliest formulation, must be considered to take the position of absolute pacifism as its normative standard of conduct."[104] The life of Shakyamuni Buddha, as conveyed in the earliest texts we have, is completely consistent with such teachings. It is inconceivable that he could have lived as a samurai, or that he would have approved of any such use of his teachings.

What Victoria says about the early Buddhist sangha enables us to develop this contrast further:

> The sangha was organized to be a non-coercive, non-authoritarian, democratic society where leadership came only from good moral character and spiritual insight. It is an order of society which has no political ambitions within the nation, and in whose ranks there is no striving for leadership. It seeks to persuade men and women to follow its way, by example and exhortation, not by force. By completely eliminating the then prevalent caste system from its ranks, Buddha Shakyamuni may rightly be considered one of history's first leaders not only to advocate but actually to practice his belief in the basic equality of all human beings. He clearly hoped that the religious and social ideals of the sangha would one day permeate the whole of society.[105]

How well have these ideals permeated Japanese Buddhism? Historically, Japan has been very good at adapting to foreign influences, and Buddhism is famously adaptable. This adaptability has been a double-edged sword, not only enabling Buddhism to permeate other cultures by reshaping their religious institutions to its own ends, but also allowing Buddhism to be co-opted (and even, in its birthplace, to be assimilated by the "fraternal embrace" of Hinduism, as Ananda Coomaraswamy put it). The Mahayana doctrine that samsara is nothing other than nirvana may be understood in opposite ways: the *sunya* (empty) nature of samsara may be taken as nirvana itself, or nirvana redefined in more this-worldly ways that end up rationalizing cravings, nationalism, and subservience to secular authority.

From this perspective, the basic problem with Japanese Buddhism appeared at the very beginning. Buddhism was first brought into Japan by the ruling classes, who saw it as a potent means to preserve the nation—which for them meant their own position, of course. Zen arrived several centuries later, yet it continued a pattern that by then had been set. King cites the case of Eisai (1141–1215), the "founder" of Japanese Zen, as typical. After returning from his second trip to China, during which he was ordained as a Rinzai master, Eisai found that his new Buddhism was not acceptable to the Tendai hierarchy at his home temple, Enryakuji. So he went to Kamakura, where he gained the favor of the widow of Minamoto Yoritomo, the first shogun, and she established a new temple for him. His first major writing was *Treatise on the Spread of Zen for the Protection of the Nation.* (Dogen too wrote a work, now lost, entitled *The Method of Protecting the Country by the True Dharma.*) Only later was Eisai invited back to Kyoto as an honored teacher. If the traditional stories can be trusted, establishing oneself by currying the favor of the powerful was not the way of Shakyamuni, nor the way of the early Chinese patriarchs, who only reluctantly answered the requests of emperors to become "national teachers."[106] The contact with secular authority is not in itself objectionable; according to the early sutras, Shakyamuni had numerous dealings with rulers, but always as a teacher and adviser, evidently because his Dharma was respected as an alternative authoritative law. The problem arises when Buddhist teachings and prestige are appropriated for other ends, as an ideology that supports the state and justifies class privilege.

If, as Victoria points out, Shakyamuni believed in the equality of all human beings and hoped sangha ideals would come to permeate all of society, the issue of social hierarchy is especially problematic for Japanese Zen, which came to emphasize devotion to one's lord more than one's personal path of liberation from desire and delusion. Or, more precisely, the two tended to be equated: to let go of oneself was understood to mean identifying completely with one's *daimyo*, the local feudal lord. "I have no desire to attain buddhahood," Yamamoto Tsunetomo, compiler of the seventeenth-century *Hagakure*, wrote *after* he had retired to become a monk. "The sincere resolution deeply engraved on my mind is to be reborn for as many as seven times as a Nabeshima samurai and administer our clan." However praiseworthy this may be as an example of egolessness, it still needs to be asked in what sense Yamamoto is a Buddhist monk.

King identifies an inbuilt factor in Buddhism that tended to work against its own teaching that life is sacred: a doctrine of karmic destiny. "And free as Zen may have been in some respects from the bonds of the Buddhist tradition, it was not free from the bonds of the teaching of karma."[107] Karma is a complicated issue in Buddhism, and it is too simple to say that Zen encourages us to accept such karma; yet something like that seems to be implied by the repeated exhortation to become one with our immediate circumstances. King also cites the strong sense of family loyalty and tradition, especially among the Japanese upper classes. The endorsement of one's family and occupation becomes questionable in the light of Shakyamuni's own example—not only because it may lead to violating the precept against killing, but because the sangha was originally established as an alternative to such family and caste obligations, which Shakyamuni himself had obviated by abandoning his own family and royal position.

The difficulty with accepting one's "karmic destiny" is that a collective ego ("wego") which the Japanese understanding of egolessness encouraged, is not necessarily better than the individual ego; it may even be more problematic. It is relevant, therefore, that the absolute loyalty expected by family heads and daimyo did not extend to inter-daimyo relations, for the daimyo did not consider their own compacts binding. As King points out, such agreements tended to be marriages of convenience, "a cagey betting on the winner of the next set of battles, cemented by intermarriages and hostages. Hence Japanese military history is full of temporary alliances, broken or shifted when conditions changed."[108]

It is difficult to avoid the conclusion that Eisai's relationship with the secular powers-that-be developed into a Faustian compact fatal to the original nonviolent spirit of Buddhism. Zen teachings for samurai—how to be loyal to their daimyo and how to fight better for their daimyo—elevated that social relationship above the fundamental Buddhist precept not to kill any living beings, especially humans. If it is important to recognize the problems with Western subject-object dualism, what about the dualism that pits me and my daimyo against you and yours? When we consider all the killing that has occurred on behalf of abstractions like God and some future utopian society, egoless devotion to a particular person might seem preferable—but only until we ask whether that daimyo was inspired by anything more than his (and his clan's) own lust for power, wealth, and prestige. Accepting one's karmic role in such a social system does provide a clear solution to the perennial problem about the meaning of one's life, yet we should be clear that this was not Shakyamuni's solution.

The *Code of the Samurai* exhorts that "one who is a samurai must before all things keep constantly in mind, by day and by night...the fact that he has to die. That is his chief business."[109] No one would deny that Zen should help us be able to die; but one may still be uncomfortable with the other idea implicit here, that this will enable us to kill better. The issue is, finally, an ethical one: did the warrior's code of *bushido* provide an ethic or did it serve *in place of* an ethic? That is, did it provide some moral authority tempering the power of secular authority? King quotes Roger Ames: "*bushido* being centered in this resolution to die, it is not in any strict sense an ethical system at all.... In essence, it does not represent any particular mode of conduct or normative standards." This may remind us of the bodhisattva, whose compassionate activities are not limited by the bounds of conventional morality, yet it is very different, because insofar as Zen did not provide an alternative moral perspective on the hierarchical and predatory social system, it became co-opted by it. As Ames continues: "Of course, historically, the proponent of *bushido*, the samurai, did align himself with a prevailing morality, or more likely was born into circumstances where the decision of moral alignment was predetermined." [110]

King puts his finger on the problem:

> If, as Suzuki claims, Zen is impatient with all rationalizing and ethicizing and believes only in visceral-intuitive rightness, if it can be (as already noted) "wedded to anarchism or fascism, communism or democracy, atheism or idealism or any political or economic dogmatism," serving any master that happens to be dominant at the time or place where Zen is, can it be called "Buddhist" in any meaningful sense; or is it only a subjective energy-providing technique?
>
> ...For essentially Zen, with its slight regard for scripture and literary or ritual tradition, has no means of checking its "Buddhist" quality from time to time or maintaining a consistent witness to a good or holy life-pattern. [111]

Perhaps this gives us some insight into the many scandals in U.S. Zen centers, whose teachers (mostly Japanese or Japanese trained) were discovered to have engaged in sexual, financial, and other misconduct. If King is right, the basic difficulty is that Zen training, being amoral, does not prepare teachers to deal with the moral dilemmas and temptations that their positions expose them to, especially in a non-Confucian, individualistic society.

Suzuki could not help touching on the problem of morality in the chapters on swordsmanship in his *Zen and Japanese Culture*. King quotes most of a long paragraph that encapsulates Suzuki's view:

The sword is generally associated with killing, and most of us wonder how it can come into connection with Zen, which is a school of Buddhism that teaches the gospel of love and mercy. The fact is that the art of swordsmanship distinguishes between the sword that kills and the sword that gives life. The one that is used by a technician cannot go any further than killing, for he never appeals to the sword unless he intends to kill. The case is altogether different with the one who is compelled to lift the sword. For it is really not he but the sword itself that does the killing. He has no desire to do harm to anybody, but the enemy appears and makes himself a victim. It is as though the sword performs automatically its function of justice, which is the function of mercy. This is the kind of sword that Christ is said to have brought among us. It is not meant just for bringing the peace mawkishly cherished by sentimentalists.... [This sword] is no more a weapon of self-defense or an instrument of killing, and the swordsman turns into an artist of the first grade, engaged in producing a work of genuine originality.[112]

This is not one of Suzuki's better paragraphs. According to this attempt to "aestheticize" ethics, selflessness makes the killing sword into a life-giving instrument of righteousness, for the man who has mastered the art does not use the sword; thus the opponent may be said to kill himself. "The enemy is filled with the evil spirit of killing and so he is killed by this evil spirit."[113] In the Japanese feudal era, though, were all enemies really evil? And what would happen, then, if feuding daimyo required two enlightened swordmasters to fight? Would each be killed by the selfless sword of the other?

King too finds such apologetics unconvincing. He is left "almost speechless" by the logic, as if a blow that kills were ethically indistinguishable from the brushstroke of a calligraphy master. "There is a vague and imprecise hope that the Zen-inspired sword is, indeed, functioning as an instrument of 'justice'—one presumes in the conceptual, moralistic sense of the word. But it is apparently not absolutely necessary that it be so to make such deeds beyond and above ordinary ethical judgments."[114]

In sum, insofar as the Zen experience "transcends" concepts and ethics, and emphasizes oneness with one's situation, its Japanese practitioners seem more vulnerable to the prevailing ideology and more likely to be co-opted by the dominant social system. Instead of providing a moral and spiritual perspective on secular authority, Zen ends up sacralizing secular authority.

Zen Nationalism

Despite such passages suggestive of co-optation, it is not entirely clear whether Suzuki himself fell into this trap. His twelve years in the United States and Europe (1897–1909) provided him with an international perspective on the emperor system, state Shinto, militarism, and the self-righteous "Japanese spirit" they propagated.[115]

Unfortunately, the same cannot be said for most of his colleagues in the Zen world, who did not benefit from such a lengthy internationalization. Suzuki's teacher Shaku Soen, a progressive, university-educated *roshi* who portrayed Buddhism as a "universal religion" at the Chicago World Parliament of Religions, actively supported the Russo-Japanese War (1904–05) and justified it in terms embarrassing to read today:

"War is not necessarily horrible, provided that it is fought for a just and honorable cause, that it is fought for the upholding of humanity and civilization. Many material human bodies may be destroyed, many humane hearts be broken, but from a broader point of view these sacrifices are so many phoenixes consumed in the sacred fire of spirituality, which will arise from the smouldering ashes reanimated, ennobled, and glorified."[116]

Thus have all wars been justified by their apologists. When Tolstoy wrote to Soen asking him to cooperate in appealing for peace, Soen refused and visited the war front to encourage the troops, declaring that

> war against evils must be unflinchingly prosecuted till we attain the final aim. In the present hostilities, into which Japan has entered with great reluctance, she pursues no egoistic purpose, but seeks the subjugation of evils hostile to civilization, peace, and enlightenment.... I came here with a double purpose. I wished to have my faith tested by going through the greatest horrors of life, but I also wished to inspire, if I could, our valiant soldiers with the ennobling thoughts of the Buddha, so as to enable them to die on the battlefield with the confidence that the task in which they are engaged is great and noble. I wished to convince them of the truths that this war is not a mere slaughter of their fellow-beings, but that they are combating an evil, and that, at the same time, corporeal annihilation really means a rebirth of soul, not in heaven, indeed, but here among ourselves.[117]

Harada Sogaku (1870–1961), the abbot of Hosshin-ji, made the identification between Zen and war complete and explicit: "Forgetting [the difference between] self and others in every situation, you should always become completely one with your work. [When ordered to] march—tramp, tramp; [when ordered to] fire—bang, bang; this is the clearest expression of the highest Bodhi-wisdom, the unity of Zen and war."[118]

What is most discomforting about these words is not that Soen and Harada support war but that they invoke Buddhism to justify and promote it. In Soen's case, a terminology appropriate to Armageddon is used to excuse a war of colonial expansion. In Harada's case, the nonduality of self and other is used in a way that flatly contradicts the basic spirit of Shakyamuni's teachings. The issue is complicated by the European colonization of Asia, which made the Japanese fearful for their own independence. The Russo-Japanese War, for example, was started in reaction to Russia's imperialist moves into Manchuria and the Liaodong Peninsula. What is not complicated, however, is the unquestioned identification of Zen ideology with nationalistic aims. If both Soen and Harada were politically and historically benighted, or at least uncritical, one wonders how much Zen anti-intellectualism played a part in this. Again, the problem is not so much that they were products of their time but that Japanese Zen contributed to making and keeping them so.

In "The Zen of Japanese Nationalism" Robert Sharf argues for a close relationship between such Zen ideology and *nihonjinron*, the popular pseudo-science devoted to demonstrating the uniqueness (and usually the superiority) of Japanese culture and spirit. Sharf believes this association holds true not only for the Zen religious establishment but for the philosophical proselytizers whose views have been most influential in the West. In his examination of D. T. Suzuki's writings, he devotes a long section to nihonjinron themes, which he traces back to 1935 when Suzuki began publishing a series of Zen books still largely unknown outside Japan. This section is less persuasive, however, in the light of Kirita's more detailed study of Suzuki's social and political views. For example, during World War II Suzuki's non-Buddhist writings were concerned to find a uniquely Japanese spirituality in Buddhism, especially in its Pure Land sects, yet this did not lead him to exalt the Japanese people or offer them as an example for the rest of the world to follow. Here is a typical passage:

> The Japanese are highly sentimental and lacking in logic, have difficulty in forming an independent judgment on the right and wrong of things,

are only concerned about being ridiculed by others, and are reluctant to enter into unknown and unexplored areas, and if they should dare to do so, they do it recklessly and without any plans made in advance.

This is not nihonjinron. However, some of Sharf's other targets are more difficult to defend. Suzuki's lifelong friend the philosopher Nishida Kitaro "was himself guilty of the most spurious forms of nihonjinron speculation," such as repeatedly characterizing Japanese culture as one of "pure feeling," more emotional, aesthetic, and communal than (and, by implication, superior to) the intellectual, rationalistic, and scientific cultures of the West.[119] In 1944, a difficult year for all Japanese, Nishida declared that contemporary Buddhists "have forgotten [the] true meaning of the Mahayana. Eastern culture must arise again from such a standpoint. It must contribute a new light to world culture. As a self-determination of the absolute present, the national polity *(kokutai)* of Japan is a norm of historical action in such a perspective. The above-mentioned true spirit of the Mahayana is in the East preserved today only in Japan."[120] This must be taken in the light of Nishida's support for the Greater East Asian Co-Prosperity Sphere and for the Pacific War.

Such a nihonjinron attitude was evidently shared by Hisamatsu Shin'ichi (1889–1980), who also believed that only Japanese have the aesthetic and intellectual sensibility necessary to fathom Zen, despite the fact that this truth was universal:

> I have long spoken of "Oriental Nothingness."… I qualify it as Oriental because in the West such Nothingness has never been fully awakened, nor has there been penetration to such a level. However, this does not mean that it belongs exclusively to the East. On the contrary, it is the most profound basis or root source of man; in this sense it belongs neither to the East or West. Only as regards the actual Awakening to such a Self, there have been no instances in the West; hence the regional qualification "Oriental."[121]

Sharf recounts a well-known conversation between Hisamatsu and Suzuki recorded at Harvard University in 1958:

HISAMATSU: Among the many people you've met or heard of (in the West) is there anyone who you think has some understanding of Zen?

SUZUKI: No one. Not yet anyway.

HISAMATSU: I see. Not yet. Well then, is there at least someone you have hope for? (Laughter)

SUZUKI: No. Not even that.

HISAMATSU: So, of the many people (in the West) who have written about Zen there aren't any who understand it?

SUZUKI: That's right.

HISAMATSU: Well, is there at least some book written (by a Westerner) which is at least fairly accurate?

SUZUKI: No. Not to my knowledge.[122]

Taken out of context, this conversation is perhaps misleading. Suzuki had high hopes for Zen in the West, while recognizing that its acceptance there would take time. Nonetheless, if Zen experience is indeed the essence of all religion, as Suzuki so often claimed, his evaluation cannot help but be depressing for Western Zen students. Yet there is more than one way to understand their dialogue. It may be that Occidental culture is so rationalistic and so infected by subject-object dualism that all Westerners are spiritually obtuse. It is also possible that the problem is on the other side as well: that a supposedly universal experience has in fact come to be defined primarily in Japanese terms.

Sharf concludes by situating the nihonjinron impulse in its historical context, as one intellectual reaction to the radical and destabilizing transformation of Japan initiated by the Meiji reformation:

Nihonjinron is in large part a Japanese response to modernity—the sense of being adrift in a sea of tumultuous change, cut off from the past, alienated from history and tradition. Since the Meiji reforms, Japanese intellectuals have been confronted with the collapse of traditional Japanese political and social structures, accompanied by the insidious threat posed by the hegemonic discourse of the West. In response, the Japanese would formulate a conception of Japaneseness that would, in part, insulate themselves from Western universalizing discourse. This was accomplished through insisting that the essence of Japanese character lay in a uniquely

Japanese experience of the world, an experience that was thus conveniently out of the reach of foreigners.[123]

Even if this overstates the case, it touches on something important. The Meiji restoration remains an ambiguous legacy. Traumatized by being brutally forced open to the rest of the world, Japan was acutely aware that it needed to adopt Western technology as quickly as possible, if only to defend itself from the imminent colonization that devastated the rest of Asia. Not only Japan's self-confidence but its very self-identity was badly shaken. It is not surprising, then, that Zen and the samurai spirit were understood to exemplify the superior soul of the Japanese—which happened to fit nicely into a concern that arose in certain quarters of the West to find a superior "other" with which to flog itself. We may sympathize with Japan's need to establish its own identity on the world stage, and with Japanese intellectuals' need to avoid the "hegemonic discourse" of the West. Nonetheless, the resulting self-understanding of Japanese Zen Buddhists cannot be accepted uncritically.

What else can we learn from this example of co-option of Buddhist principles? For a start, we are reminded that there is nothing in the Buddhist teachings themselves that ensures how they will actually be used. This issue becomes especially problematic when Buddhism is introduced into a new culture. If Buddhism takes root, it changes that culture, but it is also changed by it. There is no way to predict which will be changed more. In the case of Japan, a comparison with the Theravadan societies of South and Southeast Asia suggests that Japanese Buddhism might be more Japanese than Buddhist; at least, the differences are more obvious than the similarities. Chan Zen, as we have seen, has an antimonian side that paradoxically makes it more adaptable and susceptible to new ethical and cultural codes.

As Buddhism infiltrates the West, this is a lesson to be heeded if the meaning of the teachings, e.g., of karma and rebirth, is not to be distorted. We must be alert to the difference between their original context and their new context. For example, traditional Buddhist emphasis on personal liberation can easily plug into North American concern to free oneself from social bonds and responsibilities. Ostensibly, this concern can seem similar to the sangha of renunciants that Shakyamuni established, but individual freedom tends to mean something quite different in a technological society preoccupied with making and spending money. Is one contemporary equivalent to medieval Japanese militarism North American consumerism? It is not yet clear how much American Buddhism is in danger of itself becoming commodified.

There is, however, another lesson to be learned from the sad tale of Japanese Buddhist militarism. In one way, such nationalistic co-option is the fate to be expected of a spiritual tradition that has insufficiently addressed the problem of collective social dukkha caused by institutionalized greed, ill will, and delusion. Today the most powerful god, the one that most people are willing to kill and die for, is not Jehovah or Allah but the nation-state. All the casualties of medieval Japanese wars can hardly be compared with the tens of millions sacrificed at the altar of the modern state, now accountable to nothing higher than itself. I think it is unlikely that Western Buddhism will be seduced by this deity, but it remains to be seen what role Buddhism can play in exposing what is probably the most pernicious ideology of the modern world. Again, this highlights the need for Buddhist social theories that develop the collective and institutional implications of the Dharma.

What does all this mean, in particular, for those of us who have found a spiritual home within Zen Buddhism? The Zen tradition emphasizes that the student should surpass the teacher. This is an area where Western Zen must surpass Japanese Zen, learning from its limitations—without any naivete that Western practitioners will thus be able to transcend all the delusions of our own culture. As we remain eternally grateful for the achievements of the Sino-Japanese Zen tradition, and for the efforts of so many generations of its teachers on behalf of their students, let us do what we can to extend and develop that teaching to meet the social challenges of today.

CHAPTER 8

Remaking Ourselves

On the Duality between Nature and Technology

As human beings our greatness lies not so much in being able to remake the world as in being able to remake ourselves.

—Gandhi

W E CAN SAFELY SUPPOSE that Gandhi was not thinking about genetic engineering when he emphasized the importance of remaking ourselves. Today, however, we have access to new ways of remaking ourselves, and the rest of the biosphere as well. What criteria should we use to evaluate them?

In the case of modifying our own genotype, for example, enthusiasm about this alternative way to reduce some types of dukkha (most obviously, by treating hereditary genetic diseases) is overshadowed by concern about its evident dangers. In addition to the problem of accidents, which are inevitable and may be disastrous, there is the issue of who will control this technology, and for what ends. Given the domination of market principles today, will we end up with an elite of supersmart, superhealthy, and superbeautiful people who control the rest of us? Some scientists are already discussing the likelihood of such a future, and not all of them see it as something to be worried about.[124]

Given both its promise and its dangers, then, how are we to evaluate such extraordinary new possibilities? Up to now, at least, new technologies have usually been judged by distinguishing between nature and artifact, between the "world of born" and a "world of made" (e. e. cummings), in order to take sides. Either we are fascinated by new technological possibilities, which seem to allow us greater control over our destiny, or we are suspicious of those possibilities and nostalgic for a more "natural" order. To a large extent, our understanding remains paralyzed by this antithesis—which highlights the possible importance of a non-Western perspective. What can a Buddhist social theory contribute here?

What both of these alternatives presuppose is an acute bifurcation between nature and culture, a dualism that is not only peculiarly Western but perhaps even fundamental to Western civilization. Our preoccupation with this dualism may be traced all the way back to our Greek origins, to its distinction between *phusis* and *nomos,* nature and convention (which, by recognizing the the latter as construct, allows the possibility of restructuring society and our natural environment). Is this conceptual antinomy a liberating discovery, because it deprives social and ideological structures of their inevitable and "natural" character, or is it another constraining thought construction? Or both? Such questions reveal how inescapable the dualism has become for us: even the attempt to understand it becomes expressed in terms of it.

Much of the Western tradition can be understood as an increasing self-consciousness about the difference between nature and convention/culture, and the dialectic whereby each alternately becomes preferred to the other. Hesiod (eighth century B.C.E.), who stands perhaps not far inside the threshold of literacy, already distinguishes between the traditional agricultural life he praises (in the Golden Age of the past) and the technological innovations that Protagoras and Anaxagoras would later praise (which they and many since them think may lead to a golden age in the future). Already we see the pattern: those who yearn for nature evoke the past, while those who privilege culture (including technology) have high hopes for the future. Then, as today, nobody is satisfied with the present.

The fifth century brought not only the democratic and imperialistic aspirations of Periclean Athens but also the first plans for reorganizing society along more rational lines. As Democritus expressed it, nature is not simply what is inborn, for it may be implanted with education and training. Perhaps the most enthusiastic proclamation of human ability to control and transform the natural is found in Sophocles' *Antigone,* which includes what may be the first recorded warning that this power is a mixed blessing. Like many other conceptual tensions, that between *phusis* and *nomos* was addressed but not quite resolved by Plato: the simpler life of earlier pastoral society was more conducive to goodness and happiness, yet it lacked philosophy—itself a product of the growing alienation between social custom and natural order.[125]

The Cynics may be viewed as one radical reaction to this split. In response to the unsatisfactory *nomos* that their reconstructing Greek society offered, they preferred to live naturally, dog-like *(kunikos)*. Unfortunately, the attraction of such a lifestyle is at the same time a condition of its impossibility. Once convention has been recognized as convention, you can't go home again, for the essential condition of being truly "close to nature" is that you do not know you are close to nature. The paradox has dogged us ever since.

Closer to our time, but no less determined by this dualism, such figures as Diderot, Rousseau, Herder, Spengler, Romantic philosophers and poets contrasted the organic and genuine with the artificial and conventional, seeking sincerity and spontaneity in place of sterile rationality. On the other side, Kant, Hegel, Marx, Condorcet, and Comte (to mention only a few) expressed almost unbounded optimism in the progressive capacity of human beings to understand and control the laws of their own development. More recently, Freud emphasized the necessity for the socially constructed ego and superego to control the anomic urges of libido instinct; Herbert Marcuse and Norman Brown celebrated eros unbound. Today we debate whether the Internet is liberating or alienating, while postmodern environmentalists such as Neil Evernden and Max Oelschlaeger attempt to abandon the concept of "nature," but only as a strategy to recuperate the saving power of a wild and sacred otherness.[126]

One could even argue that the historical dialectic between nature and culture/technology *is* the Western tradition, which would explain why our ways of thinking about such issues "naturally" (that word again!) tend to bifurcate into those opposed possibilities. When we translate this dichotomy back into the issue of how to evaluate the possibilities of bioengineering our own genetic code, the usual dualism between nature and culture/technology means that some people want to dismiss that possibility out of hand as abominable because unnatural, while others cannot understand why we are so reluctant to take charge of our (otherwise random?) genetic destiny.

From a Buddhist perspective, the dualism between nature and culture/technology may be seen to suffer from the same problem as most other dualistic ways of thinking. Earlier chapters have already examined the peculiar delusion of antithetical categories. We distinguish between them because we want one rather than the other, but their interdependence means that we cannot have one without the other, since each term has meaning only as the negation of the other. Applied to the nature/culture dualism, this suggests that today we cannot live a natural life without a rather unnatural preoccupation with avoiding many unnatural technologies. From the other side, however, our modern infatuation with technology may be brought into question by asking, Why is it so important to be "unnatural"? Why are we so preoccupied with reconstructing the conditions of our existence on the earth? Why try to take charge of our own collective destiny? These are undoubtedly silly questions for those committed to permanent technological revolution, yet they are ones we shall need to return to.

Another way to get at the problem is to generalize the question and ask what motivates our creating a dualism between nature and culture. That may be the crucial issue if we want to escape the sort of deadlock that usually ensues.

It seems to me that their bifurcation is related to the tension between two of our most basic psychological needs, security and freedom. This is more obvious on an individual level: we want to be free, but becoming free makes us more anxious and therefore more inclined to sacrifice that freedom for security, at which time we again feel a need to be free. For example, sometimes I want to be special and better than others, to stand out from the crowd; at other times I feel a need to fit in, to be part of the group and share the security of being just like everyone else. Otto Rank expressed this in terms of two opposite fears: "Whereas the life fear is anxiety at going forward, the death fear is anxiety at going backward, losing individuality. Between these two fear possibilities the individual is thrown back and forth all his life."[127]

In short, two of our most important psychological needs—for freedom and security—conflict. Is the same thing true on the collective level?

A basic but often unrecognized issue here is how we understand the meaning of our lives. When we accept our culture as natural, we are securely grounded in the roles that culture (including religious belief) determines for us, whereas when we are free to discover or construct our own meaning, we forfeit that "natural" ground. Materially, of course, something like the opposite has often been the case. In many premodern societies, the physical conditions of their survival were often precarious, so people embraced technology to control and secure those conditions. The supreme irony of the ecological crisis, from that perspective, is that our technological efforts to secure ourselves materially over the last five hundred years are what have caused the biospheric degradation that now threatens our very survival.

Collectively as well as individually, then, we have tended to alternate between yearning for the security of a "natural" grounding, and reconstructing the technological conditions of our existence. Each has its own attractions and problems. Today our ambivalence is further complicated by the fact that the technological genie cannot be put back inside his bottle. Nor would we want to return (even if we could) to some "natural" premodern society such as Tokugawa Japan, where hierarchical and exploitative political structures were presented as perfect because they conformed to "the order found in the manifold natural phenomena of heaven and earth."[128] That is not a serious option for us.

So where does that leave us? If our thinking today about new technologies such as bioengineering remains trapped within this dialectic, is there any other approach that might shed light on our ambivalence between what are often the genuine promises of new technologies and what are also often well-founded concerns about their expected and unexpected side effects?

If a dualism between nature and culture/technology has been so essential to the development of the West, we may wonder about whether the same is true for other civilizations, and the answer, so far as I can tell, is largely negative. As anthropologists have learned, most if not all cultures make some such distinction, yet other cultures differ widely in how and where they draw the line between them; nature and culture generally intertwine much more than they do in the West. By no coincidence, the English term "nature," with its extraordinarily wide range of meanings, is notoriously difficult to translate into other languages, perhaps because our dualism is not so "natural" to other cultures. For example, the main Japanese term for nature, *shinen* (or *jinen*), originally borrowed from Chinese, cannot normally be understood as one side of such a dualism.[129]

The distinction between nature and "unnatural" culture/technology is also not very Buddhist. Shakyamuni's Dharma did not distinguish between them, and insofar as some such dualism might be read into his teachings, one might even argue (if somewhat perversely) that the Buddhist emphasis may even be on the *un*natural. (An example might be the celibacy of the sangha and its withdrawal from usual social and economic activities.) Perhaps the main place where naturalness may be said to be privileged in Buddhism is occasionally in those traditions influenced by Taoism or Shinto, such as Zen. Mahayana Buddhism, in particular, emphasizes the interdependence of everything, which allows for no self-existence and which emphasizes no basic distinction between nature and non-nature. The Huayen metaphor of Indra's infinite net sees everything as reflecting everything else, without any such bifurcation.

Nor does Buddhism provide any support for those who wish to return to some (pre-agricultural?) golden age in the distant past. The Buddha could not find the beginning of our dukkha, and he was not much interested in that anyway; his sole concern was to show us how our dukkha could be ended. Nor did he express any interest in a technological solution to (some of) our dukkha, although such an approach was not much of an option for his culture anyway. Unsurprisingly, I have not been able to find any references to biotechnology in the Buddhist scriptures. More generally, it is clear that critiques that argue that technology is unnatural are somewhat unnatural to Buddhism. The Buddhist angle is different, although no less acute.

In short, our discomfort with modern technologies such as bioengineering needs to be articulated in a different way, not by simply privileging the nature side of the nature/technology dualism—and Buddhism offers us such a way. As we have seen, according to Buddhism we make ourselves and each other unhappy because of the three roots of evil: greed, ill will, and delusion. In order to become happy, these three poisons need to be transformed into their positive counterparts: generosity, compassion, and wisdom. That is because actions motivated by negative intentions tend to bring about bad consequences, while actions motivated by good intentions tend to bring good results. This, of course, is the Buddhist doctrine of karma.

It follows that one way to evaluate new technologies might be to look at the motivations behind our preoccupation with developing them. If this eagerness is motivated by our generosity, compassion, and wisdom, we can conclude that this technology is likely to bring about good results. If, however, we are motivated by greed, ill will, or delusion, we should expect the new technology to increase our dukkha, rather than reduce it.

This criterion may seem simple and even obvious, yet it contradicts the utilitarian assumptions that we normally use, or presuppose, when we evaluate a new technology. We usually ask: What will this new technology do for us? I am suggesting that we also need to ask the more Buddhist questions: Why do we really *want* to do what this new technology can do? Why is this so important to us?

Of course, the issue is rarely a simple matter of "either/or," for there is a wide spectrum between the two extremes of greed and generosity. Both individually and collectively, our motivations are usually a composite of various factors. Nonetheless, and despite all the public rhetoric about the potential to improve our lives (which cannot be denied), it is not difficult to find the three poisons influencing our eagerness to develop new technologies today. Let us again focus on the example of biotechnology. The most obvious motivation is greed, in the form of personal desire for excessive wealth and corporate desire for greater profits. Those desires have become so central to our lives, both individually and collectively, that we have become reluctant to label them "greed," but from a Buddhist perspective that term is appropriate. The recurring squabbles over patent rights for bioengineered life forms, and even for parts of the human genome, make that all too obvious. Since this problem has been so widely discussed, there is no need to go into it any further, except to emphasize how this "root of evil" works to circumvent the painstaking, long-term evaluation necessary for even the most innocuous and benign applications of genetic engineering, if serious mistakes are to be avoided. Unfortunately, the rush to make big money from bioengineered life tends to make us all into laboratory rats.

The role of ill will, the second root of evil, is less obvious, and one hopes less pervasive, yet such motivations are present in the competitive pressures that often drive researchers eager for Nobel Prizes and corporations eager for lucrative patents. As we each know from personal experience, desire thwarted or threatened tends to generate resentment and other forms of ill will.

The least obvious factor, however, may well be the most problematic one: the third root of evil, in this case our collective ignorance or delusion. The issue here is whether there may be some other, less conscious motivations behind our fascination with technologies such as genetic engineering. Do we really understand why this technology, in particular, has suddenly become so important to us? Are we simply enthusiastic about developing new ways to help people (as well as make a buck, of course), or is something else driving us here? There seems to be a psychological law that when we are motivated by something unconscious, our actions are likely to have unfortunate consequences, because what we *think* we want is not really what we want and so our efforts cannot satisfy us. That makes it all the more important for us to clarify our motivations.

As one way to approach this, let us see whether the parallel between our individual motivations and our collective ones sheds light on our modern preoccupation with technological solutions to human dukkha, bioengineering in particular.

As I mentioned in the introduction, what is most striking about our collective predicament today is how much it resembles the central problem for each of us as individuals: the sense of separation between an ego-self inside and an objective world outside. This subject-object dualism, which we tend to take for granted, is the root delusion that makes us unhappy. It causes us to seek happiness by trying to manipulate things in the objective world in order to get what we want from it, yet that just reinforces our illusion of a self inside alienated from some objective world "out there."

According to Buddhism, this ego-self is illusory because it corresponds to nothing substantial: it is *shunya,* or "empty." Instead of being separate from the world, my sense of self is one manifestation of it. In more contemporary terms, the sense of self is an impermanent—because interdependent—construct. Furthermore, I think we are all at least dimly aware of this, for our lack of a more substantial, Cartesian self means that our ungrounded sense of self is haunted by a profound insecurity that we can never quite manage to resolve. We usually experience this insecurity as the feeling that "something is wrong with me," a feeling we understand and act upon in different ways according to our particular character and situation. Contemporary Western culture conditions many of us into thinking that what is wrong with us is that we do not have enough money or enough sex, for instance. Academics (like aspiring Hollywood actors) are more likely to understand the problem as not being famous enough (not published enough, not read enough, etc.). All these different ways of understanding our lack encourage the same trap. Perceiving a lack, I therefore vainly try to ground myself by modifying the world outside me. In other words, I try to subjectify myself (make myself feel more real)by objectifying myself (finding something in the world to identify with). Unfortunately, nothing in our notoriously impermanent world can fill up the bottomless pit at the core of my being—bottomless, because there is really no-thing there that can be filled up. To put it another way, no amount of money or fame in the world can ever be enough if lack of money and fame is not really the source of my lack.

According to Buddhism, such personal "reality projects"—these ways we try to make ourselves feel more real—cannot be successful, for a very different approach is needed to overcome our sense of lack. Instead of trying to ground ourselves somewhere on the "outside," we need to look "inside." Instead of running away from this sense of emptiness at our core, we need to become more comfortable with it and more aware, in which case it can transform from a sense of lack into the source of our creativity and spontaneity.

If this describes our individual problem, is the same thing true collectively?

Can this shed any light on our contemporary attitude toward technology? Individually, we usually address the problem of our lack of self-grounding by trying to ground ourselves somewhere in the world—for example, in the size of our bank account or in the number of people who know our name. Are we collectively attempting to solve the problem of our collective lack of self-grounding in a parallel fashion, by trying to ground ourselves in the world? In this case, by objectifying and transforming the world technologically?

"Technology is not applied science," writes Donald Verene. "It is the expression of a deep longing, an original longing that is present in modern science from its beginning. This is the desire of the self to seek its own truth through the mastery of the object.... The power of technique is not to connect thought effectively to nature; it alters nature to its own purpose. Its aim is to master its being; to own it."[130]

What is that deep longing? Remember the problem of life's meaning, which, I have suggested, motivates (or contributes to) our dualism between nature and culture/technology. Despite their material insecurity, most pre-modern societies are quite secure in that the meaning of their lives is determined for them, for better *and* worse. From our perspective they may be "stuck," yet insofar as they do not know of any alternative, they are able to enjoy themselves as much as their situation allows. In contrast, our freedom to determine the meaning of our lives, and direct the development of our own societies, means we have lost such security due to the lack of any such "natural" ground for us. In compensation, has technological development become our collective security project?

Today we have become so familiar with rapid scientific and technological development that we have come to think of it as natural, which in this case means something that does not need to be explained. Yet in what sense is it natural to "progress" from the Wright brothers' biplane to a lunar landing within one lifetime? (For example, the British philosopher Bertrand Russell was already an adult when the Wright Brothers first flew; he lived long enough to watch the first moon landing on television). In response to the anxiety produced by our alienation from a more original type of "natural" condition, we try to make ourselves feel more real by reorganizing the whole world until we can see our own image everywhere, reflected in the "resources" with which we try to manipulate and secure the material conditions of our existence.

This is why so many of us have been able to dispense with the consolations of traditional religion: now we have other ways to control our fate, or at least

try to. But we must also understand how that impels us. Because the traditional security provided by religious meaning—grounding us in God and the
like—has been taken away from us, we have not been able to escape the task
of trying to construct our own self-ground. According to Buddhism, however, such projects are doomed from the start, for nothing can have self-existence. That everything interpenetrates everything else means that all things
are composed of "non-self" elements—an important truth for a species
wholly dependent on its deteriorating physical environment.

The result is that no amount of material security can provide the kind of
grounding we crave, the sense of reality we most need—a need best understood as spiritual, for that helps us to see the fundamental contradiction that
bedevils us. Unfortunately, we cannot manipulate the natural world in a collective attempt to self-ground ourselves, and then also hope to find in that
world a grounding in something greater than ourselves. Our incredible technological power means we can do almost anything we want, yet the ironic
consequence is that we no longer know what we want. Our reaction has been
to grow and "develop" ever more quickly, but to what end?… To keep evad-
ing these deepest questions about the meaning of our lives, one suspects. Our
preoccupation with the means (the whole earth as "resources") impels us perpetually to postpone thinking about where we are all going so quickly. Or are
we running so fast because we are trying to get away from something?

Another way to put it is that technology has become our attempt to own the
universe, an attempt that is always frustrated because, for reasons we do not
quite understand, we never possess it fully enough to feel secure in our own-
ership. For many people dubious of this technocratic project, nature has taken
over the role of a more transcendental God, because, like God, it can fulfill our
need to be grounded in something greater than us. Our technology cannot fill
that role because it is motivated by the opposite need: to extend our control,
which banishes all sacrality. Our success in "improving" nature means we can
no longer rest peacefully in its bosom.

Yet there seems to be a problem with my critique of this approach. Doen't
it smear all technological development with the same Buddhist brush? Instead
of deconstructing the nature versus technology duality, doesn't such a perspective risk falling into the same pro-nature, anti-progress attitude that was
questioned earlier?

In response, it must be emphasized that this evaluation does not imply any
wholesale rejection of modern technology. Remember that the Buddhist

emphasis is on our motivations. This does not necessarily mean that any particular technology is bad in itself, inasmuch as it is our problematic and confused negative motivations that tend to lead to negative consequences. To evaluate specific situations we can apply a Buddhist rule of thumb: Is our interest in developing this new technology due to our greed or ill will; and can we become clear about why we are doing this? Among other things, this means: Do we clearly understand how this will reduce dukkha, and what its other effects will be?

Such questions encourage us, in effect, to transform our motivations, in a way that would enable us to evaluate technologies in a more conscious and thoughtful fashion. One crucial issue in this process, of course, is who "we" are. Transformative technologies have often been initiated and propagated without much thought of their long-range consequences (e.g., automobiles), but sometimes they have been imposed by elites who a firm belief in their superior understanding (e.g., the exponents of nuclear power). The evaluation process I am suggesting would involve engaging in a much more thorough and wide-ranging democratic discussion of what we collectively want from a technology. This will not stop us from making mistakes, but at least they will be our collective mistakes, rather than those of elites who may have more to gain and less to lose than the rest of us. Also, this will inevitably slow down the development of new technologies, something I see as advantageous because it will allow for a more painstaking scientific and sociological evaluation, less subverted by desire for profit or competitive advantage.

What, if anything, does this specifically imply about biotechnology, the main example used in this chapter? In one way, nothing. Genetic engineering is not to be distinguished from other technologies in that they all need to be evaluated in the above fashion. In another way, however, biotechnology is special because it presents us with the most extreme version of the difficulty with technological objectification generally. The Buddhist claim that we are nondual with the world, not separate from it, means that when we objectify and commodify the world, we ourselves end up objectified and commodified, by it and in it. As the world has become reduced to a collection of resources to be managed, the physical and social structures we have created to accomplish this have ended up reducing *us* to resources—"human resources"—and we find ourselves increasingly subjected to those structures, which organize and utilize us in various ways.

Biotechnology signifies the completion of this commodification process.

Life, or at least human life, has been seen as the last bastion of the sacred in an increasingly desacralized world. Now this last resistance to commodification is being overcome, and the category of the sacred ceases to correspond to anything in our experience. There are many places and phenomena we cannot yet commodify, but in principle nothing now remains outside the scope of technological transformation into resources by a species that has yet to demonstrate it is mature enough to exercise this power in a healthy way. Until now, we have labored to ground ourselves by reconstructing our environment. Suddenly there is this new possibility: trying to ground ourselves by reconstructing ourselves—by altering our own genetic codes.

This raises, in an especially acute way, all the ethical and spiritual issues adumbrated above. If we allow market principles the same freedom to commodify that is now accepted in most other areas, this technology will become available mainly for those who can afford it, especially wealthy parents concerned about the health, intelligence, and beauty of their offspring, and wealthy individuals concerned to immortalize themselves with clones. In addition to this obvious challenge to our egalitarian aspirations, there are more "spiritual" problems. Can we trust such technologies to be controlled by people who do not understand, and therefore are unable to cope with, their own mortality and sense of lack? Do we want the genetic foundation of life itself to become another hostage to our inability to accept the conditions of our impermanent existence in the world?

In this fashion biotechnology not only creates special dangers and possibilities, it also prompts us to address such technological issues in a more conscious and open way.

More concretely, what does this mean for how genetic engineering is being conducted today? From the Buddhist perspective offered in this chapter, it seems difficult to escape the conclusion that biotechnology as it is presently being developed should be suspended, while we engage in a much more thorough democratic discussion of what we collectively want from it. The greed, competition, and delusion that motivate so much bioengineering research and application today are a recipe for disaster. Needless to say, we should have no delusions that such a public debate will happen unless we fight for it. The economic and political powers-that-be have too much of a stake in pushing biotechnology. Yet the difficulties encountered by the Monsanto Corporation, for instance, in promoting its genetically modified foods and terminator seeds suggest that there are grounds for hope.

Nevertheless, and against the view that all biotechnology is abominable because unnatural, sometime in the future we may have economic and political conditions that enable us to pursue bioengineering with more conscious and humble motivations: to reduce dukkha.

That is because—to say it again—the essential point of Buddhism is not to return to some pristine natural condition but to reduce our dukkha. Despite the obvious dangers, there is the possibility that biotechnology may do that— for example (and most obviously) by treating inherited genetic diseases. Today we cannot expect the CEOs of biotech companies to be bodhisattvas committed to the well-being of all, but we can still hope that this may someday be a world where a much more cautious approach to genetic engineering will improve the human condition more than it will threaten it.

This, however, is unlikely to occur until we learn that remaking ourselves spiritually is more important than remaking the world—which brings us back to the issue of how we are to apply the Buddhist rule of thumb in evaluating technologies. Earlier, I emphasized the importance of becoming clear about why we want to develop a new technology, but how can we become clear about something like that?

This leads me to the conclusion that we cannot evade yet another parallel between the personal and the social. As a society, we cannot expect to become sufficiently aware of our collective motivations unless we also make the effort to become more aware of our individual motivations. I suspect we will not be able to resolve our group sense of lack unless more of us individually address our personal sense of lack. If the root problem in both cases is due to our felt lack of reality, we cannot expect wholly "secular" solutions to technological problems that provide us with a spiritual challenge.

CHAPTER 9

Loving the World As Our Own Body

The Nondualist Ethics of Taoism, Buddhism, and Deep Ecology

> The Western version of mystical awareness, our version of Buddhism or Taoism, will be ecological awareness.
>
> —Fritjof Capra

I F CAPRA IS CORRECT, a contemporary Buddhist social theory needs to incorporate an appreciation of recent ecological theory. Given Buddhism's emphasis on the nonduality of self and world, we can expect its ecological implications to resonate especially with deep ecology, which most directly questions the duality between *Homo sapiens* and the earth's other species. As Capra implies, we may also benefit from looking at what Taoism has to say about these dualities and the reasons for them.

In the last few decades ethics has experienced a revolution as parameters basic since ancient Greece have been transformed. Until quite recently, ethical theory has addressed the issue of what binds us human beings together: How do we relate to other people, or to society as a whole, without using or abusing one another? Today the issue of ethical responsibility has broadened to encompass the whole eco-sphere. The crucial question has become how to relate to all beings, not only animals and plants but even apparently nonsentient beings such as tropical rain forest systems and the ozone layer. In spite of distractions such as the debate over "sustainable development" (an oxymoron?), the suspicion continues to grow that what is involved is much more than the need to preserve "our natural resources." Lynn White Jr., one of the first to consider the philosophical implications of the ecological crisis, realized that the issue is fundamentally a spiritual one: "Since the roots of our trouble are so largely religious, the remedy must also be essentially religious, whether we call it that or not. We must rethink and refeel our destiny."[131] It is becoming obvious that what is required is nothing less than a fundamental transformation in the way we have understood the relation between ourselves and the earth.

At the heart of this issue, as we have seen repeatedly in the foregoing chapters, is the self. The ecological problem seems to be the perennial personal problem writ large, a consequence of the alienation between myself and the world I find myself in. In both these dualisms, the self is understood to be the locus of awareness and therefore the source of meaning and value. This bifurcation devalues the objective world, including all of nature, reducing it to the sphere of activity wherein the self labors to fulfill itself. The alienated subject feels no responsibility for the objectified other and attempts to find satisfaction through exploitative projects that, in fact, usually increase the sense of alienation.

If so, the meaning and purpose that we seek can be attained only by establishing a more nondual relationship with the objectified other: in ecological terms, establishing a more nondual relationship with the earth, which, as I've suggested, is not only our home but our mother. In contrast to the main humanistic or anthropocentric tendency within the West, Asian philosophical and religious traditions have had much to say about the nonduality of subject and object. This chapter discusses and compares the relevant insights of Taoism, Buddhism, and deep ecology. All three of these perspectives avoid the usual is/ought problem (namely, how to infer what one should do from what is the case—a category mistake according to most modern philosophy) by transposing the issue from morality to understanding. The main problem is not evil but ignorance, and the solution is not primarily a matter of applying the will but of reaching an insight into the nature of things. Socrates is vindicated: immoral conduct is indeed due to ignorance, for if we *really knew* the good, we would do it. The catch, of course, is in the "really," for the type of knowledge necessary is neither the correct moral code nor any objective scientific understanding, but an insight that can liberate us from the dualistic ways of thinking whereby we "bind ourselves without a rope," as a Zen saying puts it.

TAOISM

The reason why we have trouble is that we have a body.
When we have no body, what trouble do we have?
Therefore: he who loves the whole world as if it were his own body
Can be trusted with the whole world.

—*Tao Te Ching*

The Taoist critique of the self opposes selfness with the realization of the Tao, which is neither a transcendental God nor an impersonal Absolute but the dynamic source from which all natural phenomena arise. Formless, invisible, soundless, immaterial, unhindered, imperturbable: the Tao is "the form of the formless, the image of the imageless," empty *(chung)* and inexhaustible.[132] The relationship between it and the many things in the world is described using such metaphors as the nave and spokes of a wheel, the space inside a pot, the door and windows to a room—whose emptiness is not a lack but necessary for the wheel, pot and room to function. We can never objectively grasp such emptiness, yet it is necessary for anything to be—or, more precisely, for anything to happen, since Taoism like Buddhism rejects a substance-based ontology in favor of an event-based process.

To experience the Tao is to realize that humans are not exceptions to this natural process, for we too are manifestations of it. Instead of being the crown of creation, at the top of a great chain of beings, *Homo sapiens* is only one of the "ten thousand things" (a phrase indicating "all things") that the Tao treats indifferently, like the straw-dogs mentioned in chapter 5 of the *Tao Te Ching* that the Chinese people made for use in ceremonies and then threw away once the ceremony was over. The ten thousand things are related not vertically, with those of lesser value supporting those of higher value, but horizontally, all being citizens in the great commonwealth that is the natural world. This attitude may make us uncomfortable—who likes to lose one's special status?—but for Mahayana Buddhism, too, all beings are equally empty, because they all lack self-existence. And what has been called the central insight of deep ecology is "the idea that we can make no firm ontological divide in the field of existence: That there is no bifurcation in reality between the human and the non-human realms."[133] If we acknowledge it as valid, this realization constitutes a revolution of consciousness perhaps no less significant than that of Copernicus and Darwin. Copernicus displaced the earth from its divinely allocated position as the center of creation; Darwin demonstrated that we too are a product of the same evolutionary forces that created other species, yet (whether or not it was his intention) that still seemed to leave humans the ultimate victors, an evolutionary epitome, in the struggle for life. Now that our privileged status becomes questionable, where do we find ourselves?

Several passages in the *Tao Te Ching*, one of which was quoted above, allude to the need to overcome subject-object duality. Another Taoist classic, the *Chuang-tzu*, a later and more discursive work, is less ambiguous in asserting that "the perfect man has no self." "If there is no other, there will be no I. If there is no I, there will be none to make distinctions."[134]

> It is because there is right, that there is wrong; it is because there is wrong, that there is right. This being the situation, the sages do not approach things at this level, but reflect the light of nature. Thereupon the self is also the other; the other is also the self.... But really are there such distinctions as the self and the other, or are there no such distinctions? When the self and the other lose their contrariety, there we have the very essence of the Tao.[135]

This denial of the duality between self and other is so strange, so counterintuitive, that we are not sure how to take it; yet the fact that it is such a common claim in the mainstream Asian traditions (and occasionally in the West too—for example, in Plotinus) suggests we should consider it quite seriously. Its ethical implications were realized early in Indian Vedanta: "He who sees all beings as the very Self and the Self in all beings in consequence of that abhors none." Vidyaranya improved on that: "The knowledge of the Self leads to the identification of oneself with others as clearly as one identifies with one's own body."[136] This brings us back to *Tao Te Ching*, which likewise recommends loving the whole world as if it were one's own body.... And what if it *is* our body? What if the discrimination we usually make between our own body and the rest of the world is in some fundamental way a delusion, as Advaita Vedanta, Buddhism, and Taoism claim? Such a realization would certainly have far-reaching ethical implications.

Everyone agrees that the most important chapter of the *Tao Te Ching* is the first one; some scholars (e.g., Chang Chung-yuan and Wing-tsit Chan) claim it is the key to the entire work and that all the chapters that follow may be inferred from it. Unfortunately this chapter is also notoriously obscure. If a nondualist interpretation of Taoism is correct, we would expect the first chapter to say something important about the relation between subject-object dualism and a more nondualistic way of experiencing the world. In fact, that is exactly what the chapter seems to be about, alternately referring to the nondual Tao (lines 1, 3, 5, and 7) and to our usual dualistic way of experiencing ourselves "in" the world (lines 2, 4, 6, and 8):

> The Tao that can be Tao'd is not the constant Tao
> The name that can be named is not a constant name
> Having-no-name is the source of heaven and earth
> Having-names is the mother of the ten thousand things
> Therefore when you do not have intention you can see the wonder
> When you have intention you see the forms
> These two things have the same origin
> Although different in name…

Without going into a detailed analysis of these lines, which would take us beyond the scope of this book,[137] they may be summarized as follows. The odd-numbered lines describe the nameless Tao, the source of heaven and earth, which is the world apprehended as a "spiritual" whole. Such Tao-experience can occur when one has no intentions *(yu)*, in which case there is no awareness of oneself as being other than the Tao. In contrast, the even-numbered lines refer to our usual dualistic way of experiencing the world, perceiving it as a collection of interacting yet discrete objects (one of them being *me*). We experience the world in this way due to "names" (i.e., language) and intentions, mental processes that are not the activities *of* a self but rather that sustain the illusory sense of a self separate from the world.

What is the problem with language and intentions? Naming divides up the world into different things; then we wonder about how they (and we!) fit together. Yet the Tao is not a collection of things, as the *Chuang-tzu* emphasizes:

> The knowledge of the ancients was perfect. How perfect? At first, they did not know that there were things. This is the most perfect knowledge; nothing can be added. Next, they knew that there were things, but did not yet make distinctions between them. Next they made distinctions among them, but they did not yet pass judgements upon them. When judgements were passed, Tao was destroyed.[138]

From the Taoist perspective (and the Buddhist, which also emphasizes impermanence), the alternative to discrete things is events and processes. Everything is in motion, in transformation, and all those movements constitute a great flux in which everything harmonizes.

We cannot appreciate this alternative until we understand the problem with intentions in contemporary society: the infinite regress of a life that treats everything as a means to something else. Today many children in Japan (where I now live and raise my son) take entrance exams for kindergarten, because the right kindergarten will help them get into the right primary school, which will help them get into the right middle school, which will help them get into the right high school, which will help them get into the right university, which will help them get hired by the right corporation. So much for childhood! In his old age the poet W. B. Yeats reflected: "When I think of all the books I have read, wise words heard, anxieties given to parents…of hopes I have had, all life weighed in the balance of my own life seems to me *a preparation for something that never happens.*"[139] As the world becomes more organized and rationalized (in Weber's sense), that perpetual deferral becomes ever more true. The Romantic yearning for a "return to nature" gains much of its attraction from the fact that in modern bureaucratized society less and less is done for its own sake.

This helps us to understand the Taoist alternative to such an intention-ridden infinite regress: spontaneity *(tzu-jan)* or "self-creativity," based on the realization that all things, including us, flourish by themselves. Today we have difficulty appreciating the crucial insight that spontaneity is not opposed to order but is an expression of it, since it arises from the unforced unfolding of that natural order. For us, spontaneity is by definition a lack of order, because our order is a function of reason—that is, something to be logically understood and imposed on things. Instead of attempting to control (ourselves, other people, the world), Taoism emphasizes *letting go.* We learn by accumulating knowledge, but we lose our self-consciousness and realize the Tao by "reducing" ourselves again and again, until we reach *wei-wu-wei*, the "action of non-action." Then, although one does nothing, nothing is left undone.[140]

The action of non-action is the central paradox of Taoism and difficult to understand—until we realize that what is being recommended is not literally "doing nothing" but nondual action without the sense of an agent-self who is apart from the action and has the experience of being the one doing it. The usual interpretations of *wu-wei*, as noninterference and passive yielding, view nonaction as a kind of action, whereas nondual action reverses this and sees nonaction—that which does not change, a stillness that is not lost—in a non-dual action. Again, it is significant that the same paradox is found in other Asian traditions that maintain the nonduality of subject and object, particularly in Mahayana Buddhism. The Taoist denies that I *act,* the Buddhist denies that *I* act, but they amount to the same thing, since each half of that duality (be it *I* or *act*) is dependent on the other. As long as there is the sense of oneself as an agent distinct from one's action, there will be a sense of action due to the relation between them. When one is the action, no residue of self-consciousness remains to observe that action objectively.

So the way to transcend the duality between subject and object is to *be* the act, in which case one realizes that it is not the self that acts but the Tao that manifests through oneself, or, better (because less dualistic), *as* oneself. Then there is wu-wei: a quiet center that does not change while activity constantly and spontaneously occurs, a situation Chuang-tzu calls "tranquillity-in-disturbance." In this way we re-achieve the simplicity of a child who is "free from marks [characteristics]" and "does not take credit" for what she does because she does not have the sense of a self that does them.[141] When we live in this fashion, all things flourish by themselves.

We seem to have drifted away from ethics, but the Taoist approach to morality follows directly from this nondualistic way of living (in) the world. The long passage quoted above from the *Chuang-tzu* begins: "It is because there is right, that there is wrong; it is because there is wrong, that there is right. This being the situation, the sages do not approach things at this level, but reflect the light of nature." The *Tao te Ching* makes the same point: "When all know beauty acting as beauty, then only there is ugliness. When all know good acting as good, then only there is not-good. For being and non-being are mutually produced."[142] This is another mode of nondualism, a critique of thinking that differentiates things into opposite categories: right versus wrong, beauty versus ugliness, being versus nonbeing, life versus death, success versus failure, and so forth. It has often been pointed out that instead of either/or—the Western logic of *tertium non datur,* literally, "a third [possibility] is not given"—Chinese thought emphasizes polarity (e.g., yin/yang). Yet the Taoist critique of dualistic thinking is more than a preference for polarities. Dualistic thinking is delusive because we want to have one term and reject the other, yet that is impossible because each term gains meaning only by being the opposite of the other. Such a dichotomizing way of thinking *about* a situation keeps us from *being* the situation. It is a classic example of the kind of conceptual thinking that needs to be "reduced again and again" (per chapter 48 of the *Tao Te Ching*)—that is, released, let go.

Yet what about the distinction we make between right and wrong, between good and evil? Isn't that dualism necessary for any ethics at all? Aldous Huxley made the case for this view:

> Evil is the accentuation of division; good [is] whatever makes for unity with other lives and other beings. Pride, hatred, anger [are] the essentially evil sentiments; and essentially evil because they are all intensifications of the given reality of separateness, because they insist upon division and uniqueness, because they reject and deny other lives and beings.[143]

For Huxley, evil is that which promotes separation, good is that which promotes unity. But then is it inconsistent to accentuate the division between even those two? Doesn't his distinction between good and evil intensify separateness and division, by rejecting and denying the life of those things we label evil? This becomes more than a logical point when we remember how much evil has been created by our desire to eliminate it. The cultural psychoanalyst Otto Rank believed that our greatest human problems and sufferings are due, ironically, to the human attempt to perfect the world. Medieval inquisitors burned thousands at the stake in order to purge Christendom of heresies spread by Satan; Stalin sacrificed millions to construct his ideal socialist state; Hitler's Final Solution to the Jewish Problem was an attempt to purify the earth. As we saw in chapter 5, these evil deeds were justified as necessary to rid the world of evil.

This helps us to appreciate the full import of the Taoist (and Buddhist) critique of dualistic thinking. *To let go of such discriminations means to let go of dualistic moral codes as well.* This is not an excuse for selfishness, for the point is that such a "reduction," if genuine, also eliminates those self-centered ways of thinking that motivate selfish behavior. Deeper than the imperfectly flexible standards of moral codes is the concern for others that springs up spontaneously within those who have realized the Tao, because such a selfless person no longer feels separate from others. That is why the way to get rid of our body (self), which causes us such trouble, is to realize that the whole world is our body, in which case we can be entrusted with the world. The Taoist critique of Confucianism follows from this:

When the great Tao declines, we have [the teaching of] benevolence and
   righteousness....
When the six family relations are not friendly, we have [the teaching of]
   filial piety and paternal affection.
When the state and its families are confused and out of order, there are
   [the teachings of] loyalty and faithfulness.[144]

For Taoism, Confucian emphasis on benevolence and righteousness is an
attempt to close the barn door of morality after the horse of natural feeling
has run away. As Nietzsche realized, such moral codes are ultimately motivated by fear, which makes us want to control both others and ourselves. As
we have seen, the alternative to that fear is nothing other than love, which, if
it is genuine, no moral code can legislate. Then what is the foundation or
basis of love? The classic example is that of a mother for her child, who was
part of her and even after birth cannot survive without her. Then perhaps
what we understand as love is the affective aspect of a nondual ontological
realization: the experience that I am not-other-than the beloved.

This is consistent with the insight that concludes Spinoza's *Ethics:* blessedness is not the reward of virtue but virtue itself. A life filled with love is blessed,
not because it leads to some other reward, but because a life of love, which
unites us with others, is blessedness itself. Similarly, a life that lacks love is not
punishment for evil but evil itself. From a nondualist perspective, we are punished not *for* our sins but *by* them. To lack love is to feel separate from the
world, and the tragedy is that this lack encourages us to do things that further
aggravate our sense of duality, leading to a life based on fear and the need to
control situations. This vicious circle can lead to a hellish solipsism, and in fact
solipsism is as good a definition of hell as we have.

Such is the Taoist perspective on personal ethics—but does Taoism have
something more to say about human society today, in the twenty-first century? Our technological "global village" is so far removed from the hamlets of
Lao-tzu and Chuang-tzu that we may doubt that they can speak to us. But
they do. The ecological crisis forces us to recognize that the crucial issue of our
time is the causal relation between the fragile biosphere and our limitless
technological drive to dominate the natural world and make it serve our own
purposes. The Taoist critique addresses this drive, for in place of the *intentions*
that keep us preoccupied with "improving" the world, always going somewhere but unable to rest anywhere, Taoism offers the action of nonaction

(wei-wu-wei) and recommends letting things be. When we apply this critique to our global situation today, its relevance becomes obvious. Our contemporary emphasis on endless economic and technological development is a collective example of the future-oriented intentionality that needs to interfere with the world, because it is unable to be one with it; and the natural world that we are destroying in the process is the sphere of wu-wei and letting things be. In place of its spontaneity and self-creativity, we are obsessed with organizing and "improving" it. When we look at the Amazon and other rain forests, we see only vast resources waiting to be exploited. To what end? Where are we trying to get so fast? Our tragedy is that growth has become an end in itself, even as that growth threatens to destroy us.

Schumacher reminds us that "an attitude to life that seeks fulfilment in the single-minded pursuit of wealth—in short, materialism—does not fit into this world, because it contains within itself no limiting principle, while the environment in which it is placed is strictly limited."[145]

If in the future we are to live together peacefully in an overpopulated world, we must come to appreciate the Taoist emphasis on simple pleasures and fewer desires.

The irony is that the more we try to control situations, the more disorder that is created—precisely what Taoism implies. This is not some mystical claim but increasingly obvious in the way our technological solutions to problems (for example, our need for large amounts of electric power) keep creating ecological disasters (Three Mile Island, Chernobyl). For that reason it is difficult to be sanguine about the technological solutions that have been proposed for such disasters. A new approach is needed, and any successful Buddhist social theory will need to embody an appreciation of the Taoist insight into the self-organizing spontaneity of the natural world.

BUDDHISM

> I came to realize clearly that mind is no other than mountains and rivers
> and the great wide earth, the sun and the moon and the stars.
>
> —Dogen

From its beginnings Buddhism, and this book on Buddhist social theory, has emphasized ethics. The eightfold path taught by Shakyamuni in his first sermon is often grouped into the three pillars of *shila* (morality), *samadhi* (meditation), and *prajna* (wisdom or insight). Shila is regarded as providing the moral and karmic foundation necessary both for lay life and for successful meditation and enlightenment. As already noted in the first chapter, five ethical precepts are commonly extracted from the eightfold path: to avoid killing, stealing, false speech, misuse of sensuality, and intoxicants. Notable from an ecological perspective is that the precept against killing protects not only humans but all sentient beings.

A simpler version of the precepts originates from a verse in the *Dhammapada*: "Renounce all evil, practice all good, keep the mind pure: thus all the Buddhas have taught." Mahayana Buddhism expanded this to emphasize the attitude of the bodhisattva, who takes on the responsibility to help all sentient beings attain salvation: "Renounce all evil, practice all good, save the many beings." The first of the four vows still recited daily in all Zen temples embodies the same approach: "Although living beings are numberless, I vow to save them all." The ten basic Mahayana precepts add five more to the Pali precepts: not to discuss the faults of others, not to praise oneself while abusing others, not to withhold the Dharma assets, not to indulge in anger, and not to defame the three treasures (Buddha, Dharma, Sangha). These five add a greater psychological sensitivity to the ways the ego-sense protects and perpetuates itself.

To these ten precepts the path of the bodhisattva adds six paramitas: generosity, morality, patience, exertion, meditation, and wisdom. *Paramita,* usually translated as "transcendental" (e.g., *dana paramita* is "transcendental generosity") or "perfection of..." (perfection of generosity, etc.), literally means "to go beyond" and refers to a character trait developed to the highest possible degree. Generosity *(dana)* is first in the list for good reason: it is the preeminent Buddhist virtue, and some teachers have said that it contains all the other virtues. Buddhism condemns the practice of performing good deeds with expectation of material reward or respect, because transcendental generosity denies the barrier between the one who gives and the one who receives. *Dana paramita* is generosity without any awareness that it is oneself who is giving, that there is an other who receives, or even that there is a gift that is given. A very similar insight is found in the *Tao Te Ching:* "Not being self-boasting, therefore one has merit." "Superior virtue *(te)* is no virtue, therefore it has virtue. Inferior virtue does not lose its virtue, therefore it has no virtue."[146] As long as I am aware of my generosity, that generosity is not complete. Something extra remains or "sticks," which therefore does not reduce the sense of self but aggravates it.

The eighth-century Buddhist poet and philosopher Shantideva reminds us of the nondualist perspective that grounds this approach to ethics: "Those who wish to bring themselves and others swiftly to salvation should perform the supreme act of converting others into oneself."[147] As this suggests, Buddhist morality cannot be comprehended apart from such a realization, which liberates us from the dukkha inherent to a sense-of-self. In order to understand Buddhist ethics, therefore, we must consider its foundation in the Buddhist understanding of the self—or, more precisely, the Buddhist deconstruction of the self.

Like Taoism, Buddhism is sensitive to how language reifies things and causes us to perceive the world as a collection of self-existing *(svabhava)* objects "in" objectified space and time. The central insight of Buddhism is a critique of this tendency: not only a denial of ego-self but a critique of all self-existing "thingness." This is the point of *pratitya-samutpada* (dependent origination), the most important Buddhist doctrine. (The Buddha emphasized that anyone who really understands pratitya-samutpada understands his teaching, and vice versa.)

In response to the problem of how rebirth can occur without a permanent soul or self that is reborn, this teaching explains rebirth as a series of impersonal processes that occur without any self that is doing or experiencing them. Our dukkha occurs without there being any self that causes or experiences the dukkha. The karmic results of action are experienced without their being any self that created the karma or any self that receives its fruit, although there is a causal connection between the action and its result.

Pratitya-samutpada was taught by the Buddha, yet some of its implications were not emphasized until the development of Mahayana. This was part of a philosophical self-deconstruction of the Buddhist teachings so influential that it has continued to reverberate through all subsequent Buddhist thought. The most important statement of this Madhyamika approach is in the *Mulama-dhyamikakarika* of the great Indian Buddhist philosopher Nagarjuna, who is believed to have lived in the second century C.E.

The first verse of the *Mulamadhyamikakarika* proclaims its thoroughgoing critique of self-existence: "No things whatsoever exist, at any time or place, having risen by themselves, from another, from both or without cause." Nagarjuna's argument brings out more fully the implications of pratitya-samutpada, showing that dependent origination should rather be understood as "nondependent nonorigination." Pratitya-samutpada does not teach a causal relation between entities, because the fact that these twelve factors are mutually dependent means that they are not really discrete entities; none could occur without the conditioning of all the other factors. That none is self-existing is the meaning of the most important term *shunya* ("empty") and *shunyata* ("emptiness"). All things are "empty" because none has any essence or being of its own, everything being dependent on everything else.

That type of logic and epistemological analysis was less appealing to Chinese Buddhists, who preferred a more metaphorical way to express the inter-conditionality of all phenomena: the analogy of Indra's net described in the Avatamsaka Sutra and developed in the Huayen school of Mahayana. In the abode of the great god Indra, there is a wonderful net that stretches infinitely in all directions. At each "eye" of the net there is a jewel that reflects all the other jewels in the net, and if one looks even more closely, one can see that every one of those infinite reflections in each "eye" is itself reflecting all the other jewels. In this cosmos each phenomenon is at the same time the effect of the whole and the cause of the whole, the totality being a vast, infinite body of members, each sustaining and defining all the others. One of the most important consequences of this interpermeation (also important for Taoism and, as we shall see, for deep ecology) is that such a world is non-teleological. In such a universe human beings cannot be considered the crown of creation, because there is no hierarchy and no center—unless it is everywhere.[148]

But what do such concepts and metaphors mean for the way we live our lives? How does one actually realize and embody such interpenetration? D. T. Suzuki described Huayen as the philosophy of Zen and Zen as the practice of Huayen. Again we return to the famous passage from Dogen's *Shobogenzo*, in which he sums up the Zen path as follows:

> To study the buddha way is to study the self. To study the self is to forget the self. To forget the self is to be actualized by myriad things. When actu-alized by myriad things, your body and mind as well as the bodies and minds of others drop away. No trace of realization remains, and this no-trace continues endlessly.[149]

"Forgetting" ourselves is how we—jewels in Indra's net—lose our sense of separation and realize that we are the net. Meditation is learning how to forget the sense of self, which happens when I become absorbed into my meditation practice. Insofar as the sense of self is a result of consciousness reflecting back upon itself in order to grasp itself, such meditation practice makes sense as an exercise in de-reflection. Enlightenment occurs in Buddhism when the usually automatized reflexivity of consciousness ceases, experienced as a letting go. When consciousness stops trying to catch its own tail, I become no-thing, and discover that I am the world—or, more precisely, that instead of being a subjective consciousness confronting the world as an object, I am a manifestation of it, interpenetrating it and interpenetrated by it. When I no longer strive to make myself real through things, I find myself "actualized" by them, as Dogen puts it.

Notice, however, what this does not mean. Such a realization involves neither a monistic dissolution of the self into Indra's net nor a transcendence of the net. The interpenetration of *all* the jewels in the net implies that there is no such Archimedean master perspective. One is nondual with the net only by virtue of one's position within it. We can appreciate different perspectives, yet there is no perspectiveless perspective. We are actualized by the myriad things, not something that transcends them. What unifies the whole net is the web of interpenetrating traces that constitutes each of the myriad jewels. As the Zen master Yasutani Hakuun has expressed it, with enlightenment "each thing just as it is takes on an entirely new significance or worth. Miraculously, everything is radically transformed though remaining just as it is." In an earlier passage from the same *Shobogenzo* fascicle, Dogen emphasizes that this experience is not an expansion of ego-self but its disappearance. "To carry yourself forward and experience myriad things is delusion. That myriad things come forth and experience themselves is awakening."[150] Instead of incorporating the world into myself, self-forgetting allows the things of the world to "incorporate" me, in the sense that there is no self-existent "me" apart from the world's web of interpenetrating traces.

Again, we seem to have drifted far from ethics, yet, again, the Buddhist approach to morality follows directly from this type of nondualistic identity with Indra's net. When I discover that I am you—that I am the trace of your traces—the ethical problem of how to relate to you is transformed. Loss of self-preoccupation entails the ability to respond to others without an ulterior motive that needs to gain something, material or symbolic, from that encounter. Of course, the danger of abuse remains, if my nondual experience is not deep enough to root out those dualistic tendencies that incline me to manipulate others. As long as there is sense of self, therefore, there will be a need to inculcate morality, just as infants need training wheels on their bicycles. In Buddhism, however, ethical principles approximate the way of relating to others that nondual experience reveals; as in Christianity, I should love my neighbor as myself—in this case because the neighbor *is* myself. This makes ethical response-ability for Buddhism not the means to salvation but natural to the expression of genuine enlightenment. It is what might be called the "nonmoral morality" of the bodhisattva, who, having nothing to gain or lose—because he or she has no self to do the gaining or losing—is devoted to the welfare of others. The bodhisattva knows that no one is fully saved until everyone is saved. When I am the universe, to help others is to help myself. To become enlightened is to forget one's own dukkha, only to wake up in—or rather *at one with*—a world of dukkha. The career of the bodhisattva *is* helping others, not because one ought to, for traditionally the bodhisattva is not bound by dogma or morality, but because one *is* the situation and through oneself that situation draws forth a response to meet its needs.

What are the ecological implications of this approach? The first precept enjoins us not to kill any sentient being; the bodhisattva vow commits us to help all beings become happy and realize their Buddha-nature. As in Taoism, this engagement denies the importance of the distinction we usually make between ourselves and other living beings. Such an attitude, which developed in early Buddhism, characterizes the popular Jataka "birth stories" that describe the lives of Shakyamuni before he became the Buddha. Many Jataka passages celebrate the beauties of forests, rivers and lakes, and, most of all, the wild creatures who are usually the protagonists of the stories. In many of the best-known tales the future Buddha sacrifices himself for "lower animals," for example, offering his body to help a weak tigress feed her hungry cubs. In this fashion the Jatakas view the world nondualistically as an infinite field of spiritual effort in which no life-form, no matter how insignificant it may seem to us, is outside the path. All beings are potential Buddhas and bodhisattvas. Each is able to feel compassion and act selflessly to ease the pain of all beings. The Jatakas also remind us that everything is food for something else, part of an all-encompassing food chain that does not end with humans.[151]

Nor is this compassion limited to animals. The Buddha is believed to have been born under trees and died under trees: to have experienced his great enlightenment under a bodhi tree, and to have spent the next week under that tree. Many passages in the Pali scriptures contain expressions of the Buddha's gratitude for trees and other plants. In one sutra, the spirit dwelling in a tree appears to the Buddha in a dream and complains that its tree had been chopped down by a monk. The next morning the Buddha gathered the monks together and prohibited them from cutting down trees, for trees too have sensate existence. Bhikkhus and bhikkhunis are also prohibited from cutting off tree limbs, picking flowers, or plucking green (still living) leaves.

In sum, the Buddhist denial of a duality between oneself and one's world helps us to understand Buddhism's emphasis on saving all sentient beings, as well as its respect for all living things. Our economic system today, preoccupied as it is with ever-increasing production and consumption, is much more exploitive of the earth than the low-tech societies that Shakyamuni was familiar with. The various environmental crises that threaten us, many of which continue to worsen, thus call for a stronger Buddhist response than found in traditional Asian Buddhism. Addressing this challenge must be one of the top priorities for any Buddhist social theory. Here contemporary Buddhism can benefit from the insights of deep ecology about the duality between *Homo sapiens* and the rest of the biosphere.

Deep Ecology

The same dualism that reduces things to objects for consciousness is at work in the humanism that reduces nature to raw material for mankind.
—Michael Zimmerman

Deep ecology developed out of a critique of reform environmentalism, which attempts to mitigate some of the worst cases of pollution, wildlife destruction, and short-sighted development schemes. The shortcomings of this approach, working within the framework of conventional political processes, soon became evident. Such environmentalism tends to become technical and oriented to short-term public policy issues like resource allocation, without questioning more basic assumptions about the value of economic growth and development.

One of the earliest and best-known examples of a transformation to a deeper ecological approach was the naturalist Aldo Leopold, who in the 1920s and 1930s underwent a dramatic conversion from a resource "stewardship" mentality to what he termed an "ecological conscience." He presented his new understanding in his 1949 book *Sand County Almanac,* which argued for "biocentric equality" because "we are only fellow-voyagers with other creatures in the odyssey of evolution." To adopt an ecological conscience "changes the role of *Homo sapiens* from conqueror of the land-community to plain member and citizen of it." Leopold claimed that "the biotic mechanism is so complex that its working may never be fully understood"; the essential mysteriousness of life processes undercuts the possibility of its successful domination and control by humans. He went on to formulate an egalitarian "land ethic": "A thing is right when it tends to preserve the integrity, stability, and beauty of the biotic community. It is wrong when it tends otherwise."[152]

Leopold's subversive ideas were not appreciated for a generation, because they were too radical. Like Taoism and Buddhism, they challenge some of our most deeply rooted assumptions about the natural world, human beings, and the relationship between them. These assumptions may be summarized in four basic propositions:

1. People are fundamentally different from all other creatures on Earth, over which they have dominion (defined as domination).
2. People are masters of their own destiny; they can choose their goals and learn to do whatever is necessary to achieve them.
3. The world is vast, and thus provides unlimited opportunities for humans.
4. The history of humanity is one of progress; for every problem there is a solution, and thus progress need never cease.[153]

According to this anthropocentric worldview (which can no longer be considered merely Western, since it has spread around the globe), human beings dominate nature because we are superior to other life-forms; the earth is primarily a collection of natural resources waiting to be exploited, and technology can provide substitutes for those resources that are not infinite. Other beliefs tend to be associated with the above assumptions: for example, that the goal of life is comfort and convenience, and that technology and scientific progress can meet all our needs. Historically, this set of values has not been concerned about the quality of the environment—or, better, of the ecosphere. The emphasis has been on individualism, with little awareness of the value of the human community, much less the biotic "land community" that Leopold described. The overriding impulse has been to harness science and technology in the exploitation of nature—energy, minerals, forests—to serve the growing economy.[154]

With its present-day global reach this worldview is more dominant than ever—yet it does not go unchallenged. Two important perspectives outside the Western tradition have already been discussed. There have also been strong minority strands within the West: literary traditions such as romanticism and pastoralism; alternative Christian views of nature like that of St. Francis of Assisi; the lifestyles of indigenous peoples such as Native Americans; and less dualistic scientific models such as quantum mechanics and, of course, ecological biology itself. Within Western philosophy, two figures have been particularly important for those who want to challenge anthropocentrism (although both are controversial): Baruch Spinoza (1632–77) and Martin Heidegger (1889–1976). Like Taoism and Buddhism, the philosophies of Spinoza and Heidegger deny the self-existence of anything, including us.

For Spinoza, all beings are equal as manifestations of the one Substance, which for him has two modes, God and Nature. Although some passages in Spinoza's ethics state that we can treat other species as we like, the Norwegian philosopher Arne Naess has pointed out that this is inconsistent with the main implications of his metaphysics. For Spinoza, "all particular things are expressions of God; through all of them God acts. There is no hierarchy. There is no purpose, no final causes such that one can say that the 'lower' exist for the sake of the 'higher.' There is an ontological democracy or equalitarianism which, incidentally, greatly offended his contemporaries, but of which ecology makes us more tolerant today."[155]

More recently, Martin Heidegger has made an influential critique of the Western philosophical tradition since Plato. In Heidegger's view, the West's humanistic approach is responsible for the present technocratic mentality that espouses domination over nature. The essence of technology is found in the tendency to perceive all beings as objective, quantifiable, and disposable raw material that is valued only insofar as it enhances our power. This understanding is both the culmination of Western civilization and the triumph of nihilism. In response, Heidegger offers a "new way of thinking" in which we dwell in the world with other beings, not as their master but by letting beings be, so they can display themselves in all their glory.[156]

There are obvious similarities between Spinoza and Huayen Buddhism, and between Heidegger and Taoism, but before addressing them it will be helpful to generalize the argument by looking at what Warwick Fox considers the "central intuition" of deep ecology. "It is the idea that we can make no firm ontological divide in the field of existence: That there is no bifurcation in reality between the human and the non-human realms."[157] As an ontological claim, this denial of a bifurcation between the human and nonhuman realms is based on more than intuition. It follows from the essential ecological insight into the interrelatedness of everything. As John Muir said, when we try to pick out anything by itself, we find it hitched to everything else in the universe. Yet there is still something lacking in that way of expressing it.

"To the Western mind," observes Neil Evernden, "interrelatedness implies a causal connectedness. Things are interrelated if a change in one affects the other.... But what is actually involved is a genuine intermingling of parts of the ecosystem. There are no discrete entities."[158]

Nagarjuna could not have put it better, for this is precisely his point: the doctrine of interdependent origination leads us to the same conclusion. This means that Buddhism and ecology follow the same development. We usually begin with an understanding of the world as a collection of discrete beings, the most important being us (Buddhism begins with the individual ego-self; ecology, the collective "*wego*-self"—that is, *Homo sapiens*). Buddhist teachings and ecological science lead to the realization that beings are not discrete. All our experience and all life-forms are interrelated; to isolate anything is to destroy it. Each living being is a dissipative structure—that is, it persists only due to a continual flow of energy into the system. Yet even this insight is incomplete, because if everything is interrelated, then there are no discrete things to be related together. Again, we end up with Indra's infinite and inter-penetrating net, where each particular jewel is nothing other than a reflection of all the others, and where each particular "thing" is what the whole universe is doing at this place and time.

What is perhaps most distinctive about deep ecology is the axiological corollary it derives from the above. This has been expressed most famously in the first (and most important) of the eight principles of the Deep Ecology Platform, initially formulated by Naess and George Sessions in 1984: "The well-being and flourishing of human and nonhuman Life on Earth have values in themselves. These values are independent of the usefulness of the nonhuman world for human purposes." Naess has developed this basic perspective into two "ultimate norms," or ethical principles that cannot be proven yet may be intuited. The first is *Self-realization*, which goes beyond the self defined as an isolated ego striving for sense gratification or for its own individual salvation. According to Naess we must stop seeing ourselves as competing egos and learn to identify not only with other humans but with other species and even inanimate objects in the nonhuman world. The second ultimate norm is *biocentric equality:* all things in the biosphere have an equal right to live and blossom and to reach their own individual forms of unfolding and self-realization within the larger Self-realization. This basic intuition is that all organisms and entities in the ecosphere, as parts of the interrelated whole, are equal in intrinsic worth.[159]

Before examining these norms, a clarification is necessary. Naess has always been careful to distinguish the Deep Ecology Platform from his own ecological philosophy, because he believes the deep ecology platform can be logically derived from various, even incompatible religious and philosophical premises. It would be a mistake, therefore, to identify Naess's two norms as canonical for deep ecology, although some deep ecologists overlook the distinction between the platform and his own views. This distinction is particularly important for Self-realization and identification, since some writers have elaborated these concepts in ways that critics have shown to be problematic.

The biggest controversy has been over Naess's emphasis on identification with the nonhuman world. What does it mean? How can one identify with other species? Perhaps the best explanation is found in Naess's essay "Identification As a Source of Deep Ecological Attitudes":

> There is a process of ever-widening identification and ever-narrowing alienation which widens the self. The self is as comprehensive as the totality of our identifications.... Identification is a spontaneous, non-rational, but not irrational, process through which the interests of another being are reacted to as our own interest or interests.[160]

Since this is still vague, it is not surprising that critics, especially ecofeminists, have identified problems. In an extended critique, Val Plumwood distinguishes three different accounts of the self in her reading of Self-realization through identification: indistinguishability, which denies boundaries in the field of existence; the expansion of the self, which is an enlargement and extension of the ego-self; and transcendence of the self, which universalizes in a way that devalues personal relationships in favor of an abstractly conceived whole. All of these, she argues, involve an uncritical acceptance of rationalist and masculinist assumptions.[161]

Whether or not these criticisms apply to other deep ecologists, Naess's own writings reveal a sensitivity to precisely these problems. In his very first essay on deep ecology, written in 1973, he was careful to characterize it in relational terms: "Rejection of the human-in-environment image in favor of the relational, total-field image. Organisms as knots in the biospherical net or field of intrinsic rela-tions." In his most important book, *Ecology, Community and Lifestyle,* he points out that to see ourselves as intimately connected with nature is "a difficult ridge to walk: To the left we have the ocean of organic and mystic views, to the right the abyss of atomic individualism." At any level of realization of potentials, indi-vidual egos "do not dissolve like individual drops in the ocean" although "the individual is not, and will not be isolatable."[162] In an unpublished essay on "Gestalt Thinking and Buddhism," Naess prefers the Buddhist *anatmavada* (no-self doctrine) to Hindu *atman*-absolutism because he lays more stress on process than on a Vedantic union with a transcendent Absolute.

In an interview Naess has described the starting-point of his anti-Cartesian attitude as the desire "to overcome the entire subject-object cleavage as an axiom of modern philosophy…. It is as if I want to disappear [as an appar-ent subject]." What is the way to do this? "To enmesh yourself in what you are doing, what you experience, in such a way that the relation to your ego dis-appears, and the Self is expanded into the World."[163] The similarity between this and Zen practice is as striking as the similarity between Naess's use of gestalt internal relations and what Mahayana says about interpenetration. For Naess as with Indra's net, the way for the self to realize its nonduality with the world is for the ego-self to forget itself and "disappear." Then, instead of the world appearing as a collection of discrete objects confronting me, it is real-ized to be a vast web of traces and traces of traces that also constitute me. This answers Plumwood's feminist critique. Such a self is not indistinguish-able from the world in the way that each spoonful of porridge is indistin-guishable from the next, nor is it the result of the ego-self expanding to incorporate the world. Instead of transcending personal relationships, such a loss of self-preoccupation can only deepen them, as part of one's involvement in the world generally.

To understand such a world, the static notion of entity must be replaced with something more dynamic. When we let go of our usual way of looking at reality as a collection of self-existing entities, we end up with Buddhist insights about natural processes and events, for Buddhism too emphasizes the impermanence of things. To realize this is to see that a flower is not an entity, it is the beautiful sexual gesture of a plant. Then Naess's second ulti-mate norm, "All organisms and entities in the ecosphere are equal in intrin-sic worth," may be better expressed as "Every event is equal in intrinsic value to every other event."

This seems innocuous enough, yet it has extraordinary "moral" implications. Earlier we saw that the Huayen concept of Indra's net is non-teleological and non-hierarchical. Human beings cannot be the crown of creation, because there is none, unless it is everywhere. We have also noticed that Naess, in arguing for deep ecology, has derived the same insight from Spinoza's metaphysics: "There is no hierarchy. There is no purpose, no final causes such that one can say that the 'lower' exist for the sake of the 'higher.' There is an ontological democracy or equalitarianism." Now that entity-language has been translated into event-language, how shall we understand this? There is a famous Zen story about a sermon by Shakyamuni Buddha, when he said nothing but just twirled a flower in his hand. No one understood this except Mahakashyapa, yet what did he understand? Just "this!"—*tathata*, thusness. The entire universe exists just for the sake of this particular "flower" to bloom—and for the sake of "me" to appreciate it. Or, as deep ecologists might prefer to put it, the whole biosphere exists only for this oak tree to grow, for this river to flow, for this whale to spout.

Deep ecologists have elaborated on the meaning of intrinsic worth or inherent value. "The presence of inherent value in a natural object is independent of any awareness, interest, or appreciation of it by a conscious being."[164] This is diametrically opposed to our usual understanding of nature, yet it is deeply congruent with Taoism and Heidegger, both of which emphasize "letting things be" in order for them to flourish: not for our sake, and not even for their own sake, but for no sake at all—because questions of utility and justification no longer apply. For Heidegger, "dwelling is not primarily inhabiting but taking care of and creating that space within which something comes into its own and flourishes."[165] The teleological question "What for?" arises out of the anthropocentric attitude that perceives all beings as quantifiable and disposable raw material, and which values beings only insofar as they are good for something—in effect, good for our own purposes.

"Letting things be" challenges that basic principle of our technological and consumerist society, but it also subverts our notion of ego-self. This brings us back to the first ultimate norm that Naess derives from the nonduality between the human and nonhuman realms: Self-realization, which includes learning to identify with the whole of the biosphere. To admit that natural objects (or natural events) have an inherent value independent of any awareness or appreciation by other beings is to question our commonsense dualism between the conscious self and the objective world. If I am "in here" (inside my skin, as it were) and the world is "out there," my alienation makes value subjective: it can only be a function of my desires and my projects. Then to deny such an anthropocentric understanding of value, which deep ecology does, also leads us to question the dualism between subject and object. We have already noticed how Taoism and Buddhism deny that dualism. For Taoism all the ten thousand things, including us, are mere "straw-dogs" in themselves, because they have no reality apart from being manifestations of the Tao. Likewise, Dogen realized that his mind is "nothing other than mountains and rivers and the great wide earth, the sun and the moon and the stars." Then perhaps it is inevitable, although nonetheless a shock, that deep ecologists such as John Seed have arrived at the same conclusion:

> When humans investigate and see through their layers of anthropocentric self-cherishing, a most profound change in consciousness begins to take place.
>
> Alienation subsides. The human is no longer an outsider, apart. Your humanness is then recognized as being merely the most recent stage of your existence...you start to get in touch with yourself as mammal, as vertebrate, as a species only recently emerged from the rain forest. As the fog of amnesia disperses, there is a transformation in your relationship to other species, and in your commitment to them....
>
> "I am protecting the rain forest" develops to "I am part of the rain forest protecting myself. I am that part of the rain forest recently emerged into thinking."[166]

We are back within Indra's net: "I am that part of Indra's net recently emerged into thinking." What began as a scientific claim, about the ecological interrelatedness of species, has developed here into a spiritual claim: not just any religious claim, but the fundamental claim, or the fundamental realization, of Taoism and Buddhism.

Yet it is not wolves or whales or trees but humans who make such a claim and endeavor to realize it. This raises a question about Warwick Fox's central intuition that there is no real bifurcation between the human and nonhuman realms, for there does seem to be an important difference. We humans are the only dissipative structures that can realize that they are not separate from Indra's net; moreover, we understand that we are not parts of the net but the whole of the net, come to consciousness at this particular place and time. Or is it that we are the sole species that needs to pursue self-realization, because we are the sole species whose self-consciousness alienates it in the first place? The etymology usually given for the English word *religion* traces it back to the Latin *re* + *ligio*, "to bind back together." *Homo sapiens* seems to be the only animal that needs religion, because it is the only one deluded by an ego-self that needs to be reunified with the world.

So we can understand why Fritjof Capra thinks that the Western version of Taoism and Buddhism will be ecological awareness.[167] Deep ecology has also come to realize the importance of resolving the basically religious issue of the alienation between ourselves and the world we find ourselves "in." The individual ego-self and the species *we*go-self turn out to be different versions of the same problem, which can be resolved only by realizing that the duality between ourselves and the natural world is delusive. The increasingly frequent environmental catastrophes make it evident that such a transformation is necessary if we—not only humans, but the rich diversity that constitutes the biosphere—are to survive and thrive through the new millennium.

Afterword

A Nondual Social Theory

> One should conquer anger with kindness, evil with goodness, selfishness with generosity, and falsehood with truthfulness.
>
> —*The Dhammapada*

How WELL do the various chapters in this book form a whole, to justify the presumption of its subtitle, that they constitute a Buddhist social theory?

These essays address a wide range of social issues, but when we penetrate to the roots of the problems they analyze, in each case we end up uncovering greed, ill will, and delusion—the "three poisons" or three roots of evil according to Buddhism. A Buddhist approach to social dukkha can appreciate many salient critiques of oppression: privileged elites oppressing workers, men oppressing women, and humans oppressing the rest of the biosphere. Each of them provides an important piece of the larger puzzle. From a Buddhist perspective, hoever, those dukkha-promoting hierarchies are prominent examples of something more basic. The three poisons themselves reflect the fundamental insight and contribution of Buddhism, which is the link between our dukkha and our delusive sense of self. Understanding this link gives us purchase on the relationship today between institutionalized dukkha and our collective wego-selves.

Buddhism emphasizes the third root of evil—delusion—and especially the anthithetical dualisms with which we "bind ourselves without a rope." Buddhist compassion arises naturally from wisdom, and the root of wisdom is the realization that one's sense of self is the fundamental delusion. Today this delusion can be conceptualized in a psychotherapeutic vocabulary:

because we repress the uncomfortable awareness of our ungroundedness, we experience our emptiness as a sense of lack.

Does this repression also infect our institutionalized wegos? The ungroundedness of corporations manifests as continual pressure for profit and growth. The intrinsic insecurity of nation-states manifests as their propensity toward external aggression and internal repression, against real or imagined foes. Most generally, *Homo sapiens'* collective experience of "lack" manifests as the need to secure ourselves by achieving total control over our home and mother, the biosphere.[168]

There are many types of duality but two kinds have recurred most often in this book: bipolar categories dividing the world into conceptual opposites that are nevertheless interdependent, and the subject-object dualism that discriminates an individual or collective self from the world outside it.

This book has examined several of the the most pernicious bipolar categorizations. Chapters 2 and 3 addressed the trap of a wealth/poverty dualism that has several facets: the craving for wealth as haunted by fear of poverty, global poverty as necessary to monetize and commodify the "undeveloped" world, and poverty as a necessary benchmark for the wealthy to appreciate their own achievements; chapter 5 focused on the duality between good and evil, particularly the unfortunate paradox that "good" human attempts to eradicate evil continue to be one of the main causes of evil; chapter 6 noted a similar dualism between innocence and guilt that rationalizes our retributive justice systems; and chapter 8 traces our difficulty in evaluating new technologies back to the deeply rooted Western duality between nature and culture.

Bipolar thinking is also related to our most troublesome delusion, the duality between self and other, which becomes even more probematic when this delusion is collective and institutionalized. In chapter 2 we examined this institutional delusion as the duality between developed societies and undeveloped ones, whereby the former labor to transform the latter—"for their own good," of course. In chapters 3 and 9 I argued that human interdependence with the rest of the biosphere is incompatible with an economic system that objectifies and commodifies the earth. And the final part of chapter 5 proposed two "modes of being" distinguishing between fear, which aggravates our sense of separation from each other, and love, which brings us together. In chapter 6 our deluded self/other duality appears as our vindictive attitude toward offenders, who must be punished because unlike us, "they" are *guilty.* Chapter 7 looked at how Japanese Buddhism, and particularly samurai Zen, became co-opted by secular authority and thereby contributed to nationalism and colonialism, particularly pernicious forms of collective ego that are certainly not unique to Japan. Chapter 8 reflected on the parallel between individual subject-object duality and our collective sense of alienation from a natural ground (or grounding nature) that we technologically manipulate, hence reinforcing our sense of alienation from it. And chapter 9 examined Michael Zimmerman's claim that "The same dualism that reduces things to objects for consciousness is at work in the humanism that reduces nature to raw material for mankind."

In every case, the Buddhist solution to such probematic dualities involves realizing that this way of thinking/perceiving/acting is a construct that can be deconstructed. None of them is natural in the sense of inevitable although they often have a collective weight that grants them a life of their own and makes them difficult to identify and escape.

Examining the collective emphasis on delusive dualities helps us to understand why, in contrast to most theories of social change and attempts at social revolution, a Buddhist approach strongly emphasizes the need for personal transformation as part of collective transformation. If these dualities are the heart of our social dukkha, it becomes more obvious why we must work on both levels. Society constructs people; people construct society. We are socialized by and into these dualistic ways of thinking; and our individual ways of thinking reinforce each other to objectify and maintain institutionalized greed, ill will, and delusion.

This perspective challenges social critiques that reduce the spiritual to a deluded projection of the secular, but such a Buddhist alternative does not mean we are called upon to prepare for an apocalyptic solution, or to expect the irruption of something transcendent into this world. Rather, the type of spirituality these essays envision involves a transformed way of experiencing and living in this world, because the basic delusion of duality has been exposed. The Buddhist insight is that we can transform ourselves. It remains to be seen how well we can collectively apply this realization in transforming our dualistic and therefore dukkha-promoting institutions.

Those of us who live in the West are restrained not so much by oppressive police regimes as by various fixations of our collective consciousness: preoccupation with making money and other types of competitive success; compulsive shopping lifestyles conditioned by pervasive advertising; addictions to technological gadgets such as television, cell phones, and the Internet; as well as more traditional ideologies such as nationalism and religious fundamentalism. Exposing and undermining such mind-fixations is what is most needed, and also what Buddhism is best able to contribute to contemporary Western culture.

Today, thanks to their increasing technological powers, institutionalized forms of greed, ill will, and delusion are aggravating the world's dukkha. In response, we are all called upon to become bodhisattvas, to contribute what we can according to our situation. Our sick ecosystems and social systems do not afford us the luxury of devoting ourselves only to our own enlightenment—yet we will not be successful as bodhisattvas unless we also pursue our own awakening. Ultimately, those liberations cannot be distinguished. To wake up is to realize that I am not in the world, I am what the world is doing right here and now. When Shakyamuni became enlightened, the whole world awakened *in* him and *as* him. The world begins to heal when we realize that its sufferings are our own.

Notes

1 Loy, *Lack and Transcendence,* "Religion of the Market."

2 Herbert, *Culture and Anomie,* 156–57.

3 Quoted in ibid., 174.

4 Wagner, *Invention of Culture,* 9.

5 Becker, *Birth and Death of Meaning,* 139–40.

6 Liechty, "Principalities and Powers."

7 Ibid.

8 Anderson, *Truth about the Truth,* 16.

9 Jones, *Social Face of Buddhism,* 44.

10 See, for example, the Jambukhadakasamyutta Sutta, Samyutta Nikaya IV.38, in Bhikku Bodhi, *Connected Discourses,* 259.

11 Liechty, "Principalities and Powers."

12 Becker, *Escape from Evil,* 80–81.

13 Scott, "Criticism and Culture," 374–75.

14 Geuss, *Idea of a Critical Theory,* 56.

15 Nagarjuna, *Mulamadhyamikakarika,* 25:24.

16 Ibid., 13:8.

17 Wong, *Sutra Spoken by the Sixth Patriarch,* 95.

18 Nagarjuna, *Mulamadhyamikakarika,* 24:8–10.

19 Macy, "Greening of the Self," 180.

20 Thurman, "Edicts of Asoka," 69.

21 Batchelor, *Buddhism without Beliefs,* 113–15.

22 *Dhammapada,* v. 5.

23 Digha Nikaya 26, in Walshe, *Long Discourses,* 399–400.

24 Quoted in Chambers, *Whose Reality Counts?* 179.

25 Ibid., 179, 178.

26 "The move from hunter-gathering to farming harmed health and life-expectancy. Even today, the hunter-gatherers of the Arctic and the Kalahari have better diets than poor people in rich countries—and much better than those of many people in so-called developing countries. More of the world's population is chronically undernourished today than in the Old Stone Age." (John Gray, *Straw Dogs*, 157).

27 George and Sabelli, *Faith and Credit*, 141.

28 Simmel, "The Poor."

29 Gronemeyer, "Helping," 97.

30 Quoted in Caufield, *Masters of Illusion*, 159.

31 George and Sabelli, *Faith and Credit*, 147.

32 Polanyi, *Great Transformation*, 46.

33 Ibid., 57.

34 United Nations Human Development Report 1998.

35 Sizemore and Swearer, *Ethics, Wealth and Salvation*, 2.

36 Kosalasamyutta 167–68, in Bodhi, *Connected Discourses*, 169.

37 *Dhammapada*, v. 355.

38 Payutto, *Buddhist Economics*, 27.

39 Dalai Lama, "Dialogue on Religion and Peace," 81, 86.

40 Durning, *How Much Is Enough?* 38.

41 Dalai Lama, "Dialogue on Religion and Peace," 58–59.

42 Ibid., 127.

43 Ibid., 30–31, 173.

44 Polanyi, *Great Transformation*.

45 Dalai Lama, "Dialogue on Religion and Peace," 36.

46 Nhat Hanh, *Heart of Understanding*, 3–5.

47 *Multinational Monitor*, vol. 17, 1996: 12.

48 Mander, "Corporations As Machines," 295.

49 Charles Derber, *Corporation Nation*, p. 17.

50 Hamburg, "Inside the Money Chase," 25.

51 Information about the Bhopal disaster is from "The Bhopal Legacy: An Interview with Dr. Rosalie Bertell."

52 Grossman, "Corporations' Accountability and Responsibility."

53 Daly and Cobb, *For the Common Good*, 178.

54 Gandhi, *Autobiography*, p. 370.

55 Fish, *The Trouble with Principle*, 41.

56 Personal communication.

57 *Dhammapada*, vv. 3–5, translation altered. The Pali terms usually translated as "hatred" and "love" are *vera* and *avera*. "Absence of enmity" and "friendliness" are perhaps better equivalents for *avera*.

58 Dalai Lama, "Dialogue on Religion and Peace," 190.

59 *Time*, October 15, 2001, p. 17.

60 Sutta Nipata, vv. 1032–36.

61 This quotation was included in an email and I have not been able to trace its source.

62 Zehr, *Changing Lenses*, 36–44.

63 Wright, *Justice for Victims and Offenders*, 159.

64 Pepinsky, "Peacemaking," 305.

65 Angulimala Sutta, Majjhima Nikaya 86, in Nanamoli and Bodhi, *Middle Length Discourses*, 710–17; Cakkavatti-Sihanada Sutta (The Lion's Roar on the Turning of the Wheel), Digha Nikaya 26, in Walshe, *Long Discourses*, 395–405.

66 Cakkavatti-Sihanada Sutta, 399–400.

67 Kutadanta Sutta, Digha Nikaya 5, in Walshe, *Long Discourses*, 135.

68 Wright, *Justice for Victims and Offenders*, 7.

69 Zehr, *Changing Lenses*, 77; see also Pepinsky, "Peacemaking," 301.

70 Ratnapala, *Crime*, 73.

71 Ibid., 42.

72 Ibid., 12–13.

73 Zehr, *Changing Lenses*, 67, 66.

74 Ibid., 70.

75 Ibid., 69.

76 Ratnapala, *Crime*, 5, 93, 192. The Vinaya section of this book is much indebted to Ratnapala's book.

77 Anguttara Nikaya III.59; see also *Dhammapada*, v. 192.

78 Ratnapala, *Crime*, 76.

79 Ibid., 161ff.

80 Vinaya Pitaka V.45; see Ratnapala, *Crime*, 194–96.

81 Ratnapala, *Crime*, 77.

82 Van Ness and Strong, *Restoring Justice*, 118.

83 French, *Golden Yoke*, 74. In this section of the chapter I am much indebted to French's work.

84 Ibid., 138.

85 Quoted in ibid., 80.

86 Ibid., 77.

87 Ibid., 77, 142. Peter Cordella writes, "Within the context of liberalism, we are controlled by atomism and contract. Our unity with others is based almost exclusively on the belief that such an association will advance our self-interest. In our rational assessment of situations, we are therefore unlikely to enter into a relationship with an individual who is unable, at least theoretically, to advance our own interests. Such an unwillingness on our part excludes those with little power and few assets from engaging in contractual relations, thus creating the social problems (e.g., crime, poverty, unemployment, etc.) that have plagued the liberal democracies. In our unwillingness to involve ourselves personally with such individuals, we have surrendered community control of these problems to the state" (Cordella, "Reconciliation," 37).

88 French, *Golden Yoke*, 137.

89 Ibid., 319–325, 16.

90 Ibid., 346, 100.

91 Auerbach, *Justice without Law?* 121.

92 Wright, *Justice for Victims and Offenders*, 1–6, citing William Blackstone's Commentaries on the Laws of England, 1765–1769.

93 Zehr, *Changing Lenses*, 116.

94 Wright, *Justice for Victims and Offenders*, 112.

95 Cordella, "Reconciliation," 35.

96 Camilleri, "Human Rights," 24.

97 Toulmin, *Cosmopolis*, 212.

98 Zehr, *Changing Lenses*, 139.

99 King, *Zen*, 3.

100 Suzuki, *Essays*, 84.

101 Bellah, *Tokugawa Religion*, 188; Nakamura, *Ways of Thinking*, 505, Nakamura's italics.

102 Demieville, "Le Bouddhisme et la guerre," 353.

103 *Dhammapada*, v.201.

104 Victoria, "Modern State and Warfare," 379.

105 Ibid., 369.

106 Later there was less reluctance, according to King (*Zen*, 371): "While Buddhist monks in the southern part of China (under the Chin dynasty) successfully maintained their independence of the State, their northern counterparts did not fare as well. Faced with non-Chinese rulers, Buddhist monks offered their services as political, diplomatic and military advisers." More recent work on the Northern and Southern Schools has confirmed and elaborated on this point.

107 King, *Zen*, 33.

108 Ibid., 132.

109 Ibid., 126.

110 Ibid., 125.

111 Ibid., 190–91.

112 Suzuki, *Zen and Japanese Culture*, 145.

113 Ibid., 180.

114 King, *Zen*, 186.

115 For a detailed study of Suzuki's social and political views, see Kirita, "D. T. Suzuki on Society and the State." For an example of Suzuki's antiwar views, see Suzuki, "Why Do We fight?" A note on Shinran in *The Eastern Buddhist*, vol. 1, no. 5 (1922): 395–96, compares him favorably with Nichiren, who "inspired the militarists of some years ago when a jingoistic spirit reigned in this country." In "Buddhism and Education" Suzuki contrasts Shinto and Buddhism: "Shinto is warlike, militant, and devoid of a loving spirit; while Buddhism is just the opposite, for it teaches all-embracing love which knows no enemy of whatever nature" (36). "My firm conviction is that if Buddhism held the Japanese statesmen, militarists, and people generally in its firmer grasp, that is, if Japan had been governed by Buddhism and not by Shinto as she has been until recently, there would have been no such war as the one whose most ignominious catastrophe we Japanese are all experiencing just at present." (37).

116 Soen, *Sermons*, 211–12. The Japanese edition was published in 1906.

117 Ibid., 201–203.

118 Quoted in Victoria, "Modern State and Warfare," 65.

119 Sharf, "Zen of Japanese Nationalism," 23.

120 Nishida, "Towards a Philosophy of Religion," 36.

121 Hisamatsu, *Zen and the Fine Arts*, 48.

122 As quoted in Sharf, 30–32.

123 Sharf, "Zen of Japanese Nationalism," 36–37.

124 See, for example, Silver, *Cloning and Beyond.*

125 Sophocles, *Antigone,* lines 332–75; Plato, *Laws* 679e.

126 Everndon, *Social Construction of Nature;* Oelschlaeger, *Idea of Wilderness.*

127 Quoted in Yalom, *Existential Psychotherapy,* 141–42.

128 Wolferen, *Enigma of Japanese Power,* 337.

129 See Tellenbach and Kimura, "Japanese Concept of 'Nature.'"

130 Verene, "Technological Desire," 107.

131 Quoted in Fox, *Toward a Transpersonal Ecology,* 106.

132 *Tao Te Ching,* chapter 14, line 14.

133 Warwick Fox, "Deep Ecology: A New Philosophy of Our Time?" *The Ecologist,* v. 14, no. 56 (1984), p. 195.

134 Fung, *Chuang-tzu,* 34, 46.

135 Quoted in DeBary, *Sources of Chinese Tradition,* 69.

136 *Isa Upanisad,* v. 6; *Pancapadika* part 6, verse 285.

137 See Loy, *Nonduality,* 112–24.

138 Fung, *Chuang-tzu,* 53.

139 Quoted in Yalom, *Existential Psychotherapy,* 469.

140 *Tao Te Ching,* chapter 48.

141 *Tao Te Ching,* chapter 22.

142 *Tao Te Ching,* chapter 2.

143 Huxley, *Eyeless in Gaza,* 614.

144 *Tao Te Ching,* chapter 18.

145 Schumacher, *Small Is Beautiful,* 30.

146 *Tao Te Ching* chapters 22, 38.

147 *Bodhicaryavatara,* chapter 8, verse 120.

148 Cook, *Hua-yen Buddhism,* 2ff.

149 Dogen, "Genjo-koan," 70.

150 Yasutani, quoted in Kapleau, *Three Pillars of Zen,* 80; Dogen, "Genjo-koan," 69.

151 Rafe Martin, "Thoughts on the Jatakas," 43. For many more examples of Buddhist reverence of nature, see Kaza and Kraft, *Dharma Rain.*

152 Leopold, *Sand County Almanac,* 117, 240.

153 Catton and Dunlap, "New Ecological Paradigm," as quoted in Devall and Sessions, *Deep Ecology,* 43.

154 Devall and Sessions, *Deep Ecology,* 44.

155 Naess, *Ecology, Community, and Lifestyle,* as quoted in Devall and Sessions, *Deep Ecology,* 240.

156 Michael Zimmerman, who was among the first to point out the environmental relevance of Heidegger's critique of technology, has since argued that Heidegger's version of anti-modernism is still anthropocentric and incompatible with deep ecology in several important respects. See his *Contesting Earth's Future,* especially chapters 1 and 3.

157 Quoted in Devall and Sessions, *Deep Ecology,* 66.

158 Evernden, "Beyond Ecology," *North American Review* 213 (1978), 19.

159 Devall and Sessions, *Deep Ecology,* 66–67.

160 Quoted in Tobias, *Deep Ecology,* 261.

161 Plumwood, *Feminism,* 176ff.

162 Naess, *Ecology, Community, and Lifestyle,* 165, 195.

163 Rothenberg, *Is It Painful to Think?* 76.

164 Regan, "Environmental Ethic," 19–34.

165 As quoted in Tobias, *Deep Ecology,* 250.

166 Ibid.

167 Quoted in Fox, "Deep Ecology," 194.

168 This particular theme is developed further in *A Buddhist History of the West* (SUNY 2002), ch. 4.

Bibliography

Ali, Abdullah Yusuf, trans. *The Meaning of the Holy Qur'an.* 5th ed. Brentwood, Md.: Amana Corporation, 1993.

Anderson, Walter Truett, ed. *The Truth about the Truth: De-Confusing and Re-Constructing the Postmodern World.* New York: Tarcher/Putnam, 1995.

Auerbach, Jerold. *Justice without Law?* Oxford: Oxford University Press, 1983.

Batchelor, Stephen. *Buddhism without Beliefs: A Contemporary Guide to Awakening.* London: Bloomsbury, 1997.

Becker, Ernest. *The Birth and Death of Meaning,* 2d ed. New York: Free Press, 1971.

———. *Escape from Evil.* New York: Free Press, 1975.

Bellah, Robert N. *Tokugawa Religion: The Cultural Roots of Modern Japan.* New York: Free Press, 1957.

Bertell, Rosalie. "The Bhopal Legacy: An Interview with Dr. Rosalie Bertell." *Multinational Monitor* 18, no. 3 (March 1997).

Berthoud, Gerard. "Market." In *The Development Dictionary,* ed. Wolfgang Sachs. London: Zed Books, 1992.

Black, Eugene. *The Diplomacy of International Development.* New York: Atheneum, 1963.

Bodhi, Bhikkhu, trans. *Connected Discourses of the Buddha: A New Translation of the Samyutta Nikaya.* Somerville, Mass.: Wisdom Publications, 2000.

Braithwaite, John. *Crime, Shame and Reintegration.* New York: Cambridge University Press, 1989.

Camilleri, Joseph. "Human Rights, Cultural Diversity and Conflict Resolution." *Pacifica Review* 6, no. 2 (1994).

Catton, William, Jr., and Riley Dunlap. "New Ecological Paradigm for Post-Exuberant Sociology." *American Behavioral Scientist* 24 (September 1980).

Caufield, Catherine. *Masters of Illusion: The World Bank and the Poverty of Nations.* London: Macmillan, 1996.

Chakravarti, Uma. *The Social Dimensions of Early Buddhism.* Delhi: Oxford University Press, 1987.

Chambers, Robert. *Whose Reality Counts?* London: Intermediate Technology, 1997.

Chang Chung-yuan, trans. *Original Teachings of Chan Buddhism.* New York: Vintage, 1971.

Cook, Francis H. *Hua-yen Buddhism: The Jewel Net of Indra.* University Park: Pennsylvania State University Press, 1977.

Cordella, J. Peter. "Reconciliation and the Mutualist Model of Community." In *Criminology As Peacemaking,* eds. Harold Pepinsky and Richard Quinney. Bloomington: Indiana University Press, 1991.

"Corporate Empires." *Multinational Monitor* 17, no. 12 (December 1996).

Dalai Lama. *The Art of Happiness.* New York: Putnam, 1998.

———. "Dialogue on Religion and Peace." In *Buddhist Peacework: Creating Cultures of Peace,* ed. David W. Chappell. Somerville, Mass.: Wisdom Publications, 1999.

———. *Ethics for the New Millennium.* New York: Riverhead Books, 1999.

Daly, Herman E., and John B. Cobb, Jr., *For the Common Good.* 2d ed. Boston: Beacon Press, 1994.

DeBary, Theodore, ed. *Sources of Chinese Tradition.* New York: Columbia University Press, 1964.

Demieville, Paul. "Le Bouddhisme et la guerre." In *Melanges.* Paris: Institut des Hautes Etudes Chinoises, 1957.

Devall, Bill, and George Sessions. *Deep Ecology: Living As If Nature Mattered.* Salt Lake City: Peregrine Smith Books, 1985.

Dhammapada. Bombay: Theosophy Company, 1976.

Dogen. "Genjo-koan." In *Moon in a Dewdrop: Writings of Zen Master Dogen.* Trans. Dan Welch and Kazuaki Tanahashi. Ed. Kazuaki Tanahashi. San Francisco: North Point Press, 1985.

Drengston, Alan, and Yuichi Inoue, eds. *The Deep Ecology Movement: An Introductory Anthology.* Berkeley, Calif.: North Atlantic, 1995.

Dunning, John. *The Moral Response to Global Capitalism.* Oxford: Oxford University Press, 2003.

Durning, Alan. *How Much Is Enough?* New York: Norton, 1992.

Evernden, Neil. "Beyond Ecology," *North American Review* 263 (1978).

———. *The Social Construction of Nature.* Baltimore: Johns Hopkins University Press, 1992.

Fish, Stanley. *The Trouble with Principle.* Cambridge: Harvard University Press, 1999.

Fox, Warwick. "Deep Ecology: A New Philosophy of Our Time?" *The Ecologist,* vol. 14 no. 5–6, 1984.

———. *Toward a Transpersonal Ecology: Developing New Foundations for Environmentalism.* Boston: Shambhala, 1990.

French, Rebecca Redwood. *The Golden Yoke: The Legal Cosmology of Buddhist Tibet,* Ithaca, N.Y.: Cornell University Press, 1995.

Fung Yu-lan, trans. *Chuang-tzu, with Kuo Hsiang's Commentary.* New York: Gordon Press, 1975.

Gandhi, Mohandas K. *An Autobiography.* Boston: Beacon Press, 1957.

George, Susan, and Fabrizio Sabelli. *Faith and Credit: The World Bank's Secular Empire.* Harmondsworth: Penguin, 1994.

Geuss, Raymond. *The Idea of a Critical Theory.* Cambridge: Cambridge University Press, 1981.

Golash, Deirdre. "Punishment: An Institution in Search of a Moral Grounding." In *Punishment: Social Control and Coercion,* ed. Christine Sistare. Center for Semiotic Research, 1994.

Gray, John. *Straw Dogs: Thoughts on Humans and Other Animals.* London: Granta, 2002.

Gronemeyer, Marianne. "Helping." In *The Development Dictionary,* ed. Wolfgang Sachs. London: Zed Books, 1992.

Grossman, Richard. "Corporations' Accountability and Responsibility." Unpublished.

———. "Revoking the Corporation." *Journal of Environmental Law and Litigation* 2 (1996).

Hamburg, Dan. "Inside the Money Chase." *The Nation,* May 5, 1997.

Heisig, James W., and John C. Maraldo, eds. *Rude Awakenings: Zen, the Kyoto School, and the Question of Nationalism.* Honolulu: University of Hawaii Press, 1995.

Herbert, Christopher. *Culture and Anomie: Ethnographic Imagination in the Nineteenth Century.* Chicago: University of Chicago Press, 1991.

Hisamatsu, Shin'ichi. *Zen and the Fine Arts.* Trans. Gishin Tokiwa. Tokyo: Kodansha, 1971.

Huxley, Aldous. *Eyeless in Gaza.* London: Chatto and Windus, 1969.

Jones, Ken. *The Social Face of Buddhism: An Approach to Political and Social Activism.* London: Wisdom, 1989.

Kapleau, Philip, ed. *The Three Pillars of Zen.* Tokyo: Weatherhill, 1965.

Kaza, Stephanie, and Kenneth Kraft, eds., *Dharma Rain: Sources of Buddhist Environmentalism,* Boulder: Shambhala, 2000.

Kim, Hee-Jin. *Dogen Kigen—Mystical Realist.* Tucson: University of Arizona Press, 1975.

King, Winston L. *Zen and the Way of the Sword: Arming the Samurai Psyche.* New York: Oxford University Press, 1993.

Kirita, Kiyohide. "D. T. Suzuki on Society and the State." In *Rude Awakenings: Zen, the Kyoto School, and the Question of Nationalism,* eds. James W. Heisig and John C. Maraldo, 52–74. Honolulu: University of Hawaii Press, 1995.

Leopold, Aldo. *Sand County Almanac.* New York: Oxford University Press, 1968.

Liechty, Daniel. "Principalities and Powers: A Beckerian Reading of Walter Wink's *The Powers* Trilogy." www.ernestbecker.org/lectures [2000].

Lloyd, Henry Demarest. *Wealth against Commonwealth*. New York, Harper & Brothers, 1894.

Lopez, Donald S. *Curators of the Buddha: The Study of Buddhism under Colonialism*. Chicago: University of Chicago Press, 1995.

Loy, David, *A Buddhist History of the West: Studies in Lack*. Albany: State University of New York Press, 2002.

———. *Lack and Transcendence: The Problem of Death and Life in Psychotherapy, Existentialism and Buddhism*. Amherst, N.Y.: Humanity Books, 1996.

———. *Nonduality: A Study in Comparative Philosophy*. New Haven, Conn.: Yale University Press, 1988.

———. "The Religion of the Market." In *A Buddhist History of the West: Studies in Lack*. Albany: State University of New York Press, 2002.

Macy, Joanna. "The Greening of the Self." In *Engaged Buddhist Reader*, ed. Arnold Kotler. Berkeley, Calif.: Parallax, 1996.

Mander, Jerry. "Corporations As Machines." In *Buying America Back*, eds. Jonathan Greenberg and William Kistler. Council Oak Books, San Francisco: 1992.

Martin, Rafe, "Thoughts on the Jatakas," in Eppsteiner, Fred, and Dennis Maloney, eds., *The Path of Compassion: Contemporary Writings on Engaged Buddhism*. Berkeley: Buddhist Peace Fellowship, 1985.

Naess, Arne. *Ecology, Community, and Lifestyle: A Philosophical Approach*. Oslo: Oslo University Press, 1977; Cambridge: Cambridge University Press, 1988.

Nagarjuna. *Mulamadhyamikakarika*. In *Lucid Exposition of the Middle Way*, trans. Mervyn Sprung. Boulder, Colo.: Prajna Press, 1979.

Nakamura, Hajime. *Ways of Thinking of Eastern Peoples*. Ed. and trans. Philip P. Wiener. Honolulu: University of Hawaii Press, 1964.

Nanamoli, Bhikkhu, and Bhikkhu Bodhi, trans. *The Middle Length Discourses of the Buddha*. Somerville, Mass.: Wisdom Publications, 1995.

Nhat Hanh, Thich. *The Heart of Understanding*. Berkeley, Calif.: Parallax Press, 1988.

Nishida, Kitaro. "Towards a Philosophy of Religion with the Concept of Pre-established Harmony As a Guide." Trans. David A. Dilworth. *Eastern Buddhist*, n.s., 3, no. 1 (1970).

Oelschlaeger, Max. *The Idea of Wilderness*. New Haven, Conn.: Yale University Press, 1991.

Payutto, P. A. *Buddhist Economics: A Middle Way for the Market Place*. Trans. Dhammavijaya and Bruce Evans. 2d ed. Bangkok: Buddhadhamma Foundation, 1994.

Pepinsky, Harold. "Peacemaking in Criminology and Criminal Justice." In *Criminology as Peacemaking*, eds. Harold Pepinsky and Richard Quinney. Bloomington: Indiana University Press, 1991.

Plumwood, Val. *Feminism and the Mastery of Nature*. London: Routledge, 1993.

Polanyi, Karl. *The Great Transformation.* Boston: Beacon, 1957.

Premasiri, P. D. "Religious Values and the Measurement of Poverty: A Buddhist Perspective." Written for the World Faiths Development Dialogue with the World Bank, Johannesburg, South Africa, 12–14 January 1999.

Ratnapala, Nandasena. *Crime and Punishment in the Buddhist Tradition.* New Delhi: Mittal Publications, 1993.

Regan, Tom. "The Nature and Possibility of an Environmental Ethic." *Environmental Ethics* 3 (1981).

Rothenberg, David. *Is It Painful to Think? Conversations with Arne Naess.* Minneapolis: University of Minnesota Press, 1993.

Sbert, Jose Maria. "Progress." In *The Development Dictionary,* ed. Wolfgang Sachs. London: Zed Books, 1992.

Schumacher, E. F. *Small Is Beautiful.* New York: Harper and Row, 1975.

Scott, David. "Criticism and Culture." *Critique of Anthropology* 12, no. 4 (1992).

Sharf, Robert. "The Zen of Japanese Nationalism." *History of Religions* 33, no. 1 (August 1993).

Silver, Lee. *How Cloning and Beyond Will Change the Human Family.* New York: Avon, 1998.

Simmel, Georg. "The Poor." *Social Problems* 13 (1965).

Sizemore, Russell F., and Donald K. Swearer, eds. *Ethics, Wealth and Salvation: A Study in Buddhist Social Ethics.* Columbia: University of South Carolina, 1990.

Soen, Shaku. *Sermons of a Buddhist Abbot: Addresses on Religious Subjects.* Trans. D. T. Suzuki. New York: Weiser, 1971.

———. *Zen for Americans.* 1906. Reprint, LaSalle, Ill.: Open Court Press, 1974.

Stoneman, Colin. "The World Bank and the IMF in Zimbabwe." In *Structural Adjustment in Africa,* eds. Bonnie Campbell and John Loxley. New York: St. Martin's Press, 1989.

Sutta Nipata. Vol. 1, Ajita-manava-puccha, "Ajita's Questions." http://www.accesstoinsight.org/canon/khuddaka/suttanipata/snp5-01a.html.

Suzuki, D. T. "Buddhism and Education." *Eastern Buddhist* 8, no. 1 (May 1949), 36–45.

———. *Essays in Zen Buddhism.* First Series. New York: Harper and Row, 1949.

———. "Why Do We Fight?" *Eastern Buddhist* 1, no. 4 (November–December 1921): 270–81.

———. *Zen and Japanese Culture.* Princeton, N.J.: Princeton University Press, 1959.

Tellenbach, Hubertus, and Bin Kimura. "The Japanese Concept of 'Nature.'" In *Nature in Asian Traditions of Thought: Essays in Environmental Philosophy,* eds. J. Baird Callicott and Roger T. Ames. Albany: State University of New York Press, 1989.

Thurman, Robert A. F. "The Edicts of Asoka." In *The Path of Compassion: Contemporary*

Writings on Engaged Buddhism, eds. Fred Eppsteiner and Dennis Maloney. Berkeley, Calif.: Buddhist Peace Fellowship, 1985.

Tobias, Michael, ed. *Deep Ecology.* San Diego: Avant, 1985.

Toulmin, Stephen. *Cosmopolis: The Hidden Agenda of Modernity.* New York: Free Press, 1990.

United Nations. Human Development Report 1998 (New York: United Nations Development Program, 1998).

———. Human Development Report for 1999. http://www.undp.org/hdro/ overview.pdf.

Van Ness, Daniel, and Karen H. Strong. *Restoring Justice.* Cincinnati: Anderson Publishing, 1997.

Verene, Donald Phillip. "Technological Desire." In *Research in Philosophy and Technology,* ed. Paul T. Durbin, vol. 7. London: JAI Press, 1984.

Victoria, Brian. "Japanese Corporate Zen." *Bulletin of Concerned Asian Scholars* 12, no. 1 (1980).

———. "The Modern State and Warfare: Is There a Buddhist Position?" *1990 Anthology of Fo Kuang Shan International Buddhist Conference.*

———. *Zen at War.* New York: Weatherhill, 1997.

Wagner, Roy. *The Invention of Culture.* Englewood Cliffs, N.J.: Prentice-Hall, 1975.

Walshe, Maurice, trans. *The Long Discourses of the Buddha: A Translation of the Digha Nikaya.* Boston: Wisdom Publications, 1995, 2, 3.

Weber, Max. *The Protestant Ethic and the Spirit of Capitalism.* London: Allen and Unwin, 1930.

Wolferen, Karel van. *The Enigma of Japanese Power: People and Politics in a Stateless Nation.* London: Macmillan, 1989.

Wong, Mou-lam, trans. *Sutra Spoken by the Sixth Patriarch on the High Seat of "The Treasure of the Law."* Hong Kong: Buddhist Book Distributor, n.d.

Wright, Martin. *Justice for Victims and Offenders.* Milton Keynes, Open University Press, 1991.

Yalom, Irvin D. *Existential Psychotherapy.* New York: Basic Books, 1980.

Zehr, Howard. *Changing Lenses: A New Focus for Crime and Justice.* Scottsdale, Pa.: Herald Press, 1990.

Zimmerman, Michael. *Contesting Earth's Future: Radical Ecology and Postmodernity.* Berkelely: University of California Press, 1994.

———. "Towards a Heideggerian Ethos for Radical Environmentalism." *Environmental Ethics* 5 (1983).

Index

M
Macy, Joanna, 31
Madhyamika Buddhism, 26
Mahaghosananda, 35
Mahayana Buddhism, 31, 181–83
  and the bodhisattvas, 4
  and deep ecology, 191
  and the duality between nature and
    technology, 161, 166
  and economic globalization, 77
  Huayen school of, 161, 183, 188, 192
  and Japanese samurai Zen, 145, 153
  teaching of no-self, 39
  and Taoism, 16, 173, 177
Malaysia, 91
Manchuria, 152
mandalas, 28
Mao Zedong, 106
Mara, 28
Marcuse, Herbert, 159
marriage, 38
materialism, 28, 77, 180
Matsushita, 91
meaning, crises of, 13–14
media, 45, 92
medical care, 31, 32, 55, 59
Medieval Europe, 14, 62
meditation, 26, 77, 87, 181, 183–84
  and dukkha, 35
  right, 34
Mediterranean Sea, 13
Meiji reformation, 154–55
mental formations, 133
meta-narratives, 3, 4
metaphysics, 4–6, 17
  the Buddha's lack of interest in, 23
  and deep ecology, 188, 192
  and retributive criminal justice systems,
    123, 140
Middle way, 73
mindfulness, 26, 34, 35, 113
miniaturization, 2–3, 38
Mitsubishi, 91–92
Miyazaki, Hayo, 112–13
modernity, 8, 115
modes of being, 113–14, 118–19, 196

moha (delusion), 28, 130. *See also* delusion
Mohammed, 112
monarchies, 17, 56–57, 61, 126–30, 140
monastic orders. *See also* bhikkhunis
    (nuns); bhikkhus (monks); Sangha
    (community of monks)
  and celibacy, 38
  and dukkha, 32–33
  and poverty, 55
  and retributive criminal justice systems,
    125
Monsanto, 168
*Moral Response to Global Capitalism,
    The* (Dunning), 79
morality, 96, 172, 181
  and deep ecology, 192
  and dukkha, 34, 36
  and economic globalization, 74–78
  and karma, 7, 74
  and noble wealth, 57
  "nonmoral," of the bodhisattvas, 185
  and poverty, 56–58, 67–69
  and retributive criminal justice systems,
    130–36
  and Taoism, 178
  and Zen Buddhism, 48, 143–44, 149–51
mother, symbolic, 4
Muir, John, 189
Mulamadhyamikakarika, 25, 182–83
multicultural societies, 31, 103
Muslims, 2, 44, 104, 106, 115–17

N
Naess, Arne, 51, 188–92
Nagarjuna, 24–25, 82–83, 189
nationalism, 116, 145, 151–56, 197
nation-states, 93, 97
  and Japanese samurai Zen, 156
  and retributive criminal justice systems,
    140–142
Native Americans, 119, 188
natural selection, 9
nature. *See also* ecology
  and culture, duality between, 48, 157–69
  and Taoism, 176

About Wisdom

WISDOM PUBLICATIONS, a not-for-profit publisher, is dedicated to making available authentic Buddhist works for the benefit of all. We publish translations of the sutras and tantras, commentaries and teachings of past and contemporary Buddhist masters, and original works by the world's leading Buddhist scholars. We publish our titles with the appreciation of Buddhism as a living philosophy and with the special commitment to preserve and transmit important works from all the major Buddhist traditions.

To learn more about Wisdom, or to browse books online, visit our website at wisdompubs.org.

You may request a copy of our mail-order catalog online or by writing to:

Wisdom Publications
199 Elm Street
Somerville, Massachusetts 02144 USA
Telephone: (617) 776-7416
Fax: (617) 776-7841
Email: info@wisdompubs.org
www.wisdompubs.org

THE WISDOM TRUST

As a not-for-profit publisher, Wisdom is dedicated to the publication of Fine Dharma books for the benefit of all sentient beings and dependent upon the kindness and generosity of sponsors in order to do so. If you would like to make a donation to Wisdom, please do so through our Somerville office. If you would like to sponsor the publication of a book, please write or e-mail us at the address above.

Thank you.

Wisdom is a nonprofit, charitable 501(c)(3) organization affiliated with the Foundation for the Preservation of the Mahayana Tradition (FPMT).